I0812844

IMAGES
of America

WATERTOWN

IMAGES
of America

WATERTOWN

Donna M. Dutton

ARCADIA
PUBLISHING

ISBN 978-0-7385-0922-8

Published by Arcadia Publishing
Charleston, South Carolina

Printed in the United States of America

Library of Congress Catalog Card Number: 2001091084

For all general information contact Arcadia Publishing at:
Telephone 843-853-2070
Fax 843-853-0044
E-mail sales@arcadiapublishing.com
For customer service and orders:
Toll-Free 1-888-313-2665

Visit us on the Internet at www.arcadiapublishing.com

CONTENTS

Preface 6

Introduction 7

Acknowledgments 8

1. Public Square 9
2. The Roswell P. Flower Memorial Library 27
3. Thompson Park 33
4. Trolleys 41
5. Schools 45
6. Urban Renewal 55
7. Industry and Business 71
8. Churches 93
9. A Potpourri of Memories 111

Preface

In 2000, when the city of Watertown celebrated the bicentennial of the first settlement, many people mentioned that we should put together a book to showcase our history. When Arcadia contacted me in reference to compiling a publication about the community, I saw it as an opportunity for our city to pay tribute to our rich heritage. We have a wonderful history left to us by those who came before. In the pages that follow, I have tried to share with you some of this legacy in photographs and captions. However, not all of our history can be recorded in these few pages. My hope is that this book properly honors all the men and women—not just the famous—whose strong work ethic and perseverance carved out a community from a wilderness and whose fortitude and foresight had a lasting influence on the development of our city.

—Donna M. Dutton
City Clerk and Historian
City of Watertown

INTRODUCTION

The settling of Watertown in 1800 began a 200-year legacy that continues today. The New England pioneers who chose our area did so based on foresight of creating an industrial center, which would draw its power from the mighty Black River. These men have been described as men of strong feeling, vivid imagination, and dauntless courage. They, along with their families, faced many obstacles when they arrived. The terrain was rough and uncleared. The western end of the present public square was 12 or 15 feet higher than the eastern end, while the center was a depression that has been described as being large enough for a comfortable skating rink. There was a stream of water having its source south of Clinton Street and running across Stone Street in front of the Arcade, crossing the western end of the square on its way to the river. Yet within a few years, out of this unsightly spot evolved one of the most beautiful public squares to be found in any city of its time.

The naming of Watertown as the county seat led to much progress in the hamlet. Lawyers, including Benjamin Skinner, Egbert TenEyck, Amos Benedict, and Samuel Whittlesey, set up practice here. Six hotels were constructed. The Failing Hotel, first known as the Traveler's House, was built in 1808 at the corner of Main and LeRay Streets. During the War of 1812, the soldiers used it as a barracks. Court Street became both a residential and business street. Small mills and factories sprang up and businesses extended along Factory Street. John Safford, Tuttle & Sill, and Otis & Duane launched new stores. Other well-known names, such as Norris, Woodruff, Hungerford, Paddock, and Fairbanks, also engaged in businesses.

The development of waterpower was the force that started the wheels of progress for the community. Factory Village, which later became Factory Square, had its real beginning when the Black River Cotton and Woolen Manufacturing Company was built in 1813.

Watertown became an incorporated village in 1816 and continued to prosper. Businesses, industries, and the population all doubled by 1824. Growth continued, with the decade between 1850 and 1860 seeing the largest amount of building construction. This was due in part to rebuilding after a devastating fire but also due to new building expansion. The Davis Sewing Machine Company employed about 200 people. The Watertown Steam Engine Company had assets estimated at $1 million. The paper-making industry was flourishing. H.H. Babcock's carriage factory and Watertown Spring Wagon Company were two of the many businesses that were helping Watertown to thrive. The railroad was of tremendous importance to the economy. People marveled at the telephone, the electric light, and even "street name plates" that the city installed.

The next 100 years of history included the story of our veterans who went to wars and the citizens who helped with the war effort from home. Watertownians took pride in their community and, at one time, Watertown was named "the Ideal American City." Over the years, the economic climate has affected business and industry. However, some of today's businesses have their roots in our early history. Although the city is much different from the hamlet of 1800, we can take pride in the rich heritage that was left for us and for future generations.

ACKNOWLEDGMENTS

I would like to express my sincere appreciation to several people who helped in many ways to see this project to fruition. Special thanks goes to Deputy City Clerks Elyse Frezzo and Carol Van Dusen, who proofread and helped with the picture selection. Elyse also helped to research information for the book. My gratitude goes to Bob Brennon, who offered his military knowledge; to Rande Richardson, Carolyn Perkins, and Rev. Dora Schneider, who supplied information and photographs for the chapter on churches; and to Ken Mix for his assistance with the Public Square and Thompson Park chapters. The book would not have been possible without the help of the *Watertown Daily Times* library staff. I am grateful to Esther Daniels for the incredible amount of assistance she gave me. The photographs that I was able to obtain from the *Watertown Daily Times* helped to tell the story. Special thanks also goes to Fred Rollins, executive director of the Jefferson County Historical Society, and to Mary Weldon, curator of collections. Their enthusiasm for allowing the use of photographs from the society's collection for inclusion in this book was greatly appreciated. I would like to thank all the volunteers in the City Historian's Room. Their indexing project made it much easier to access the information that was needed.

One

Public Square

Henry Coffeen purchased a tract of land that extended to the Black River from the present Public Square when he visited the site in 1799. In 1800, he returned with his family, traveling along the old French road, from the Mohawk to Steuben's cabin, through Boon's two settlements to High Falls, and then through Martinsburg, Lowville, Denmark, Harrisburg, and Champion. His Mohawk neighbor Zachariah Butterfield and Vermont resident Hart Massey joined him and all three built cabins near what became Public Square.

Public Square, then known as the Mall, came into existence in 1805 when Hart and Isaiah Massey, Henry Coffeen, Zachariah Butterfield, Jonathan Cowan, Jesse Doolittle, Aaron Keyes, and Medad Canfield, with surprising foresight, deeded the land for public use. These men, mostly of New England origin, thought of the Mall as a common such as those that graced many New England villages. This helped to enhance the development of a business center by creating an area around which businesses could locate. Later, Cowan sought to take back some of the land. Judge Nathan Williams ruled against him.

Following the 1849 fire, most of Public Square was replaced with heavy masonry construction. The parks at the center of the square were laid out in 1853 with a fountain at the center and two ovals at either end. Cattle roamed throughout Public Square in the early days, making it necessary to put up posts and circle the park with a chain fence. The first flagpole was placed on Public Square at the beginning of the Civil War and stood 122 feet tall. It was made using a single tree from a local forest. Public Square was first paved in 1894. In 1906, the chain fence and posts were removed and curbing was placed about the parks enclosing a line of trees.

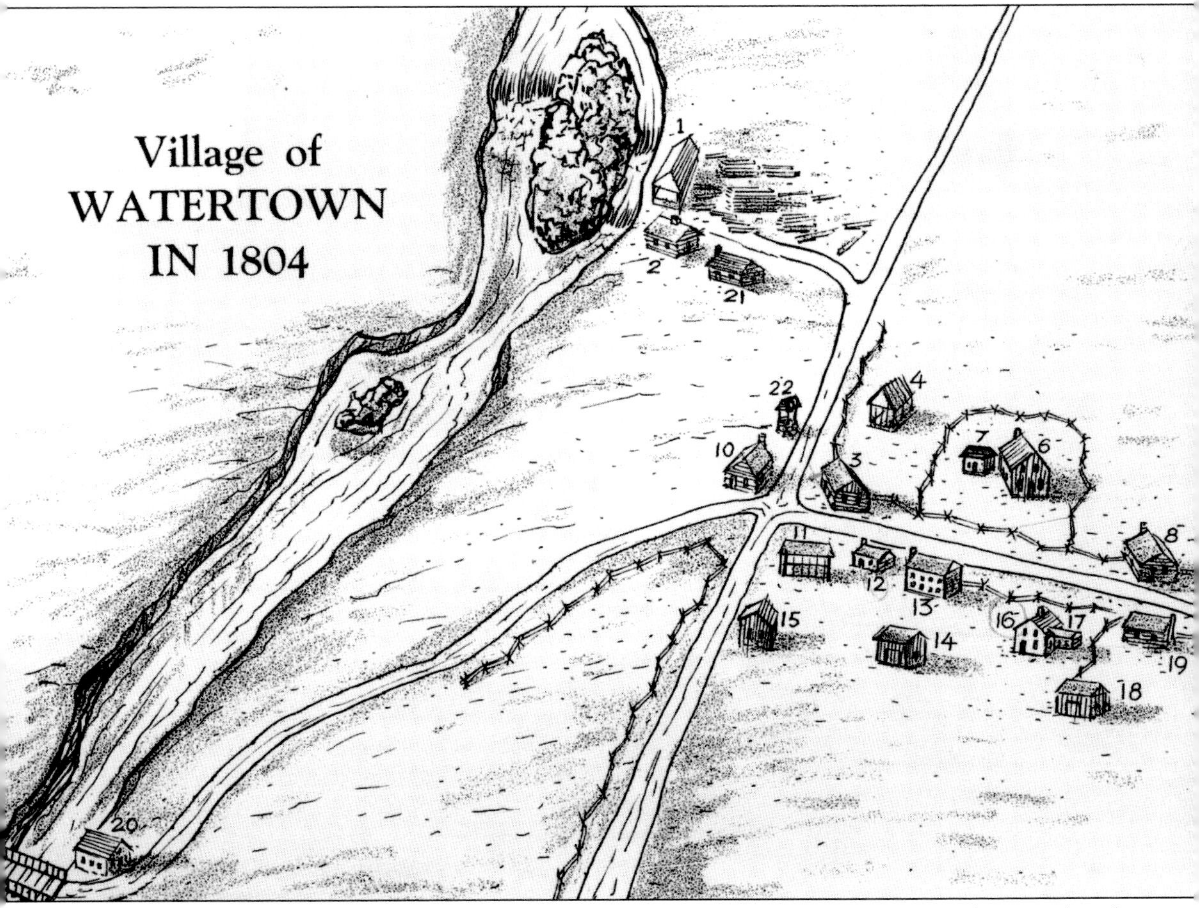

This is a map sketched by Gordon Dexter from an original by D. Huntington. The 1804 hamlet was made up of several log cabins and rough framed structures. The beginnings of Public Square can be seen at the crossroads between No. 3 (Judge Coffeen's home), No. 10 (a log house built by Zachariah Butterfield), and No. 11 (a framed structure built in 1803 by Aaron Bacon). Other buildings of note are No. 1, Cowan's sawmill, which had the only hydraulic works on the river; No. 7, Watertown's first cooper shop, operated by Aaron Keyes; No. 12, Dr. Isaiah Massey's tavern; Nos. 16 and 18, Hart Massey's home and barn, which were used for the first school; and No. 22, which indicates the spring that furnished water for the hamlet.

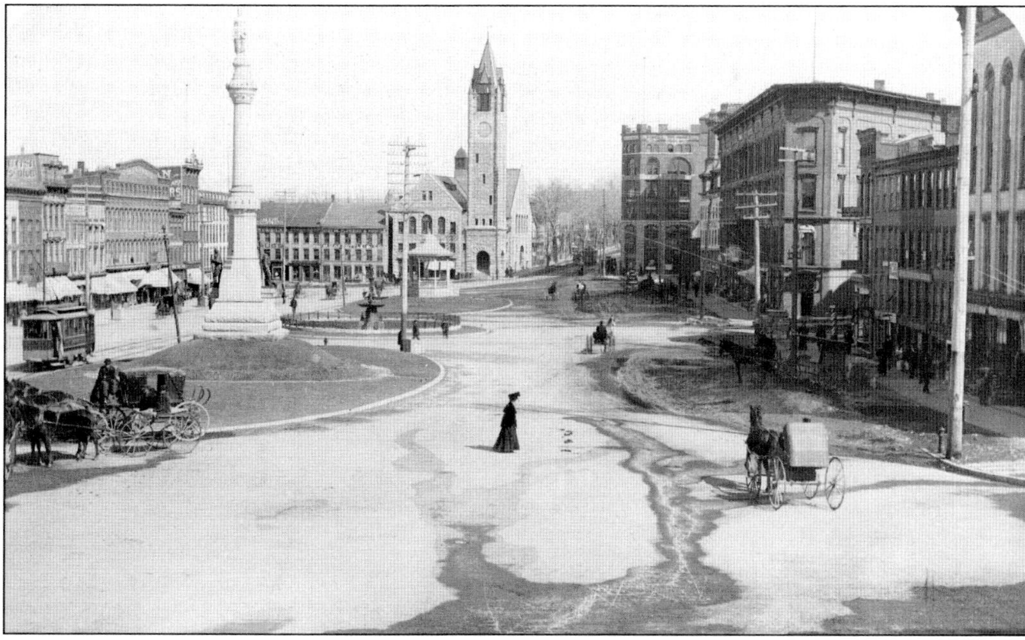

Carriages and trolleys coexisted in the early days of Watertown. A trolley can be observed in the distance going up a tree-lined State Street. The three islands in the center of the square are well defined in this photograph. A bandstand where concerts were held can be seen on the easternmost island. This replaced an earlier open bandstand that was on the western island.

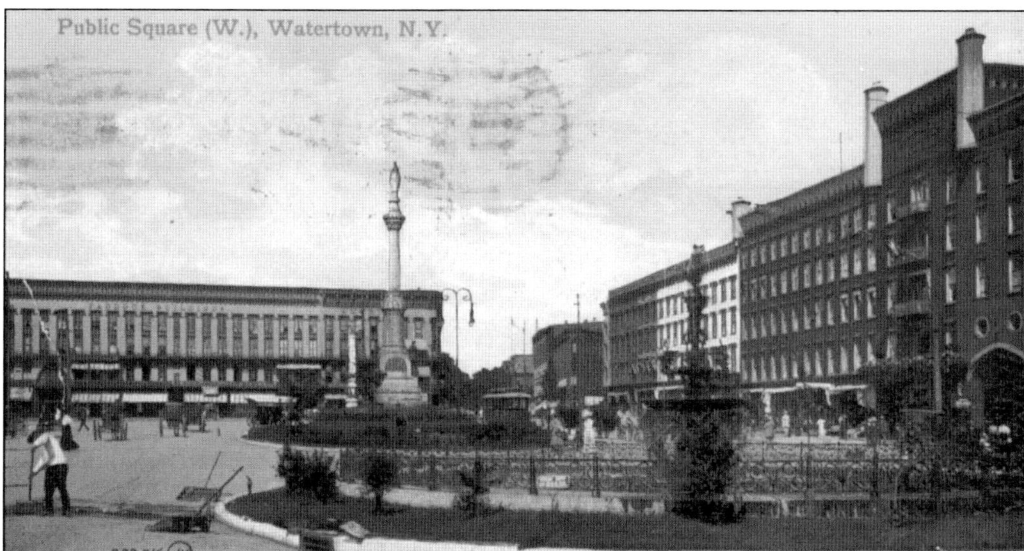

In this view, a worker can be seen sweeping the roadway around Public Square. The impressive buildings around the square include the Paddock Building and the Woodruff Hotel. The Paddock Building houses the Paddock Arcade, which is said to be one of the oldest continuously operating covered malls in the United States. Loveland Paddock built the Arcade in 1850. The Woodruff was completed in 1851 by Norris Woodruff and was one of the largest hotels in this part of New York. Some compared its dining room, with its great pillars, to that of the Astor House in New York City.

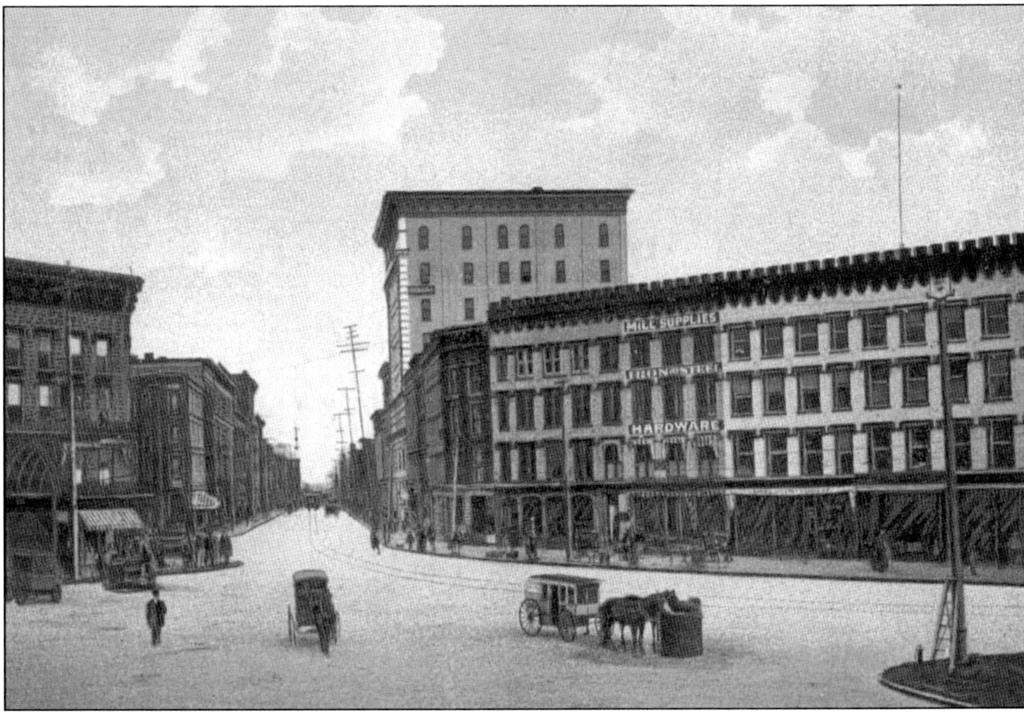

The old iron watering tank was located near the American Corner. Many a horse and rider stopped for a cool drink on a hot summer day.

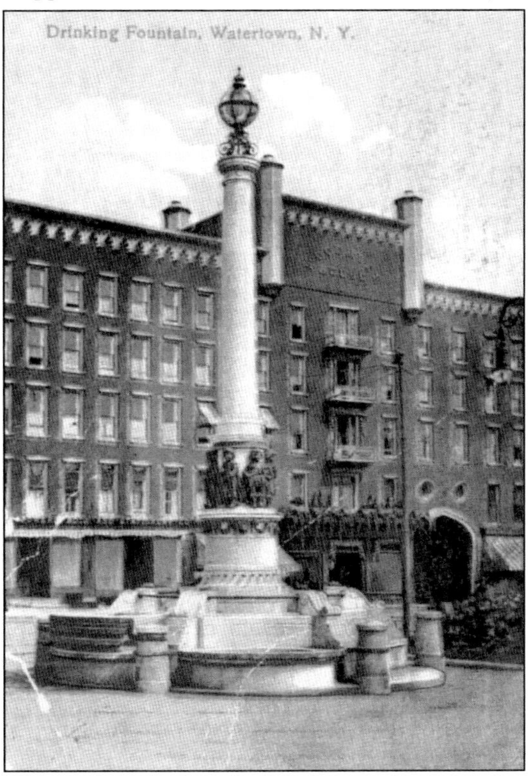

In 1906, Mrs. Roswell P. Flower gave an ornamental watering trough that replaced the old tank.

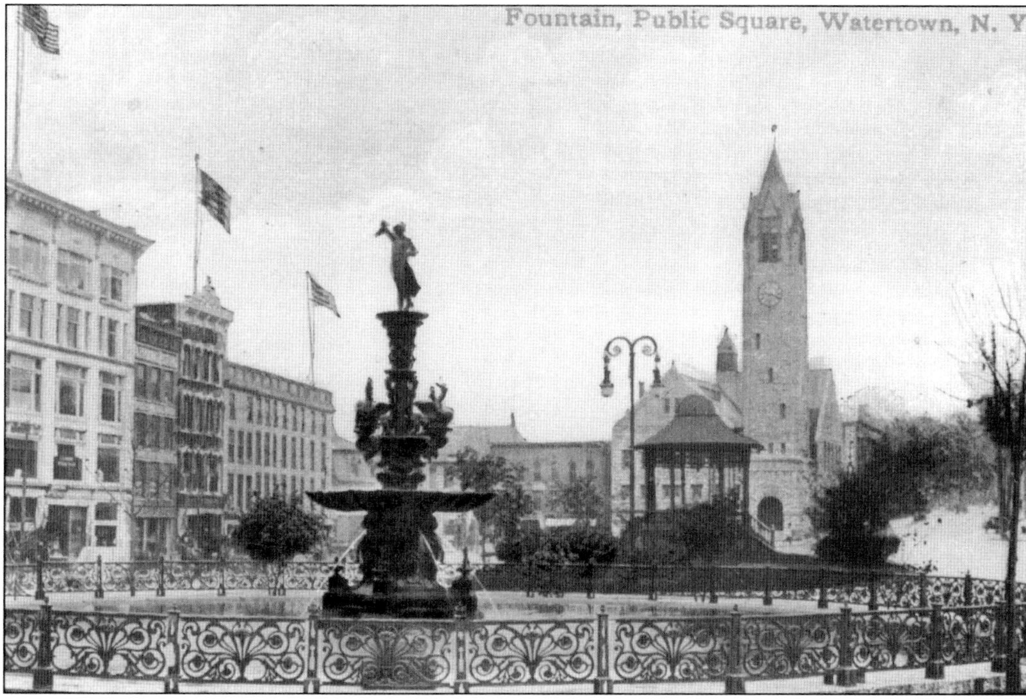

When Watertown became an incorporated city in 1869, one of the celebration events was the erecting of the fountain shown above. Its cost was under $700. The lacy iron fencing was a gift of the village women. Before this, the base was known as "Cory's Punch Bowl" in reference to Benjamin Cory, a newspaper editor who was responsible for donating the first fountain in 1855.

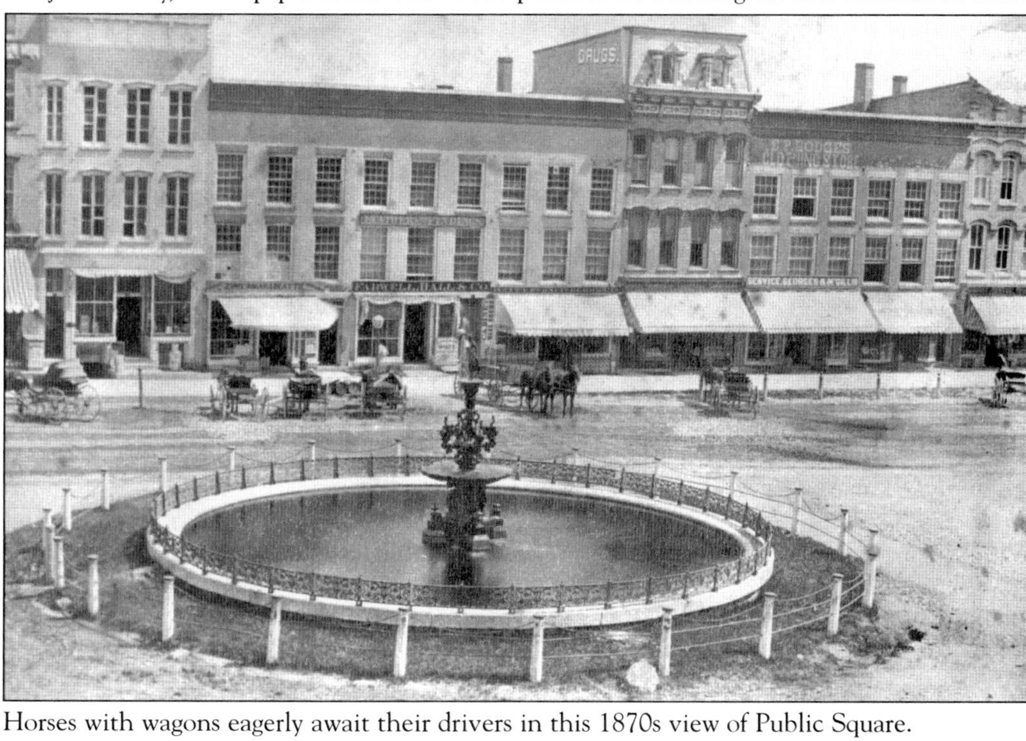

Horses with wagons eagerly await their drivers in this 1870s view of Public Square.

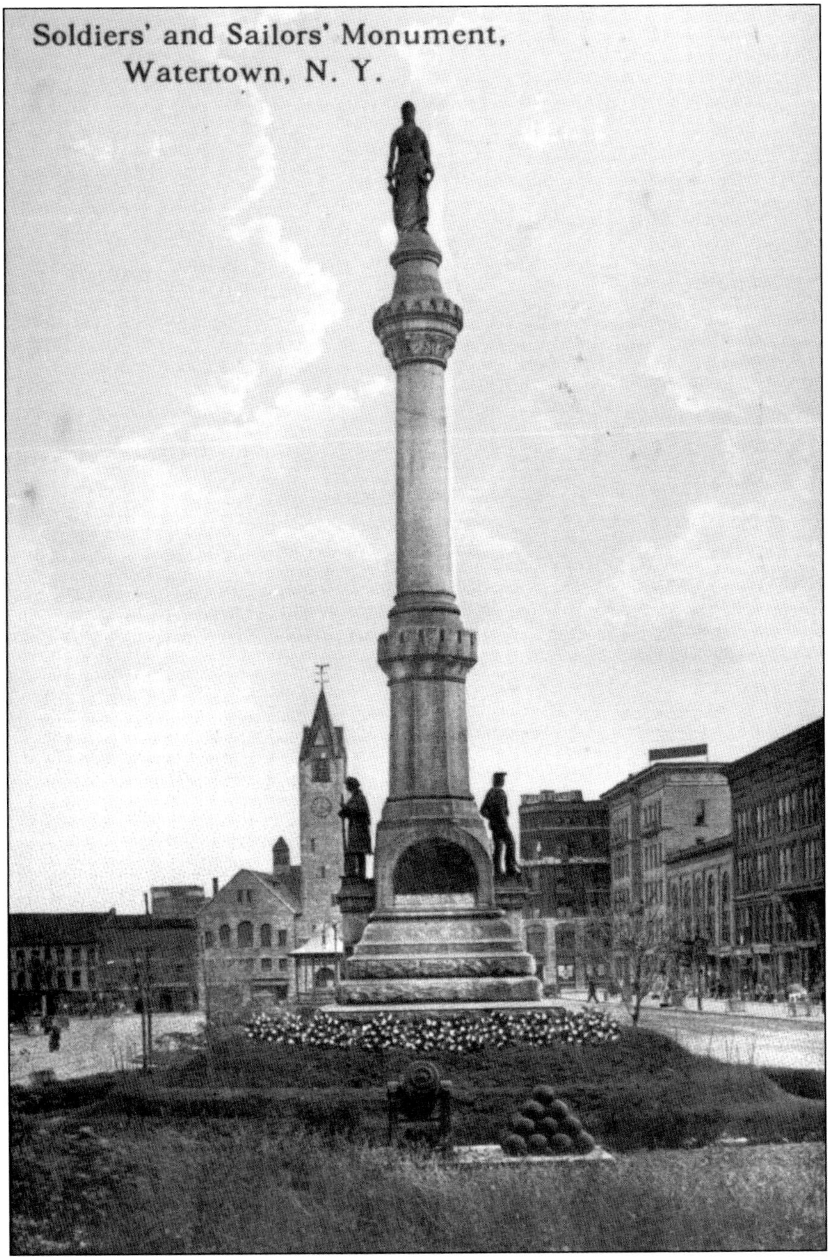

The Soldiers and Sailors Monument in Public Square was dedicated on June 3, 1891, to the men of Jefferson County "who fought and fell in defense of the union and the freedom of men." Mr. and Mrs. George Cook donated the $10,000 monument. It towers 55 feet from a 12-foot square base, which is a solid block of granite. Mounted on the cap is a round shaft, topped with the statue of Victory, a seven-and-a-half-foot-tall figure. The structure is flanked by two figures, a sailor and soldier, both in Civil War period uniforms and standing at parade rest. The night before the unveiling, the monument was covered with a large U.S. flag that was purchased in 1860 by a dozen local men. It floated from a large flagstaff in the square when each of the local regiments left for the war front. Thirty-six feet in length, the flag, which cost $115, was said to be the largest in the state at that time.

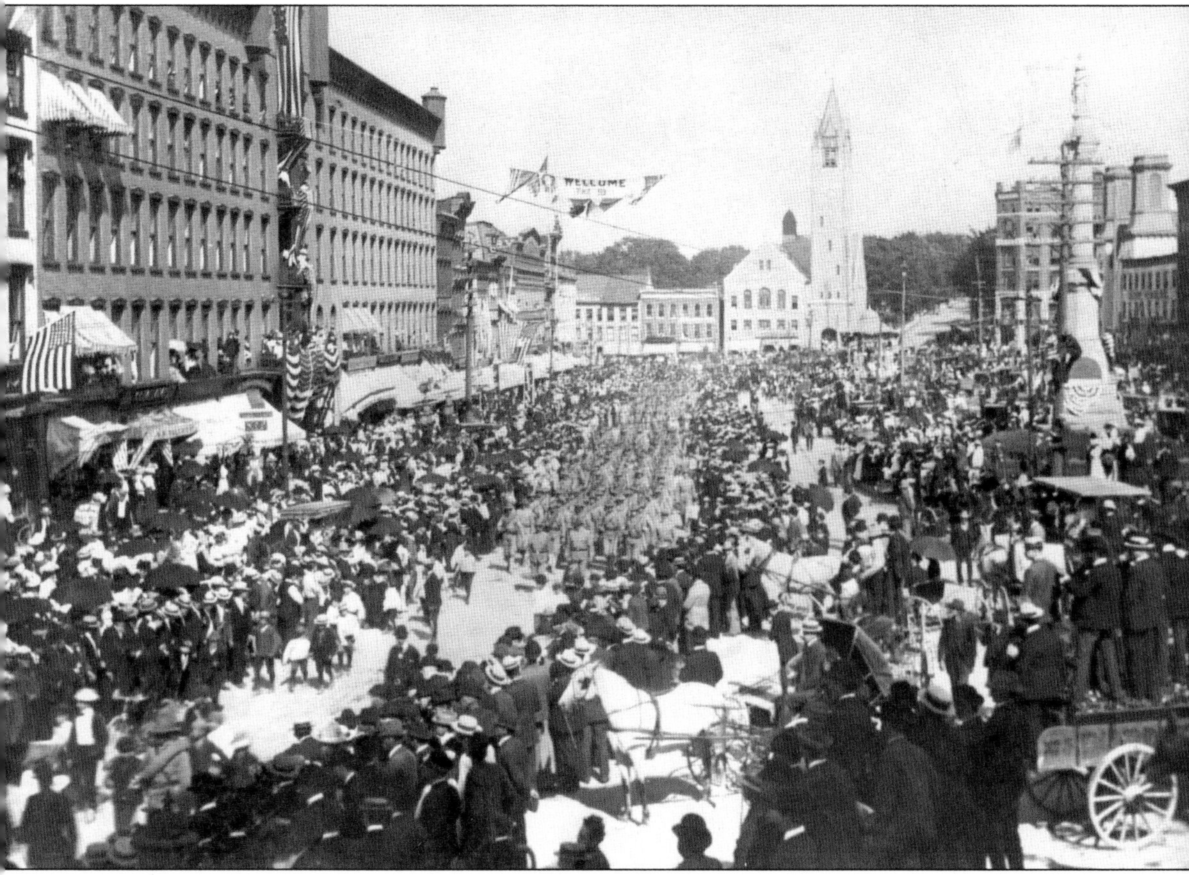

Public Square was the site of many celebrations. Here thousands are welcoming the 9th Infantry. The 9th was stationed at Madison Barracks for 14 years before and after the Spanish-American War. It arrived with three companies and a band in October 1891, and four more companies arrived the next May. It took in many local volunteers, and expansion and building at Madison Barracks reached a peak during its stay. On September 11, 1898, the 9th returned from the Spanish-American War, five months after they had left Madison Barracks for Tampa, Florida. A surrey with "the fringe on top" can be seen left of center.

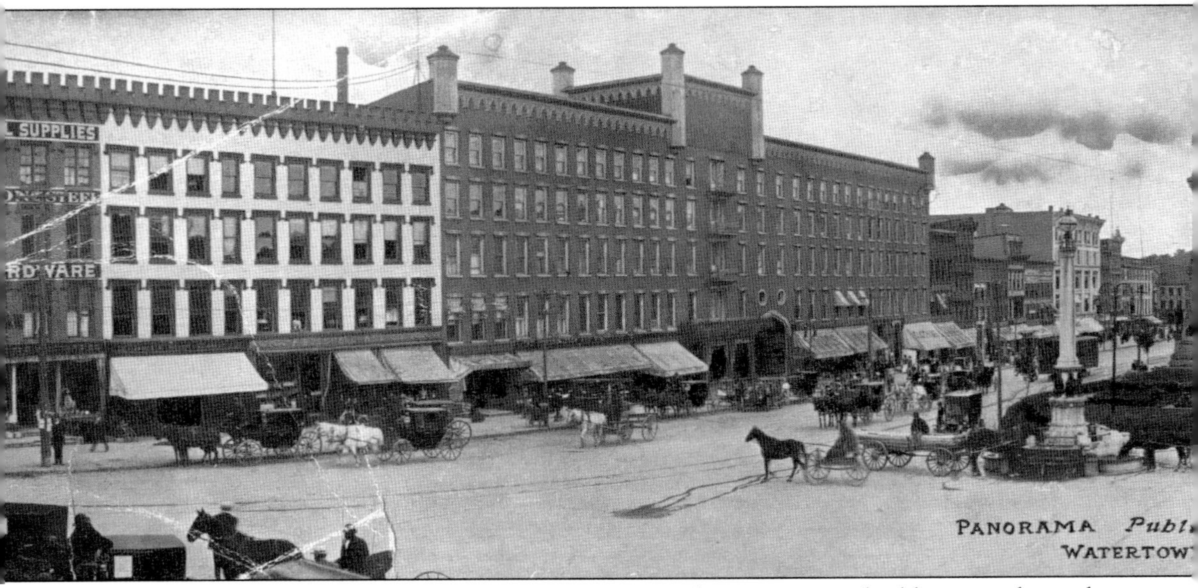

This panoramic view shows the square c. 1910. The prominent building on the right is Washington Hall. Constructed in 1853, it was one of Watertown's best-known structures for many years. On the first floor were stores. The second floor contained offices, and the third floor housed the largest hall in this section of the state, complete with stage and frescoes and

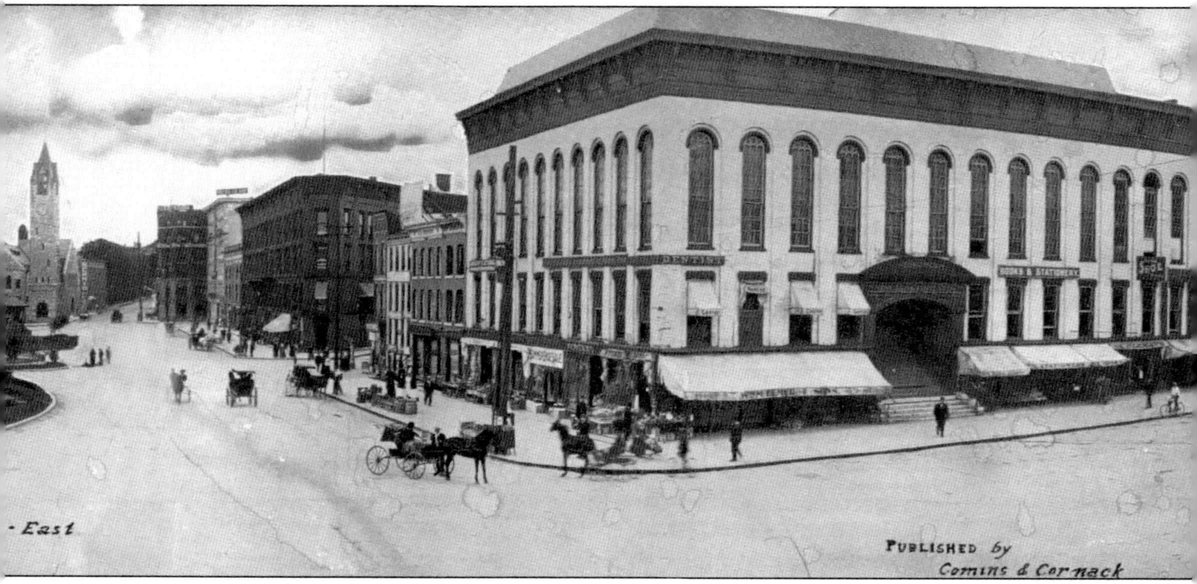

a seating capacity of 1,200. On November 6, 1857, Frederick Douglass delivered a speech here entitled "The Equality of the Races." The Woodruff House is on the left of the square. Pres. Ulysses S. Grant spoke from one of its balconies when he visited Watertown in 1873. There are numerous modes of transportation in this picture.

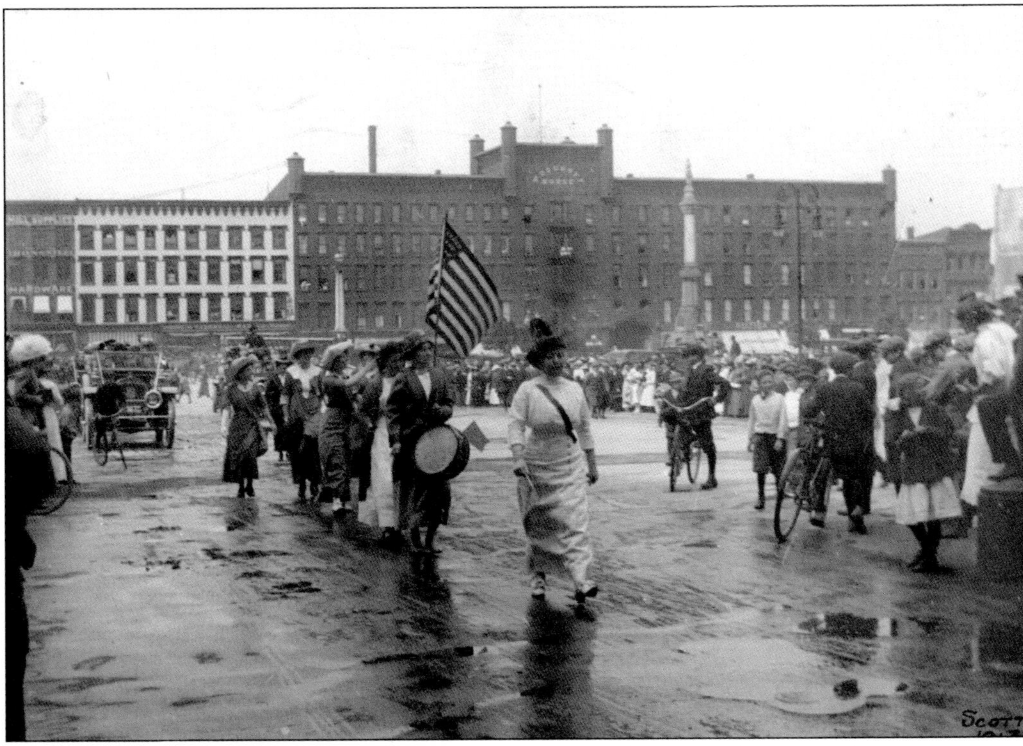

Public Square has been host to many parades during the past 200 years. Watertown's first suffragette parade was held on June 13, 1913. Six Jefferson County women filed a petition for women's suffrage on August 15, 1846.

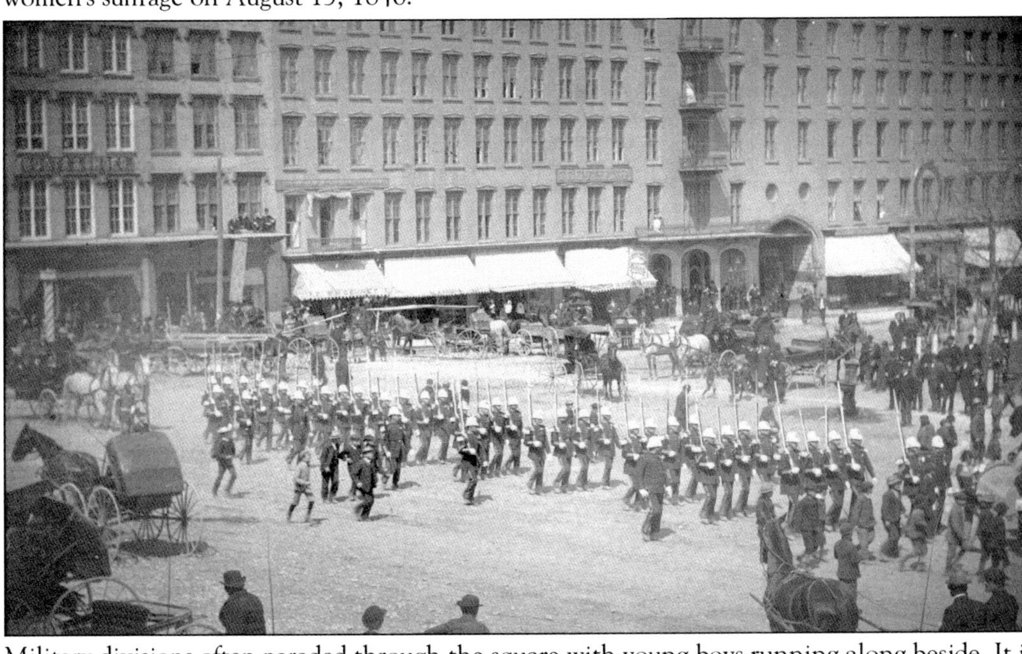

Military divisions often paraded through the square with young boys running along beside. It is believed that this particular photograph is of the 15th Infantry, which was stationed at Madison Barracks between 1899 and 1901. The 15th wore this distinctive head cover.

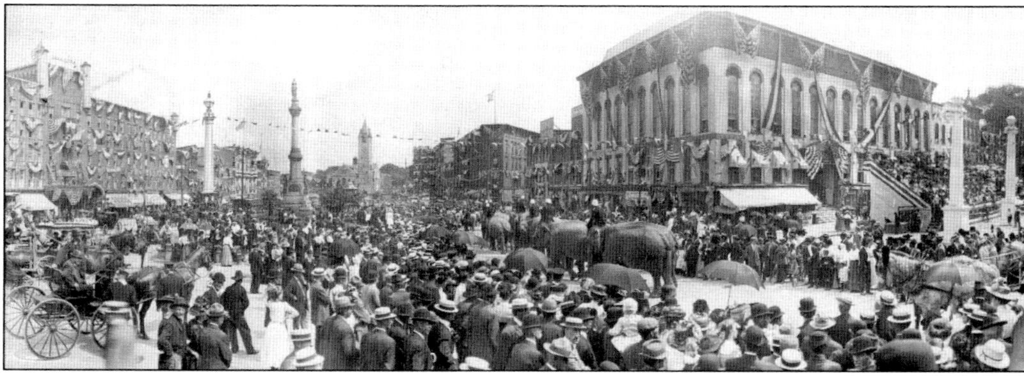

The circus came to town quite often during the early 1900s. Shown here is a firemen's parade with elephants. Circus wagons can be seen heading up toward State Street through the crowds of people.

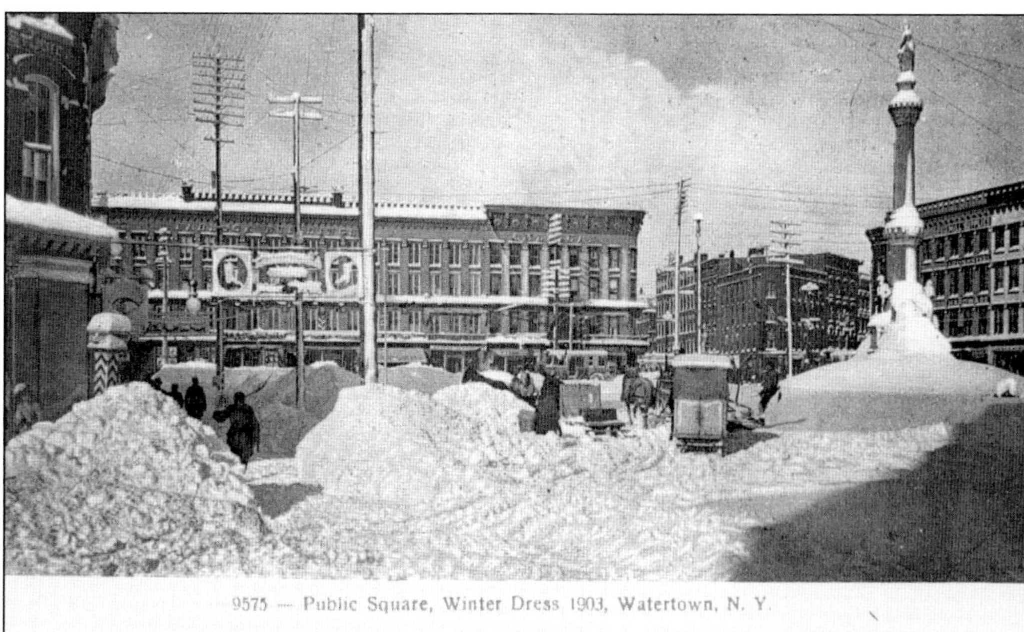

Winter snows made it difficult for horses and wagons to travel around Public Square in this 1903 photograph.

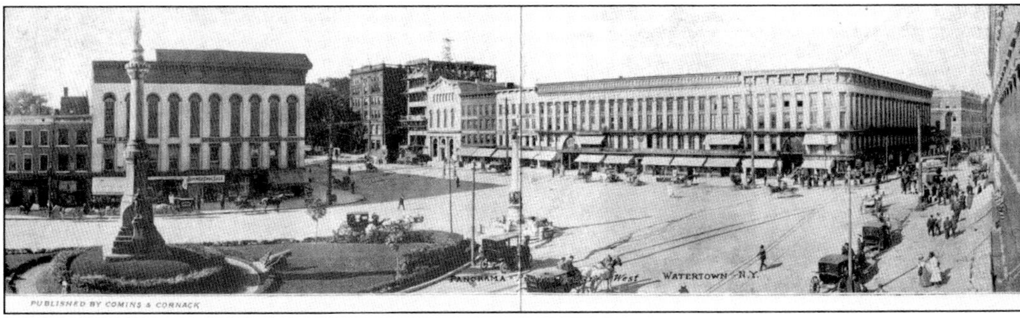

This view shows the Moore's General Store at the American Corner, the Paddock Arcade, Washington Hall, and new construction on the corner of Washington and Stone Streets.

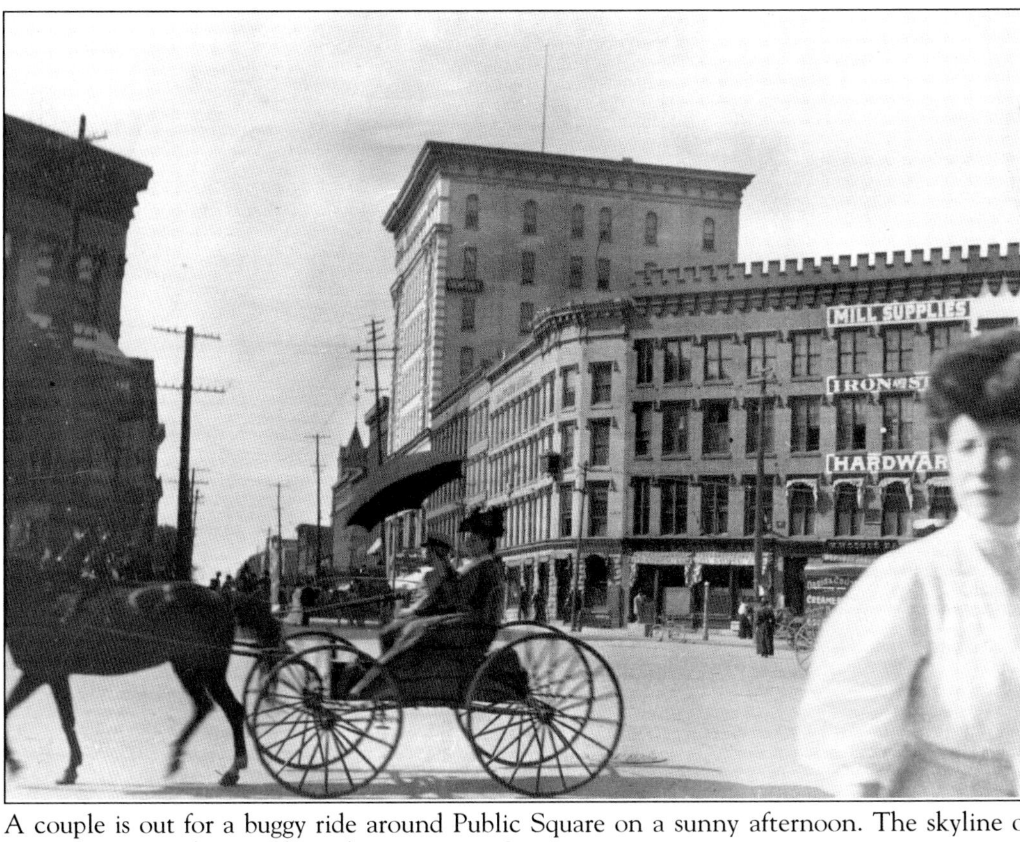

A couple is out for a buggy ride around Public Square on a sunny afternoon. The skyline of Court Street can be seen from the American Corner.

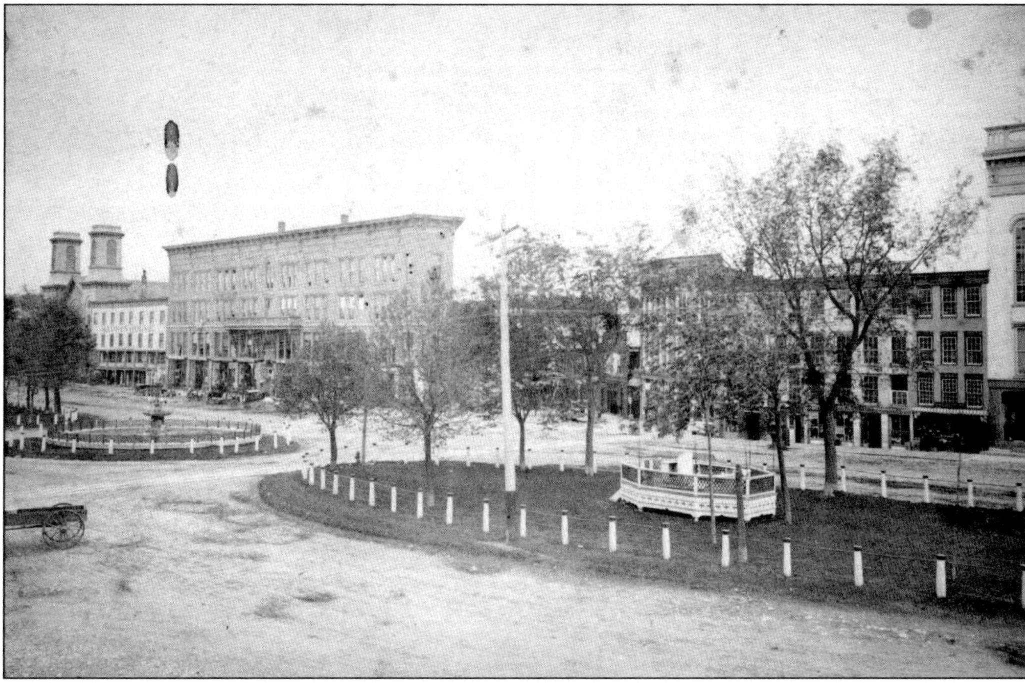

This view of Public Square is looking across from the American Corner. Franklin Street is located behind the trees, and to the far right is Washington Hall. The Harris House can be seen in the left of the picture as well as the two towers from the Universalist church.

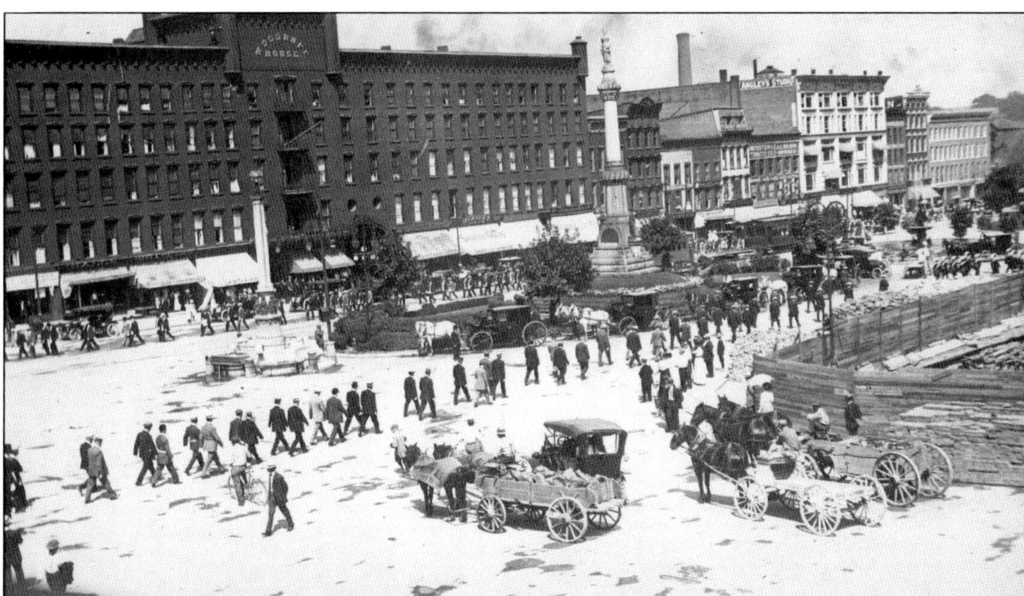

A summer parade by fraternal organizations marches by the Washington Hall demolition site in 1913.

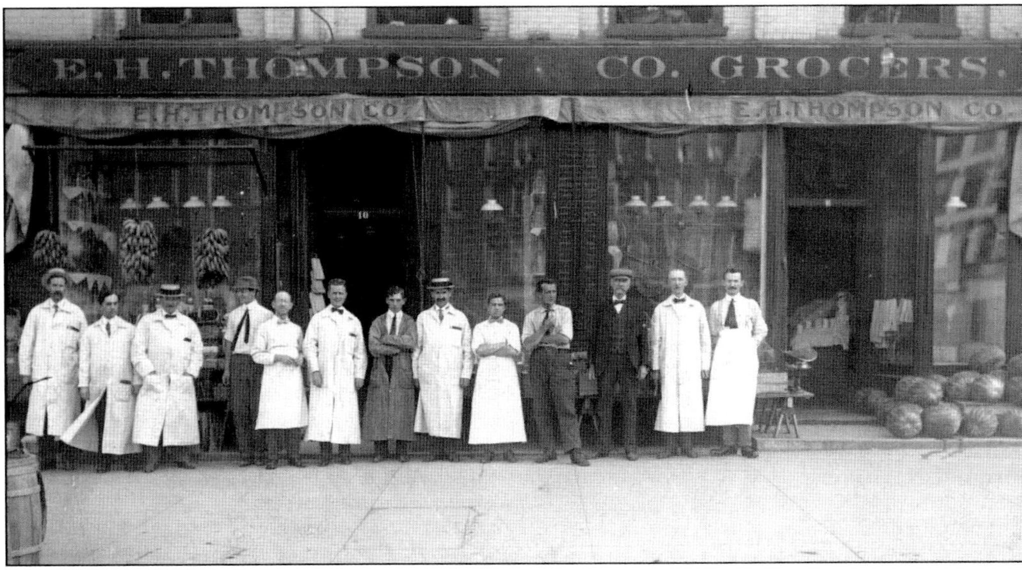

The staff members of E.H. Thompson Company Grocers pose for this *c.* 1905 photograph. At that time, this business was located at 70–71 Public Square. Later, the business moved to the Solar Building on Franklin Street.

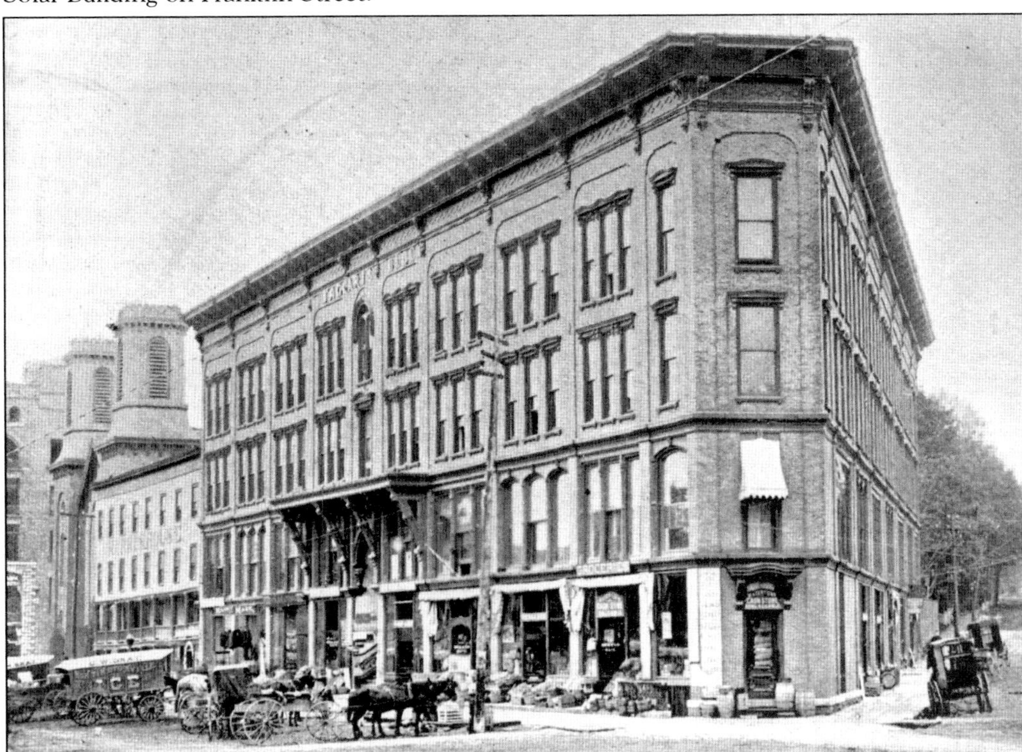

In the left-hand portion of this photograph, the Huntingtonville Ice Company's wagon waits in front of their business in the Commercial Block on Public Square. In 1892, families could purchase ice for $1.25 per month, which entitled them to 10 pounds of ice each day. Saloons paid $2.50 per ton, at one delivery.

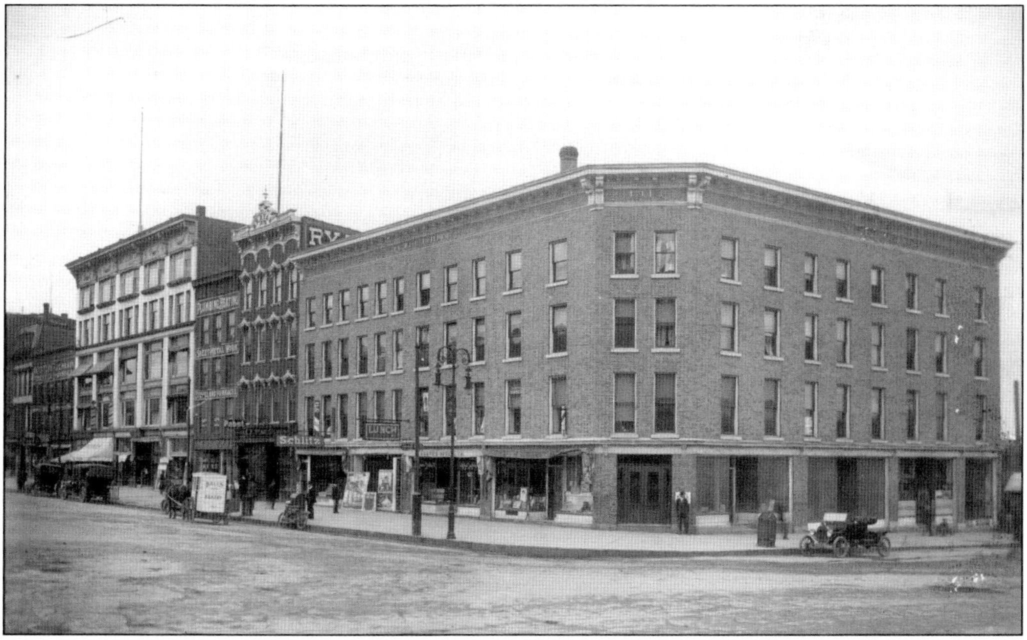

The J.B. Wise Block was constructed in 1913 and replaced the Streeter Block. J.B. Wise was a businessman and mayor of the city of Watertown. Ornate street lamps adorned Public Square at this time. The Victoria Theater operated in this building until 1958, when the building was torn down.

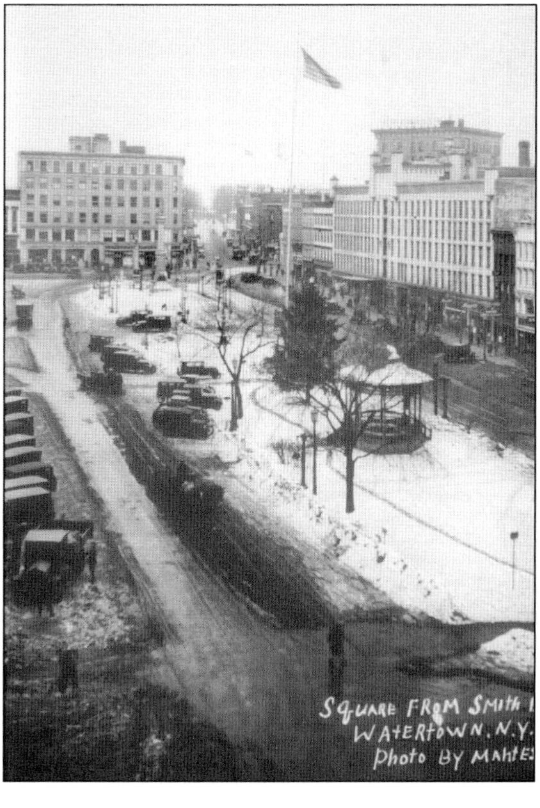

This view of the square was taken from the roof of the Smith Building, later known as the Mohican Building.

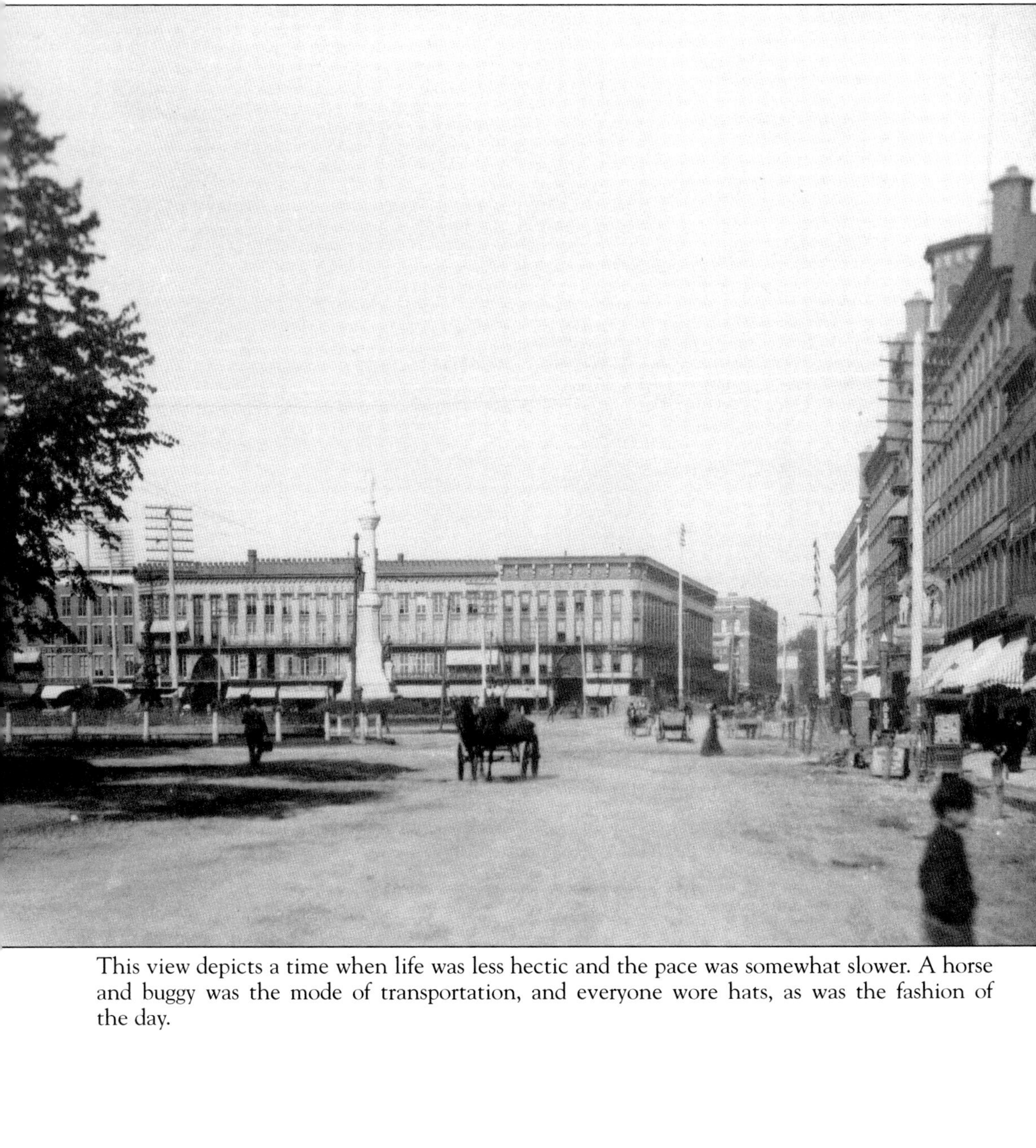

This view depicts a time when life was less hectic and the pace was somewhat slower. A horse and buggy was the mode of transportation, and everyone wore hats, as was the fashion of the day.

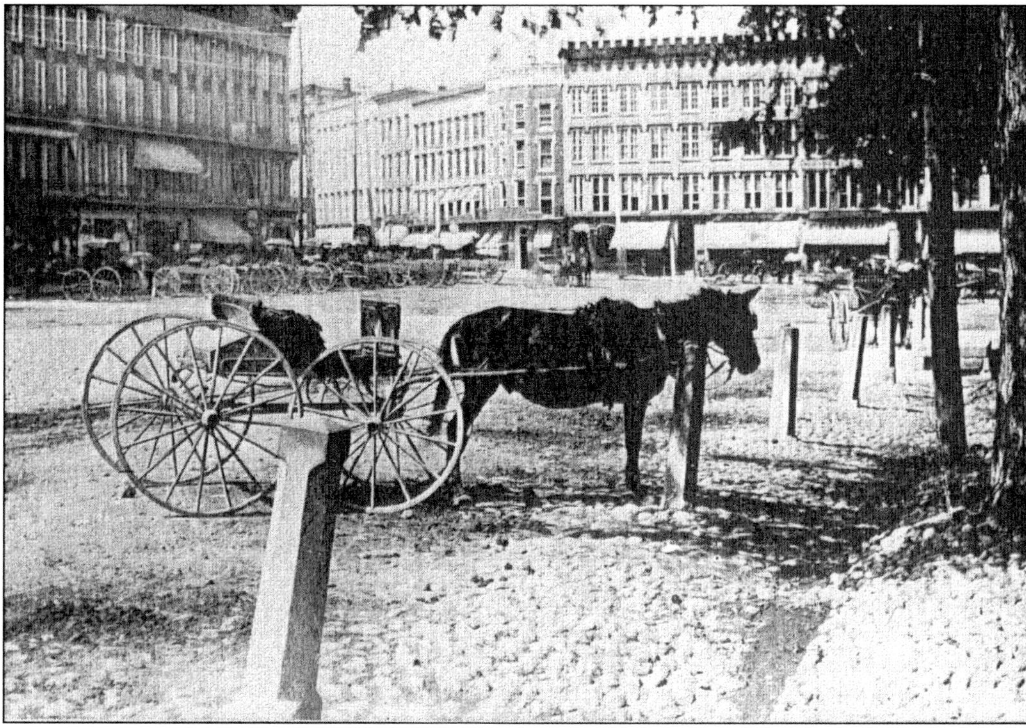

A horse is tied to a hitching post on Public Square in 1890.

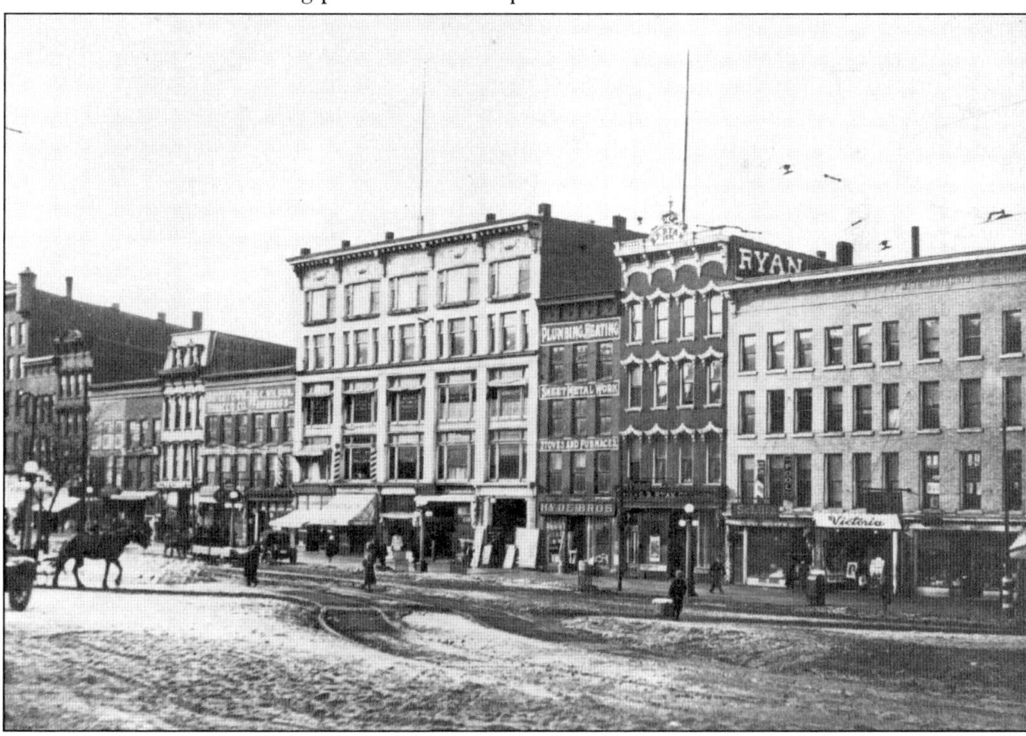

Horses and pedestrians carefully make their way through the snow- and mud-covered roadway on Public Square.

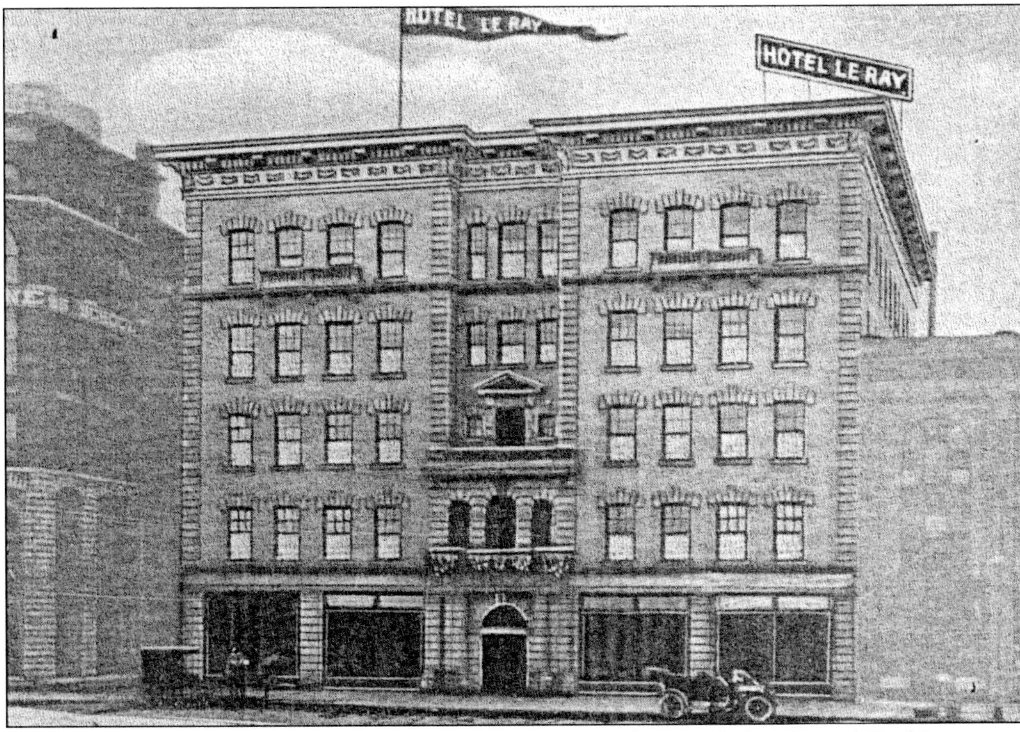

The Hotel LeRay was located on Public Square, next to the Smith (Mohican) Building.

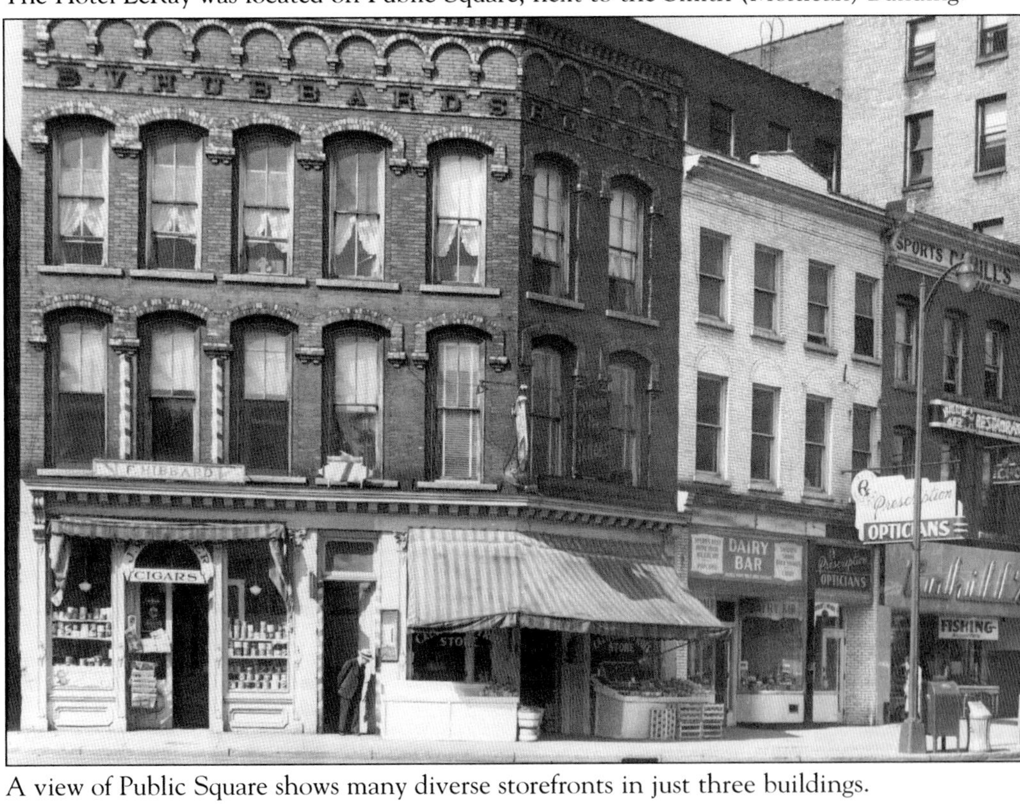

A view of Public Square shows many diverse storefronts in just three buildings.

Two

The Roswell P. Flower Memorial Library

One of the most beautiful buildings in the city is, without a doubt, the Flower Memorial Library. A citizens' movement to raise money to erect a public library was begun on April 8, 1901. At that time, Emma Flower Taylor made an offer to erect a library building and give it to the city as a memorial to her father, former Gov. Roswell P. Flower. Her generous offer was gratefully accepted. Taylor purchased the site on Washington Street and hired Addison F. Lansing, a local architect, to prepare the plans. The contract was let to John Solar, a local contractor. Taylor laid the cornerstone on July 11, 1903.

After the design of the building had been determined, the cornerstone laid, and the foundations begun, Emma Taylor invited Charles R. Lamb of New York to suggest a scheme for the interior. Lamb suggested an enlarged rotunda and the dome elevated to a heroic proportion of a full Roman, classic building. He submitted his plans for the entire treatment of the interior in color, mosaic, stained glass, mural painting, and bronze to Taylor, who accepted them without hesitation. Lamb stated that "he would wish to be responsible for everything one saw from the moment he entered the building throughout the entire interior."

The structure was built in the Grecian style of architecture, having many Roman features adapted to the standards of the time. Its dignity of style was characteristic of the man in whose memory it was built, and whose generosity was never forgotten by the citizens of Watertown.

The beautiful marble edifice, with its historical mural paintings, was completed and dedicated on November 10, 1904.

The following photographs cannot do justice to the original beauty of the building. The rotunda, with its combination of marble, gold, and bronze, stands as the central and most attractive feature of this magnificent building. The reading rooms are large and inviting and boast incredible artwork as well as exquisite architectural detail. The friezes on the mezzanine level tell a pictorial history of Watertown and Jefferson County. In fact, the Flower Memorial Library is unique, in that every historical embellishment is a record of something of importance to Jefferson County.

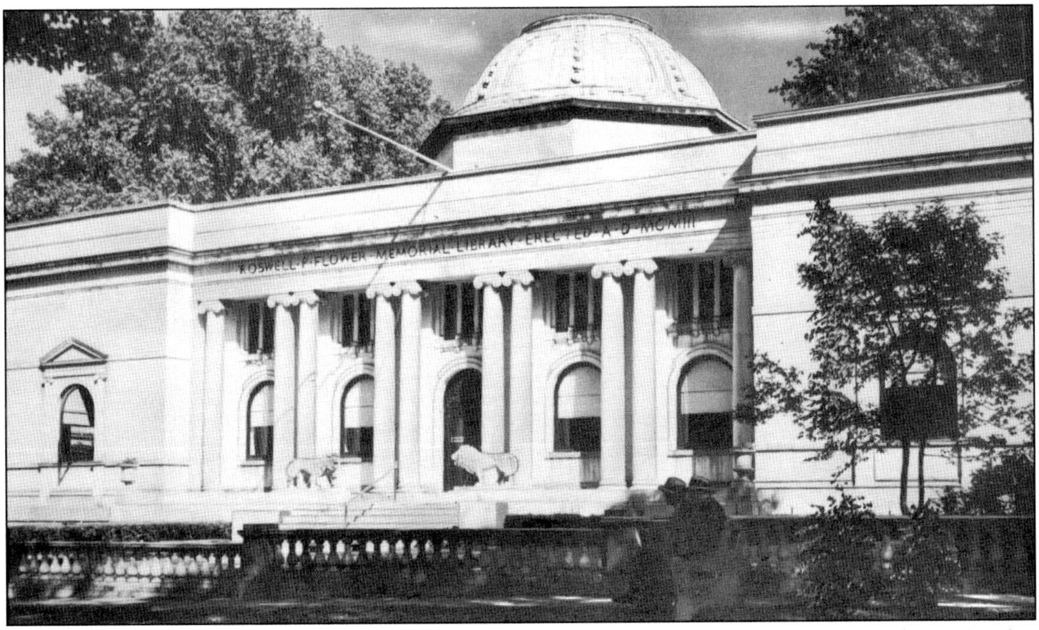

The Roswell P. Flower Memorial Library is located on Washington Street. Emma Flower Taylor had the following dedicatory bronzed inscription placed in the library: "I make this gift in loving memory of my father, to perpetuate his name and love of progress and to benefit those who delight in knowledge."

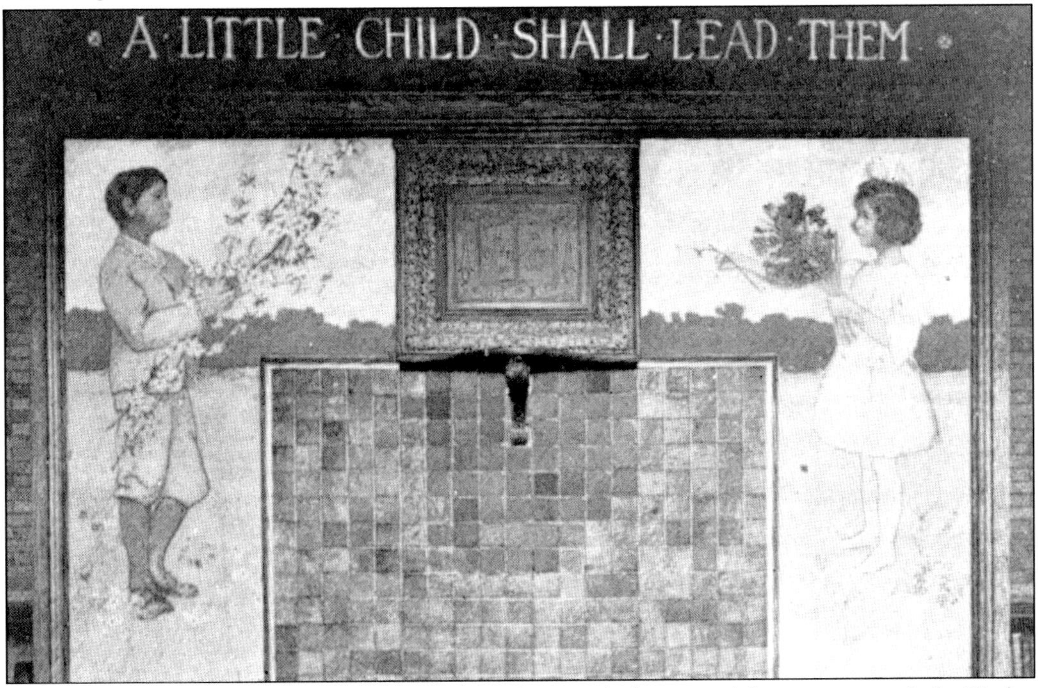

The children's room was set apart for the special use and pleasure of the young people by Taylor in memory of her eldest son, who died in infancy. His name and the dates of his life are recorded on the bronze tablet over the fireplace. On either side are the portraits of his younger brother and sister bearing spring flowers as a tribute to his memory.

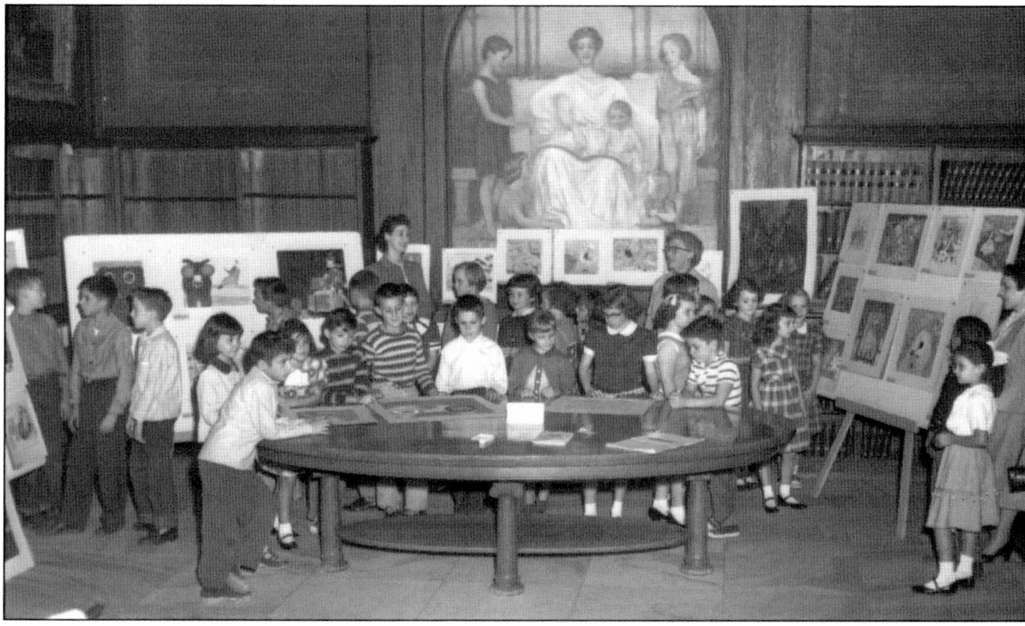

The 1955 fourth-grade class at Arsenal Street School views an exhibit of paintings in the North Reading Room loaned to the library by the Smithsonian Institution. Behind them on the wall is the painting entitled "Open Book," by Ella Condie Lamb, which shows a seated figure of a mother surrounded by her children.

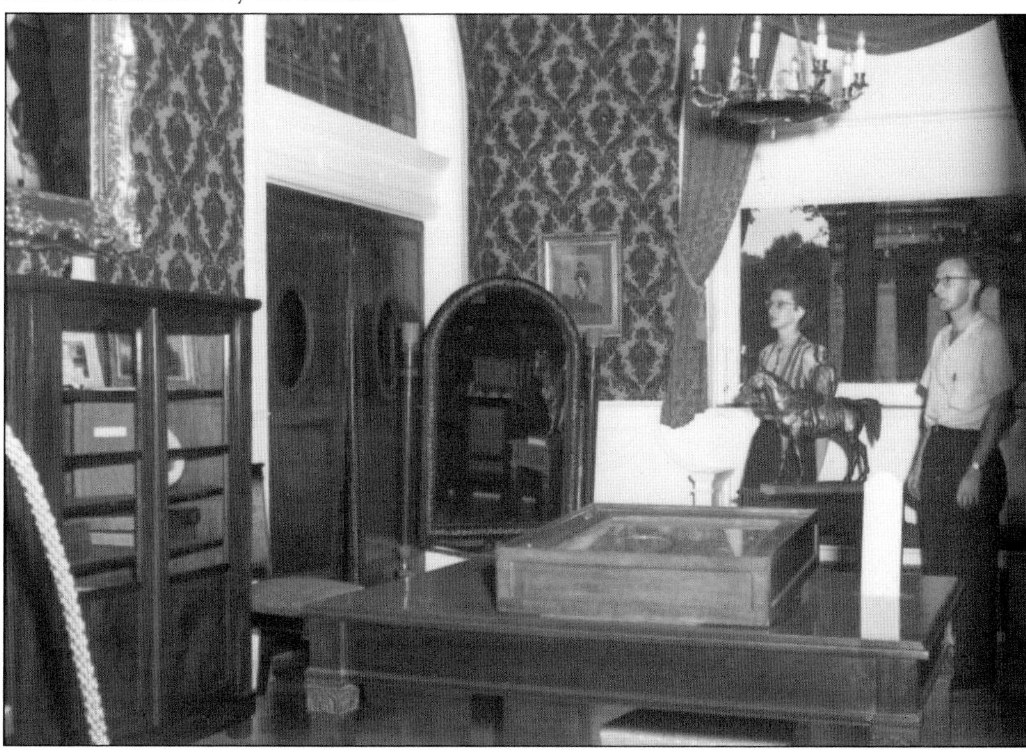

Visitors view a portrait of Napoleon Bonaparte in one of the library's conversation rooms. Reflected in the mirror at the center is a writing desk once owned by Madame Deferiet.

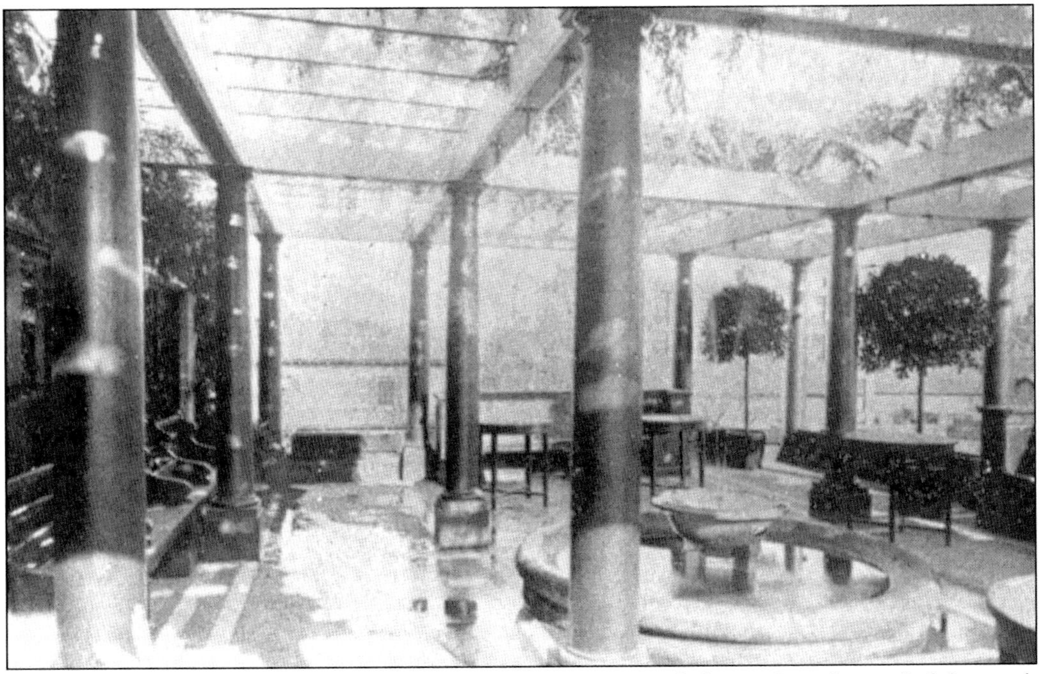

When the library was originally constructed, there was a pergola located on the roof of the stack room. There was a pleasant summer garden, shaded by a pergola and fitted with fountains, vines and bay trees, supporting columns and tables and chairs.

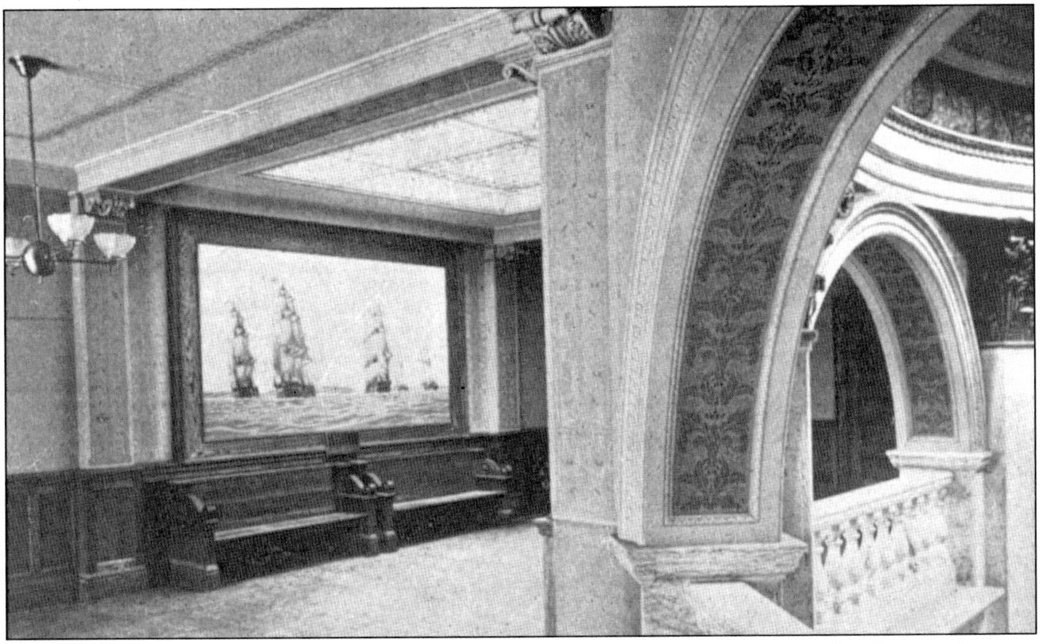

The mezzanine floor contains magnificent artwork that tells the history of Jefferson County. The French and Indian influence, the Battles of Lake Erie and Sackets Harbor, and the first public commemoration of the Declaration of Independence in Jefferson County (which was held at Independence Point on July 4, 1802) are depicted in murals and friezes throughout the second-floor rooms.

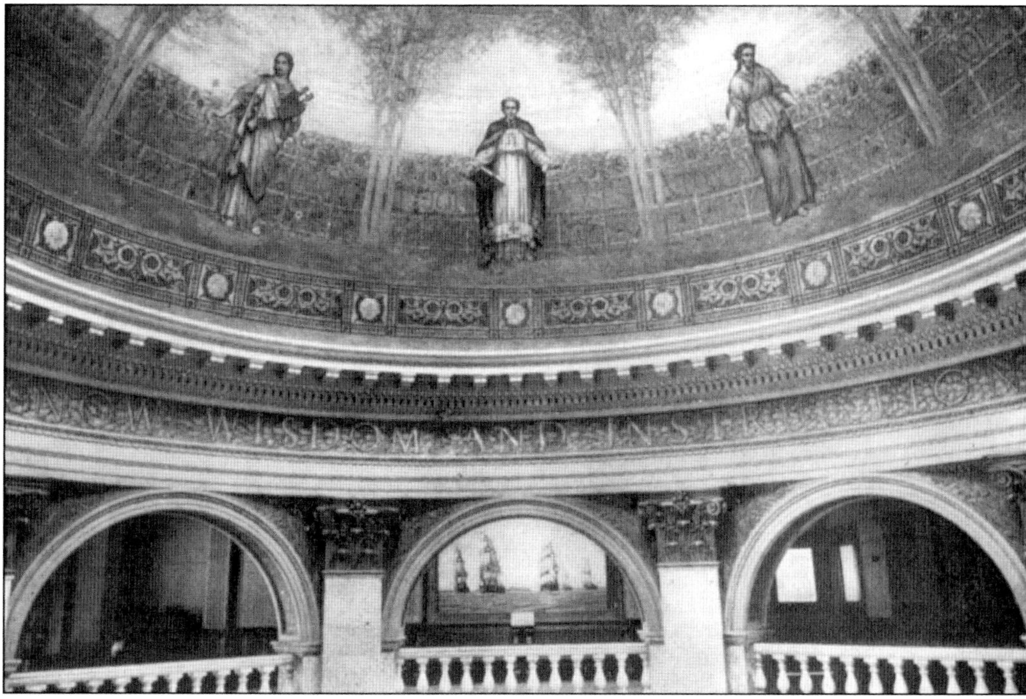

The eight figures in the dome of the rotunda personify History and Romance, Religion and Science and are separated by intermediate figures of Fable and the Drama, Lyric and Epic Poetry.

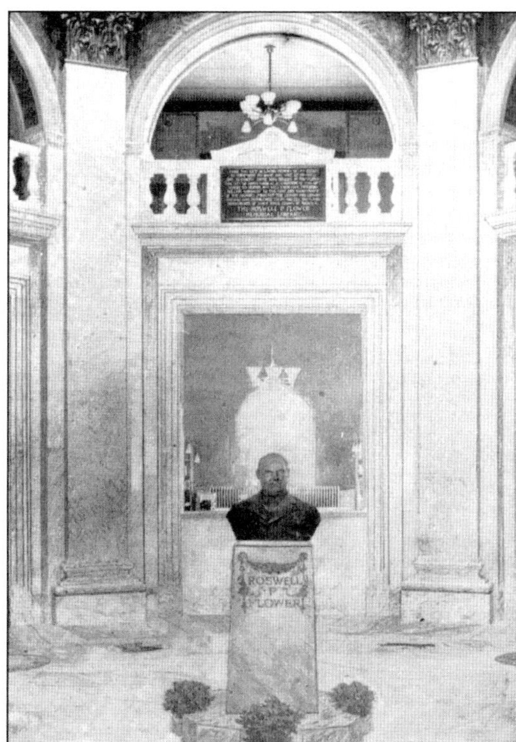

The rotunda houses the portrait bust of former Governor Flower. The sculptor was J. Scott Hartley.

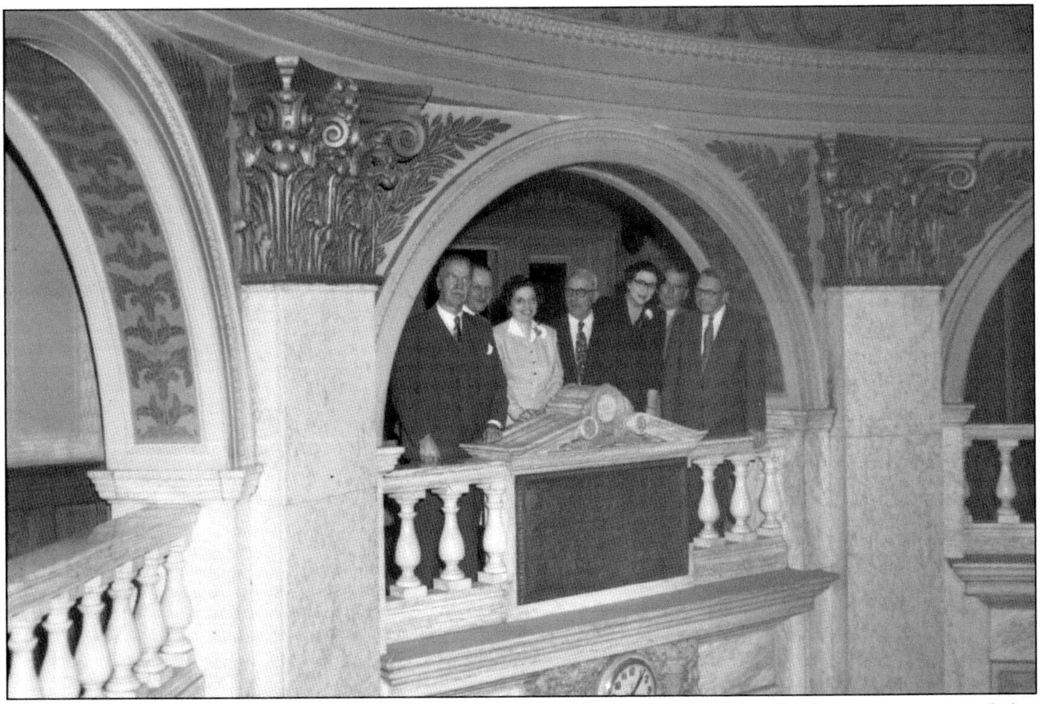

Members of the 1954 city council visited the library to celebrate the 50th anniversary of the facility. Seen here, from left to right, are Councilman William T. Field; Councilman Charles W. Hayes; Helen M. Talbert, senior librarian; Mayor John H. Newman; Mrs. Horace S. Gulick, president of the library's board; Councilman William J. Flynn; and City Manager C. Leland Wood.

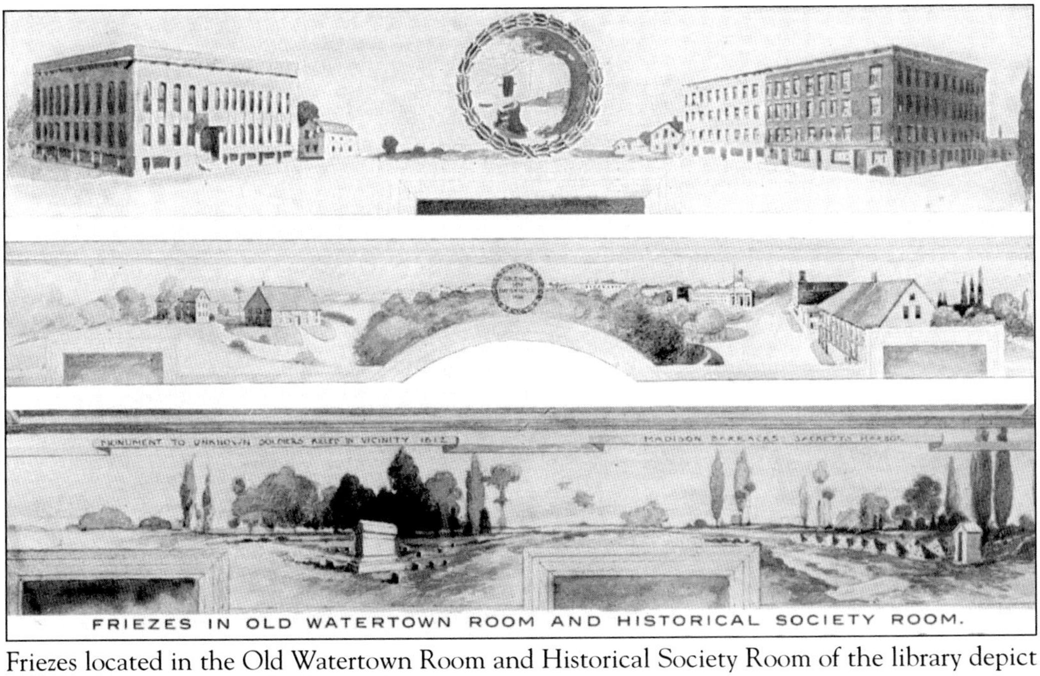

Friezes located in the Old Watertown Room and Historical Society Room of the library depict early historical scenes of Jefferson County.

Three

Thompson Park

In November 1900, the New York City *Sun* carried a story about Watertown's magnificent public park and the fact that no one knew who the benefactor was. For many months, there was speculation that it had to be either the Flower or Schley family. The only thing the citizens were certain of was that Henry Goodale was acting on behalf of an unknown donor and was purchasing about 700 acres of land around the entire pinnacle tract for park purposes. The hill was well covered with sturdy trees and seemed almost an ideal location for Watertown's park. Goodale had also announced that the Olmsted Firm, the distinguished landscape architects, had been secured to transform the large tract from a piece of wooded, hilly farmland into a park worthy of one of the largest cities. The article lists all the gifts that the Flower family had given to the community and questioned whether or not the statue of Governor Flower, which was being commissioned at the same time, should be placed in the park as a fitting tribute to him. Little did anyone know that the Flower family was not the benefactor. The gift of the park was officially given to the city on December 12, 1916, as a Christmas present. Still the citizens did not know until 1921, when a deed was transferred, that the donor was John C. Thompson, one of the organizers of the New York Airbrake Company. Thompson divided his time between New York City and Watertown and was a great supporter for Watertown. In a document found among his papers after his death, Thompson explained the reason he decided on a park donation. He felt that it would be helpful to the children by giving them a place for amusement and play, to the poorer people to give them a source of pleasure and delight, and to the well-to-do to enjoy the drives and the beauty of the foliage and scenery. He wrote, "The future alone can determine whether I have done wisely or otherwise, but at least it may be said 'he did what he could.'"

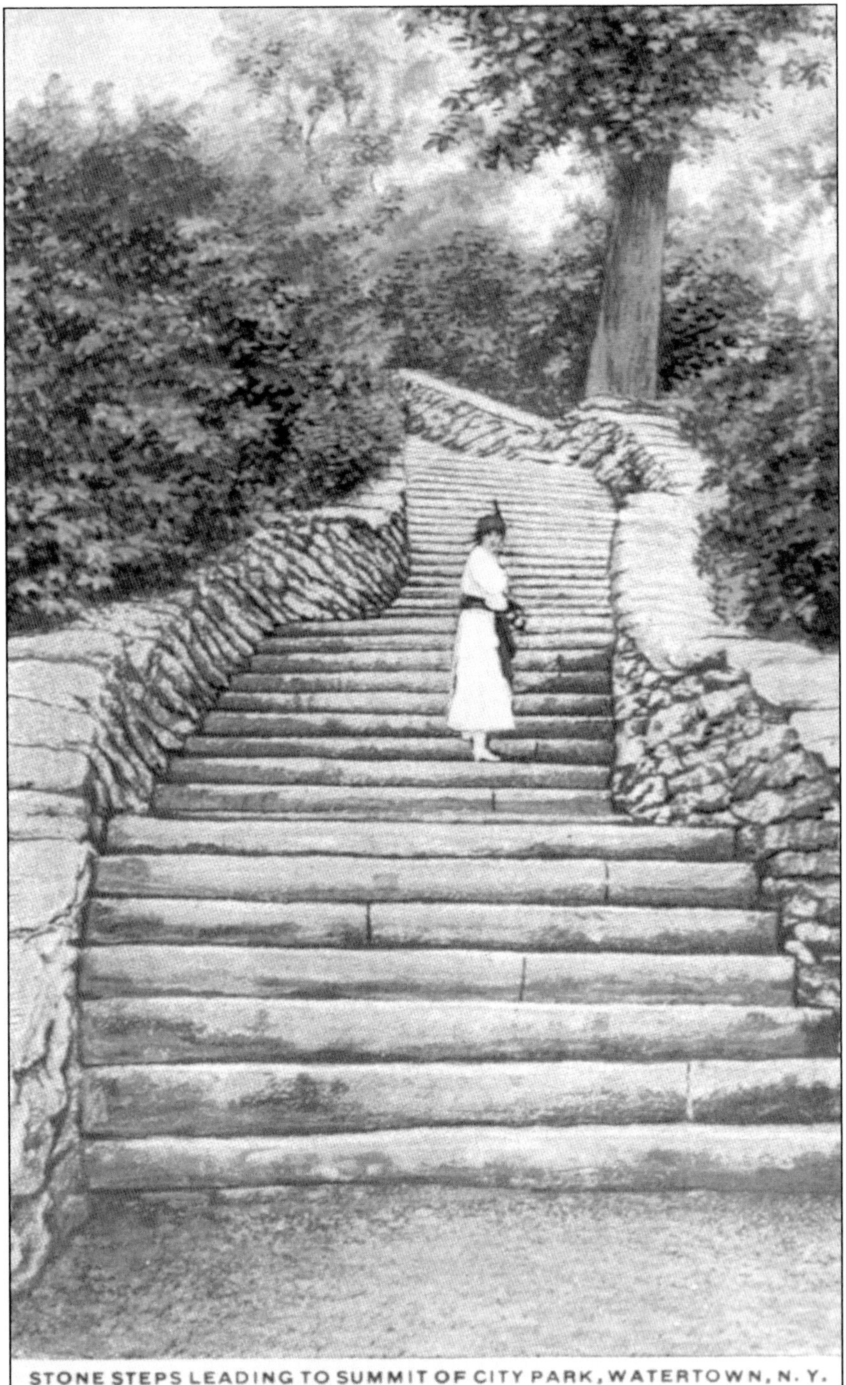

STONE STEPS LEADING TO SUMMIT OF CITY PARK, WATERTOWN, N. Y.

Stone for the steps throughout the park was gathered from the three quarries in the park. Fieldstone was collected throughout the park for the other stonework, which was done around 1902. Outside stonework that lines the southern rim of the park was done in the 1930s through a city work program. The WPA funded construction of the large stone wall that can be viewed when entering the park from the Park Circle.

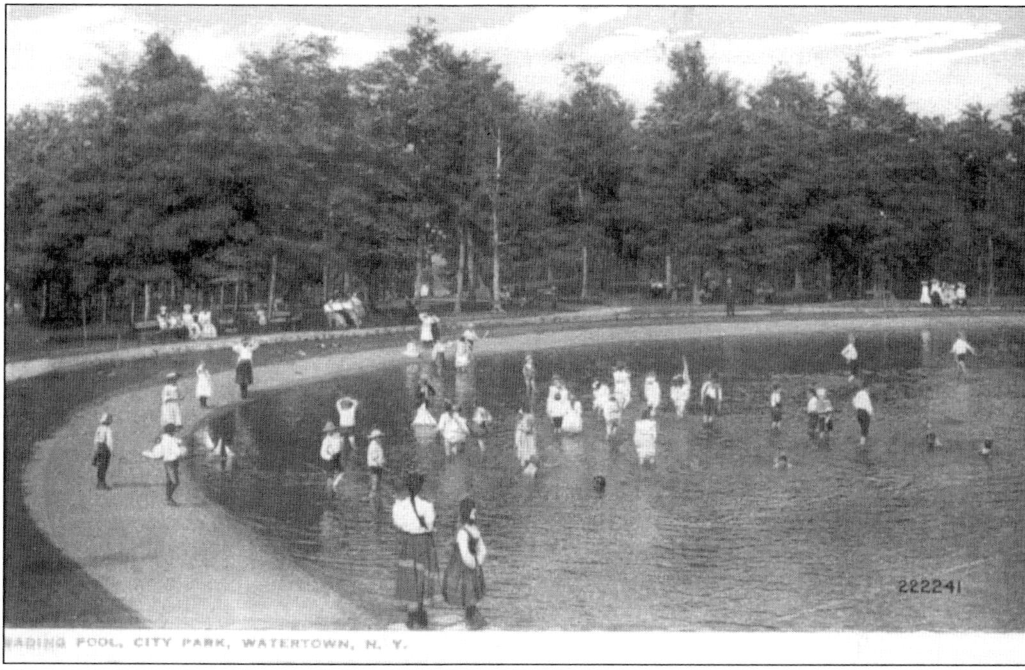

The wading pool at Thompson Park was always a busy place during the hot days of summer.

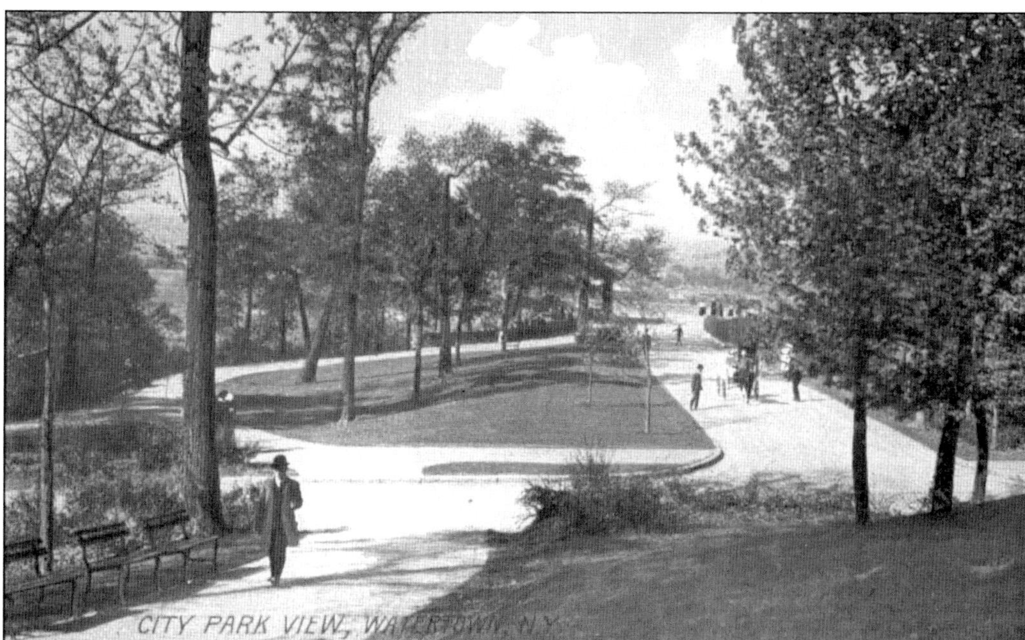

In the years before Thompson's death, the park was known as City Park. In September 1924, city council adopted a resolution naming it Thompson Park in honor of its benefactor.

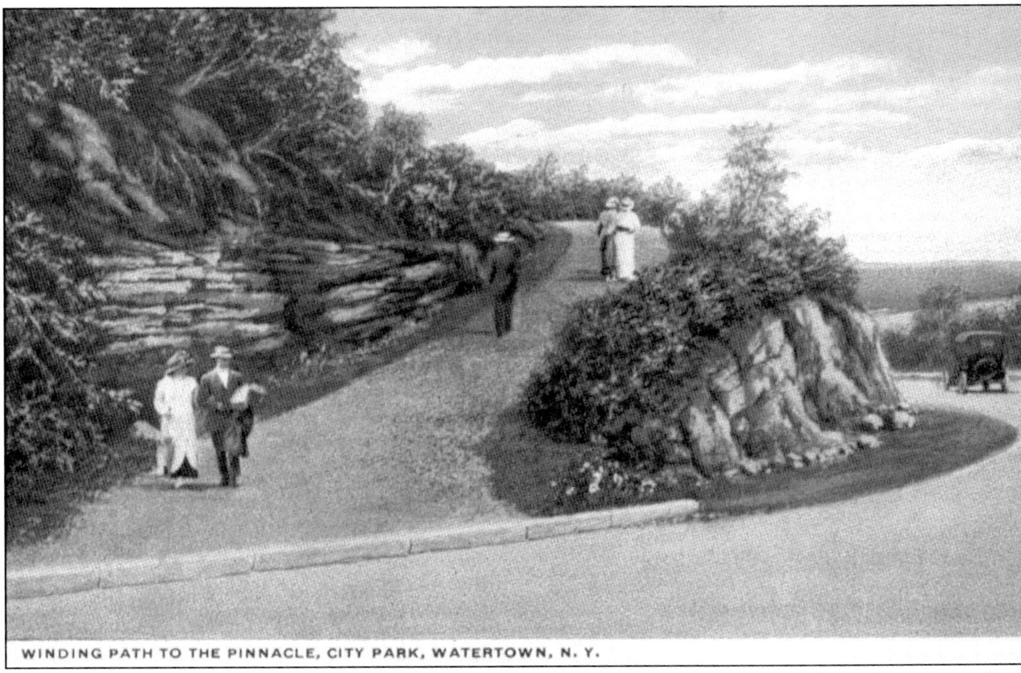

Couples enjoy a Sunday stroll along the paths leading to the pinnacle. Today, Thompson Park still maintains the beautiful outlooks, the stonework, and the walking paths that were in the original landscape design.

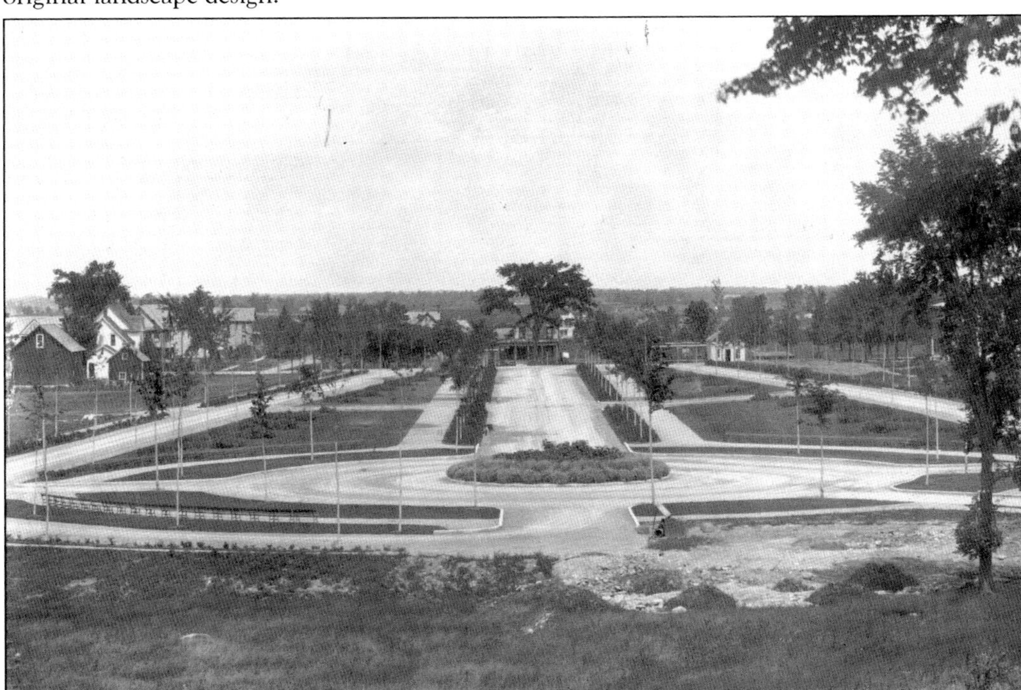

This photograph was taken on August 23, 1902, while the park was still under construction. Looking toward State Street, it shows the Park Circle. The plantings were based on the landscape architect's plans.

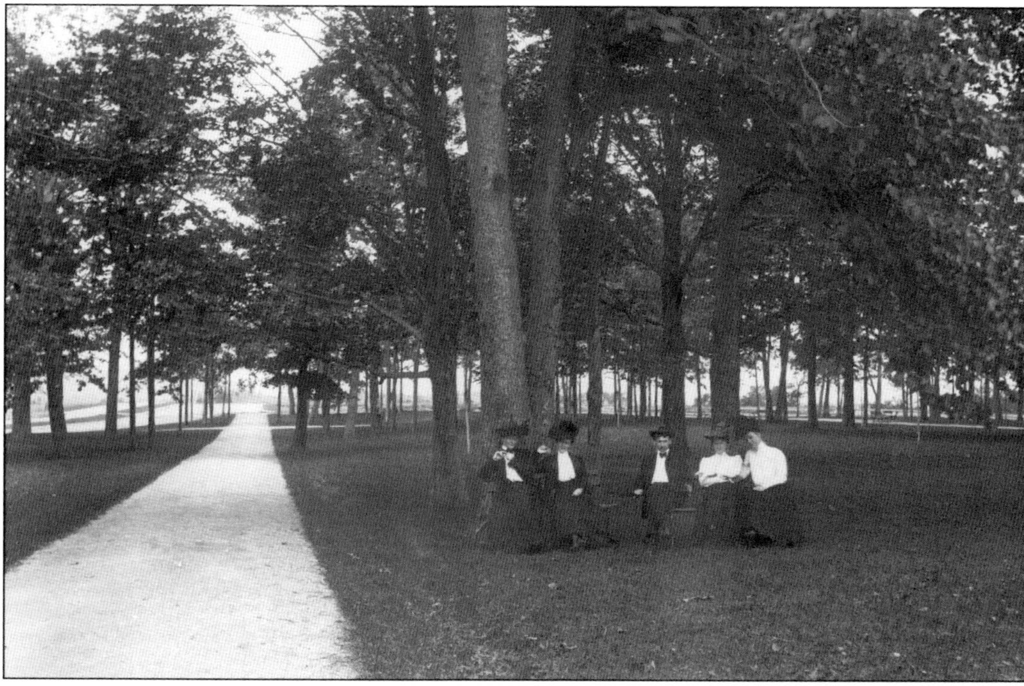

Visitors in the early 1900s always dressed up for their day in the park. The Olmsted family designed several parks across the nation, the most notable being Central Park in New York City.

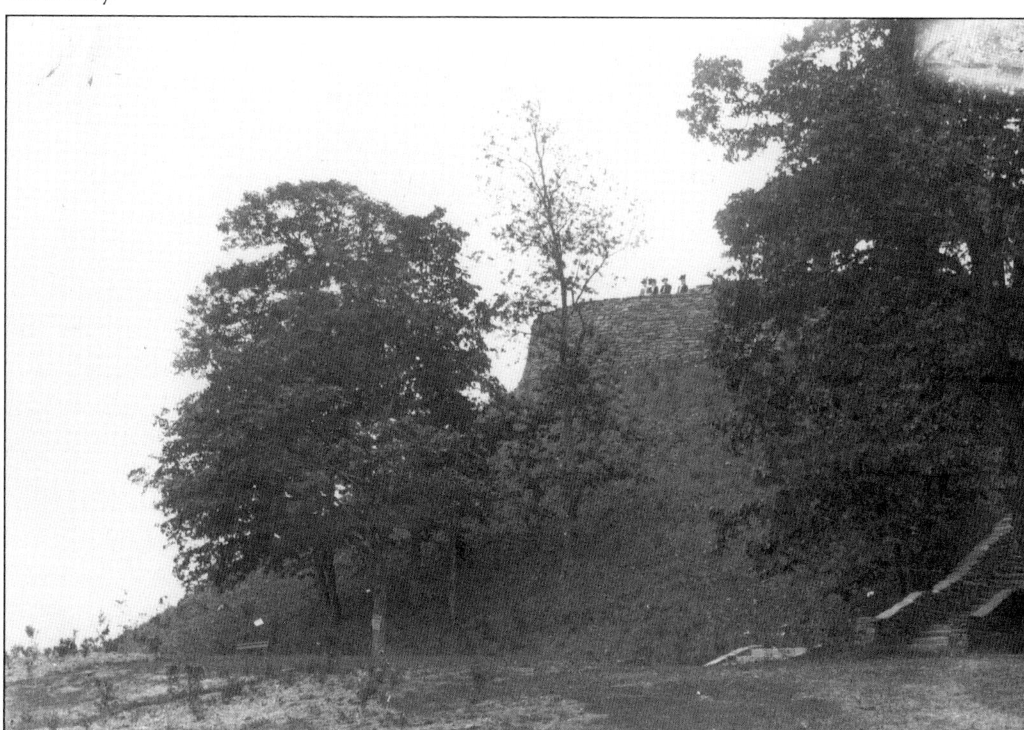

The view from the lookout was breathtaking even while the park was still under construction.

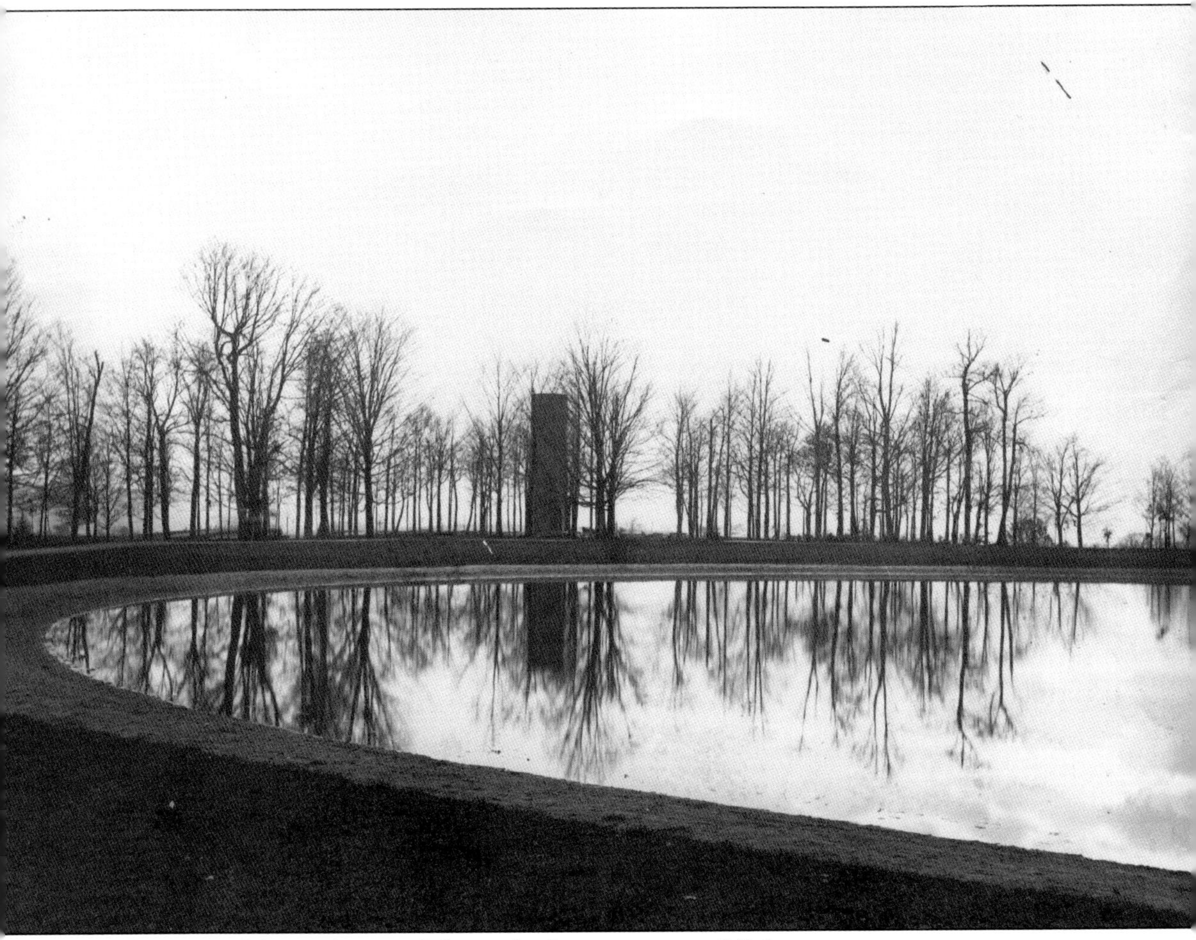

This view of the wading pool shows the bare trees on a fall day.

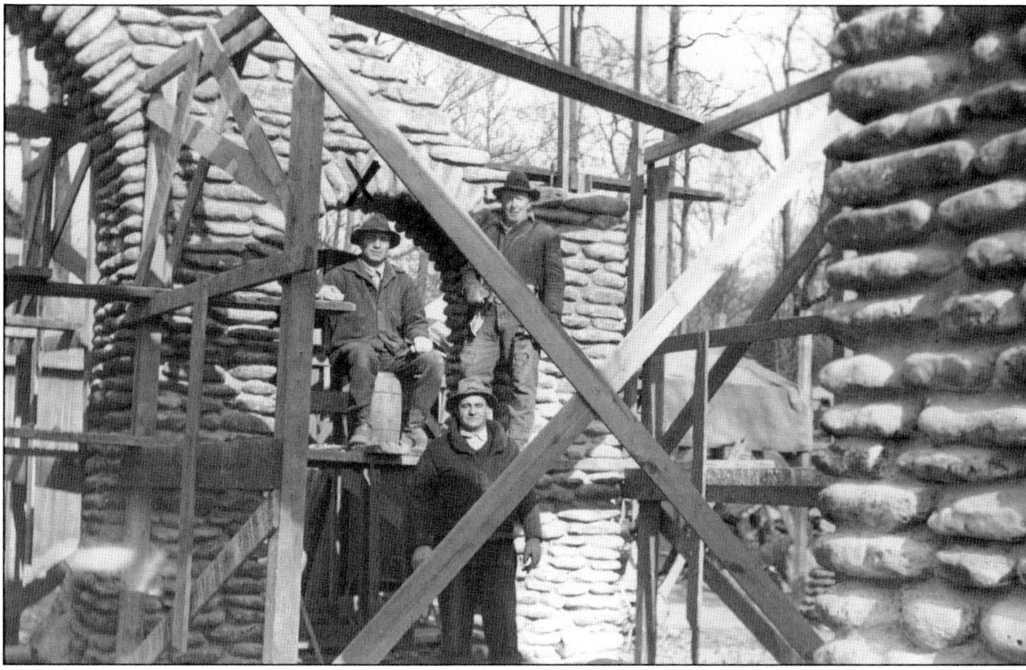

Crews are shown constructing the stonework for the pavilion.

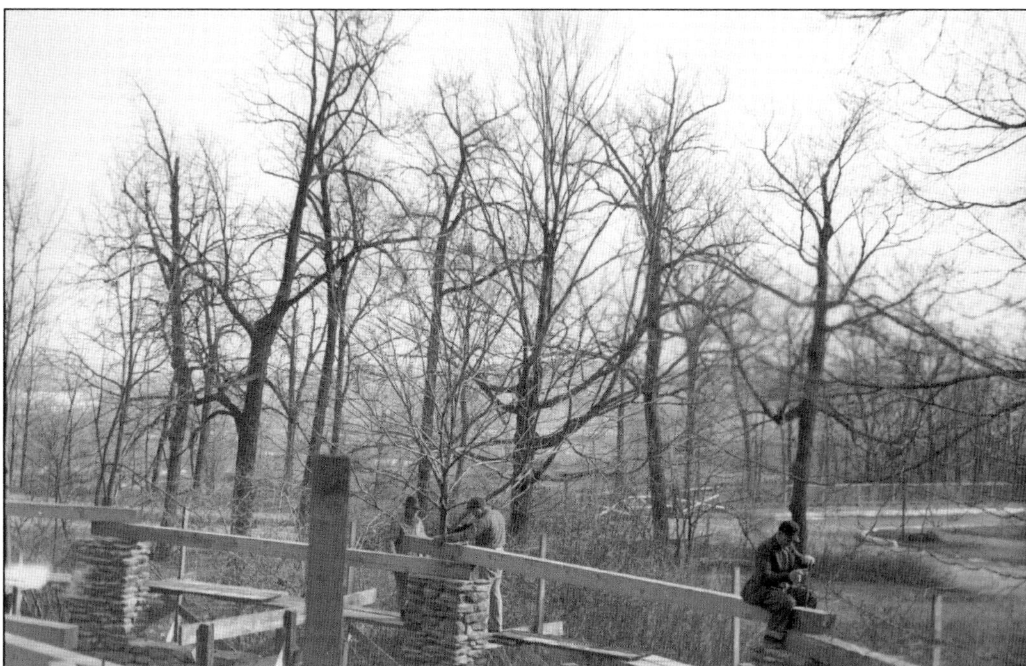

Stonework can be seen throughout the park.

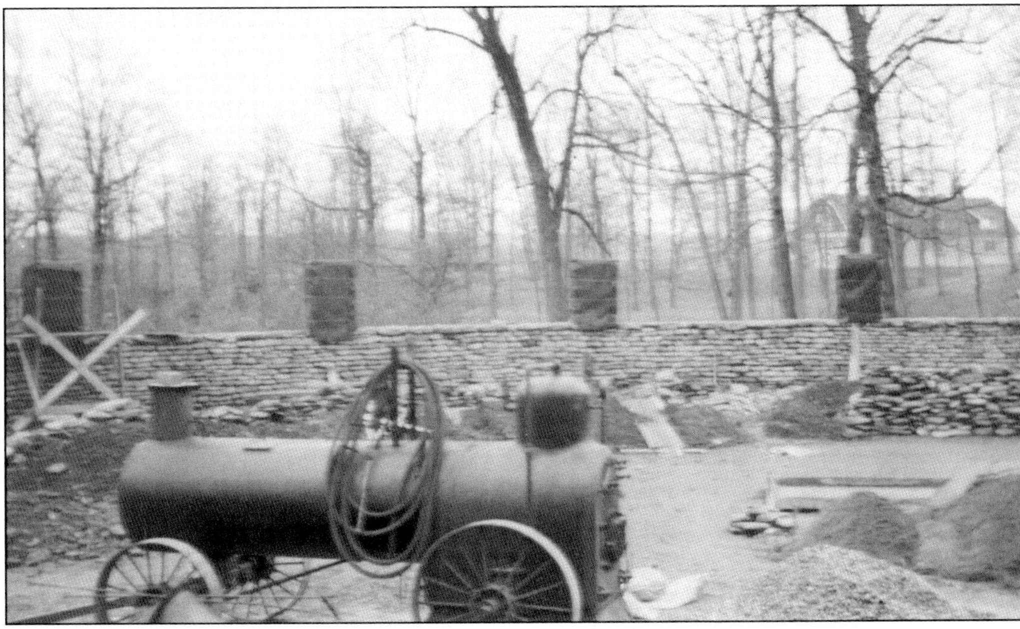

The rounded walls in the pavilion are beginning to take shape.

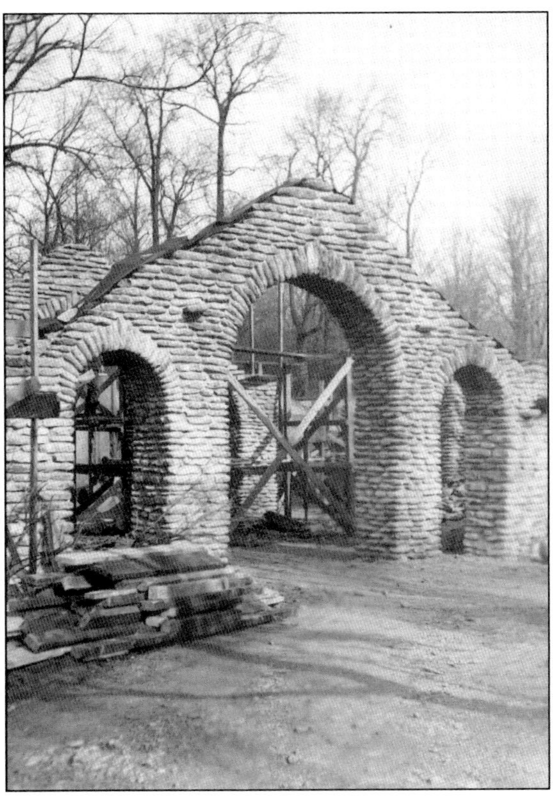

Stonemasons used designs from the landscape architect to build the stone arches for the pavilion.

Four

TROLLEYS

On May 19, 1891, the *Watertown Times* had the following announcement in the paper: "The street railway company will carry passengers and collect fares for the first time tomorrow. The cars will be open from 7 a.m. until 10 p.m., carrying passengers as far as the Watertown Steam Engine works on Main Street and as far as the line extends on State Street. The cars will start early enough tomorrow morning so the Steam Engine Works can be reached by 7 o'clock from any point on the line west of High Street and will pass a certain point every ten minutes. The fare for one continuous trip is five cents. Persons riding from Factory Square, the high school or Public Square to the Steam Engine Works must not expect to be returned unless they drop another nickel into the conductor's hand."

Further information indicates that the trolleys ran at 15-minute intervals, not 10. On the first day, they carried a considerable number of passengers in what were described as handsome cars, being the best-equipped and most expensive cars built.

Gradually the line was extended to Dexter in July 1899. During that summer, one of the regular service streetcars towed a new open-air trailer with a brightly colored awning, a device later to become popular as a summer trolley. During this same period, the line was extended up State Street to just past the Thompson Park entrance.

During the winter of 1899, schedules were held up because of the unusually high snowdrifts along the route. Some of the drifts were said to be higher than the streetcars.

The last streetcar rolled into the West Main Street carbarn at 12:35 on August 17, 1937. The streetcars, while putting up a good fight, could not compete against cars and buses as modes of transportation. For 46 years, the trolleys had carried hundreds of thousands of passengers. However, the Black River Traction Company had begun a gradual elimination of streetcars years before the final shutdown.

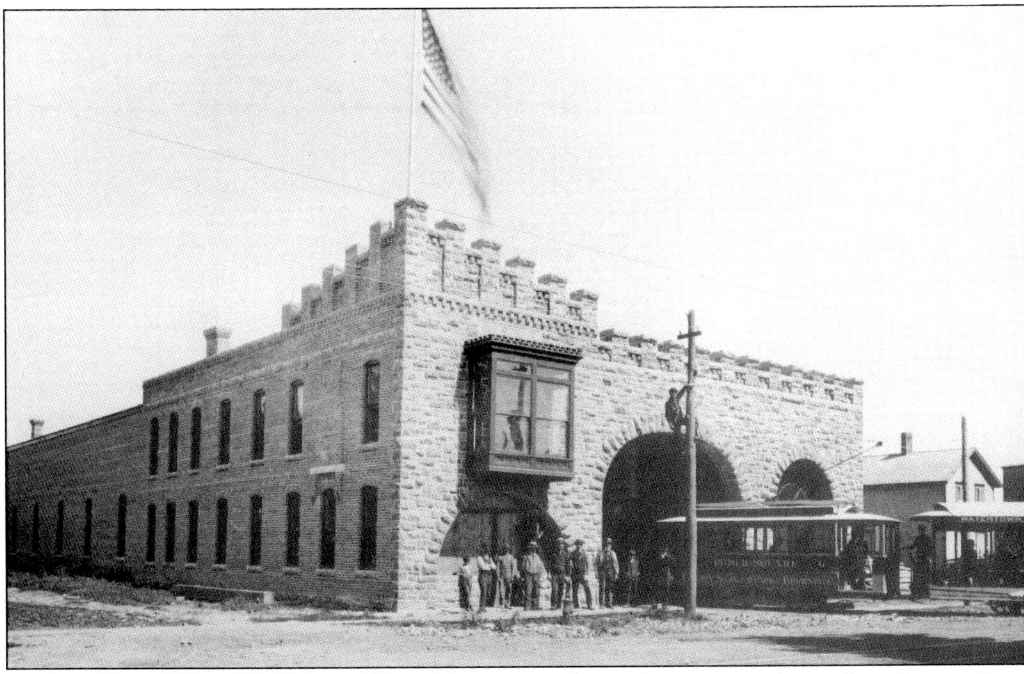

When trolley cars were first used in Watertown, the carbarns were located on lower Court Street near Jackson Street. Shortly after, an office building and barns combined with a marble front was built on the north side of West Main Street at the corner of Meade Street. This 1892 photograph shows the building that was owned by John C. Thompson and leased to the Watertown & Brownville Street Railway Company until c. 1901.

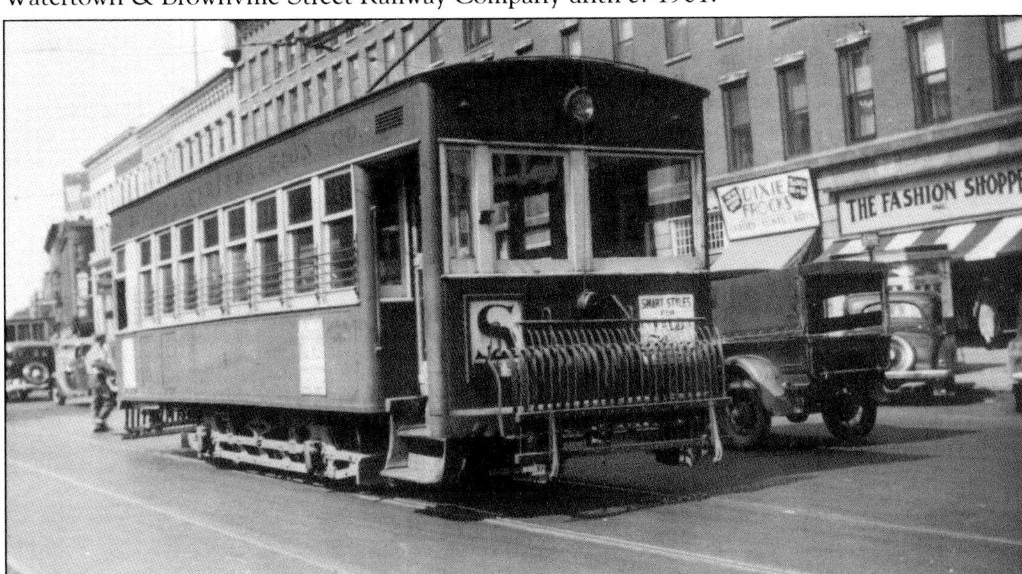

This 1935 photograph shows a car of the Black River Traction Company as it travels on Public Square. A few years prior to this, a car became stalled when the power went off. It, along with the other cars in service in the city, remained in the same position for hours. One woman declined to pay her fare, claiming that it was too cold in the car and there was too much smoke. (Photograph courtesy of JCHS.)

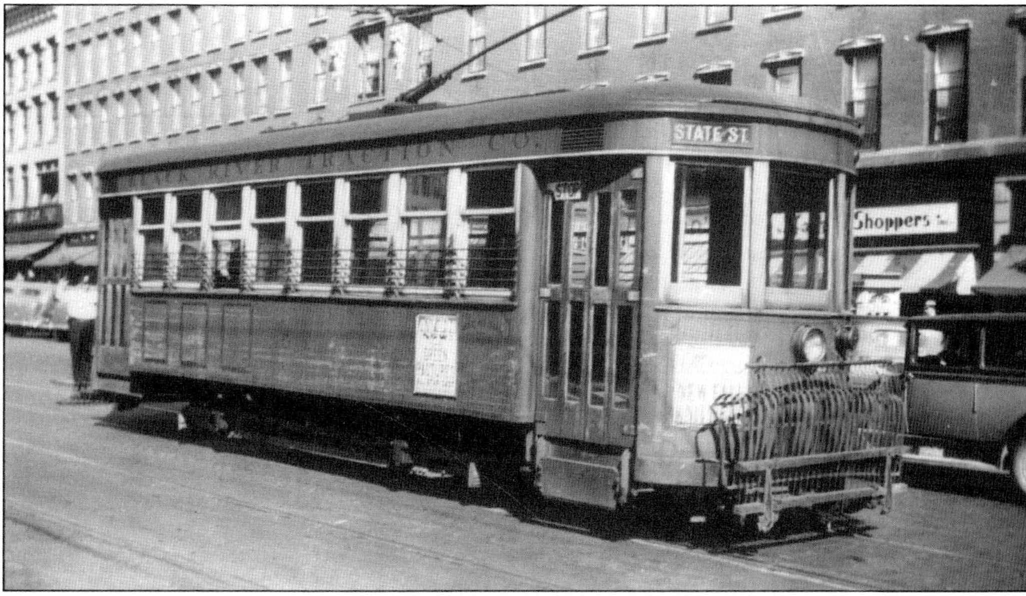

Trolley cars carried advertising for local businesses. This 1936 trolley car advertised for Herr's Fashion Shop and the Avon Theater. Window guards were installed on the cars in 1913 to keep passengers from sticking heads and arms outside. The move came after a passenger managed to get his arm hit by the Court Street Bridge. (Photograph courtesy of JCHS.)

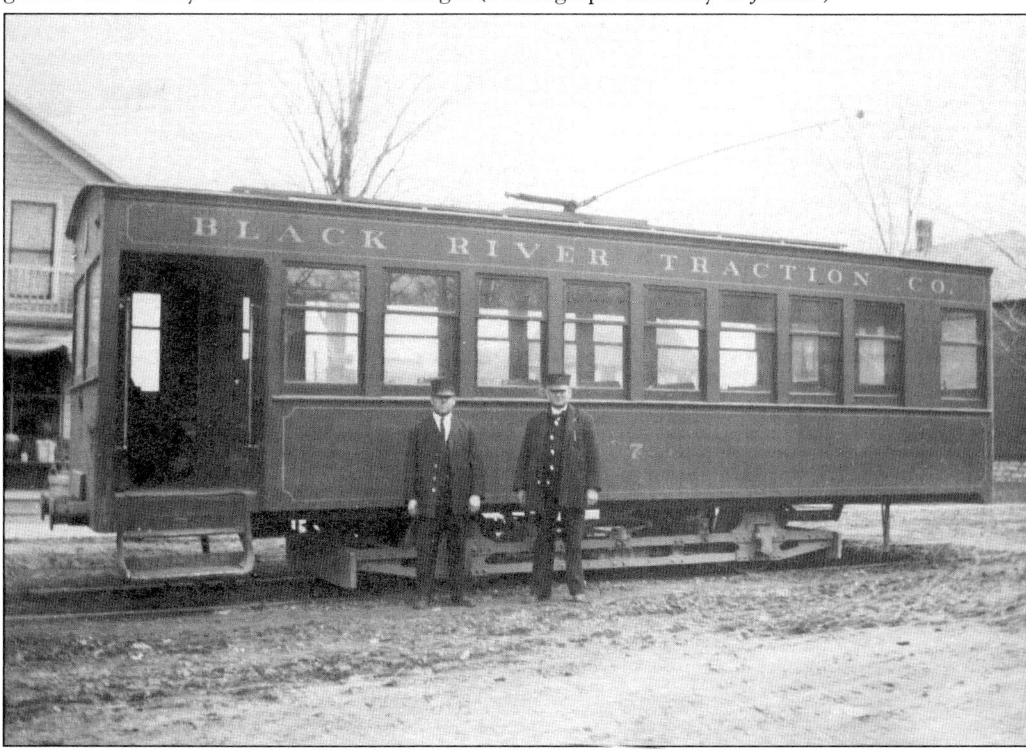

Two employees stand in front of Car No. 7 of the Black River Traction Company. City cars ran from the Thompson Park entrance to Public Square, and larger cars ran to Dexter, taking employees to work at the paper mills on the shores of the Black River.

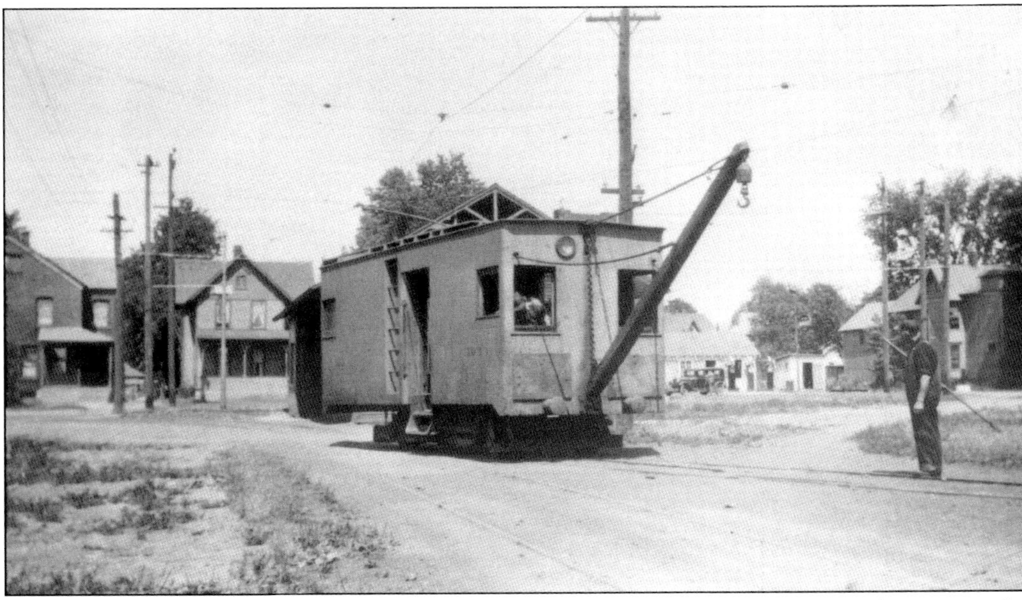

A flat-roof wooden crane car owned by the Black River Traction Company can be seen in this 1936 photograph. (Photograph courtesy of JCHS.)

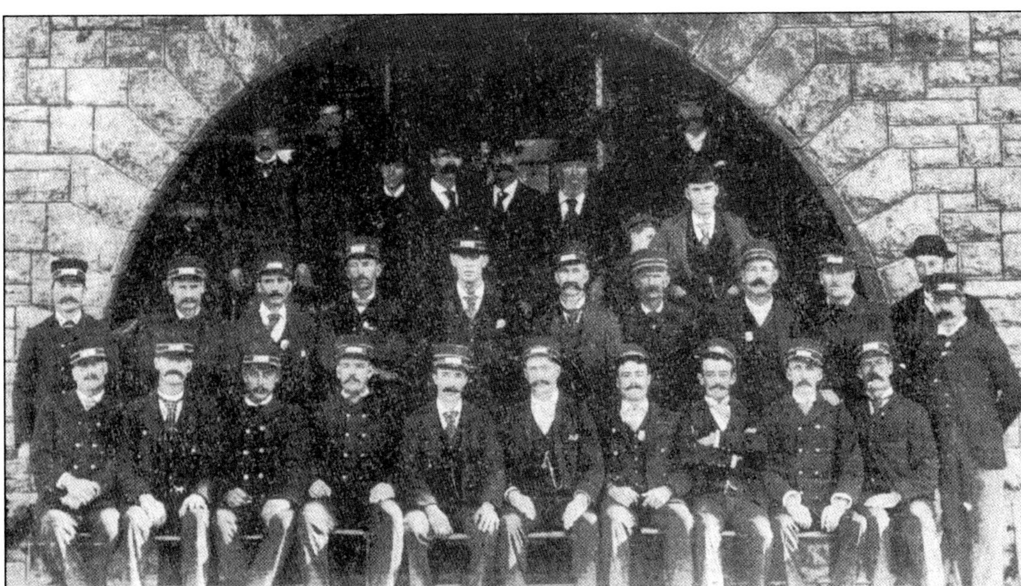

Employees of the Watertown Street Railway Company, predecessor of the Black River Traction Company, are shown in this 1893 picture. At the onset, the Watertown Company adopted a set of rules for the riders: (1) Riding or standing on the steps and platforms or getting on or off the cars when in motion was prohibited; (2) Fare was 5¢ within the city limits, with an offer of 21 tickets for a dollar; (3) No half fares were allowed. Children under four years of age rode free. Policemen and mail carriers in uniform rode free; (4) Intoxicated or disorderly people were not allowed to ride; (5) Passengers were not allowed to ride on the front platform or talk to motorman; and (6) Spitting on the floor was prohibited.

Five

SCHOOLS

Education was important to the earliest settlers of our area. The first schoolteacher in the settlement was Sally Coffeen, who began her duties when she was about 15. The first classes were held in a barn located behind Massey's Inn, near what is now Arcade Street. At about the same time, her sister Heiress Coffeen opened a school in a log house on Washington Street. In 1804, a small frame building was erected on the crest of a steep hill in the area of Public Square. It was a primitive school both inside and out. It was elevated about four feet from the ground and underpinned by logs set on end. Inside, pine boards on three sides, running the whole length, were provided for the pupils. It could accommodate about 80 students.

Solon Massey recalled in his writings for *Links in a Chain* that the first teacher in this schoolhouse was "an old man by the name of McGregor." He recalls that McGregor was a man to be remembered as one who taught by the rule. The rule, however, was made of cherry an inch in thickness, about 18 inches long, and was applied "like a triphammer in force to the tiny, soft hands of whatever child failed of the arbitrary lesson assigned as his task."

Another memorable schoolmaster was Jeremiah Bishop, who was commonly known as "long-legged Bishop." He allowed himself to become quite deep in debt, and his creditors placed him on "jail limits," refusing to imprison him so that the best interests of the community might not suffer. He was a man of science and devised a plan of ridding the Mall, the area that is now Public Square, of thistles by sprinkling salt on them so as to make them more palatable to the cows and sheep that grazed there. History notes that this plan did not work.

The Watertown Normal School was listed in the village directory as being located on Franklin Street, with Fabius Mills as principal. This school opened on September 1, 1839, and had 47 pupils. During these early years, there was also some demand for private schools. The Watertown Female Academy was established in 1824. In 1832, an academy was built on Academy Street to provide higher education for young men. The Black River Literary and Religious Institute succeeded it in 1838. This was located at the corner of State and Mechanic Streets and was a coeducational school. In May 1846, the name was changed to the Jefferson County Institute. In 1865, it was leased for a high school by the village and was used for that purpose until a high school was constructed in 1904 on Sterling Street.

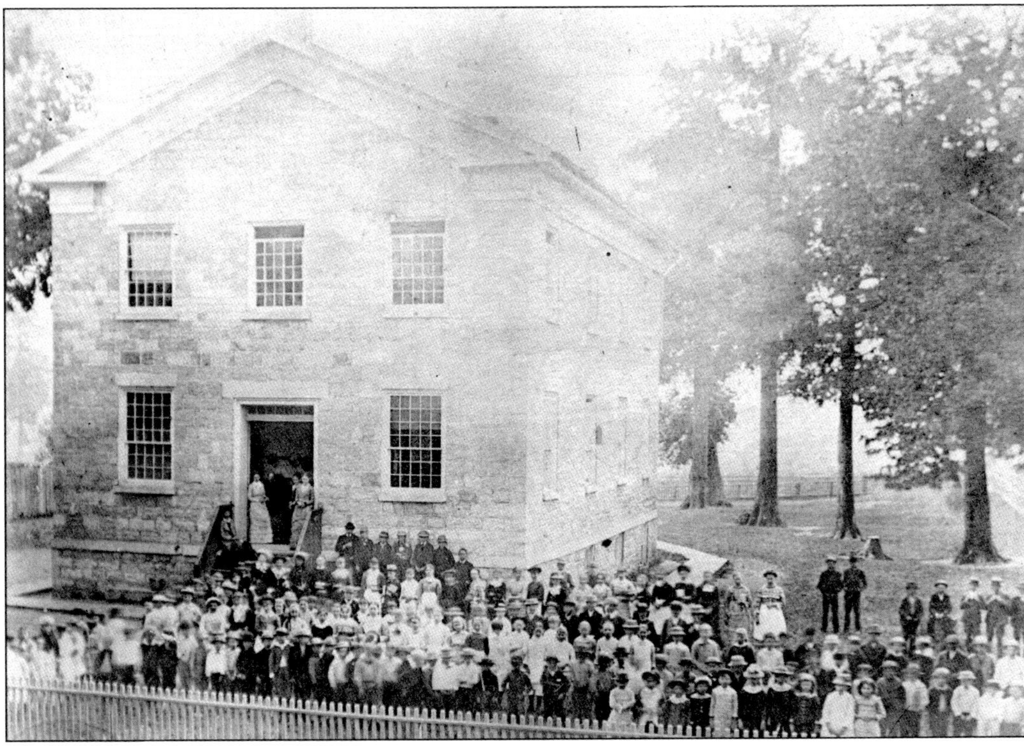

Academy Street School classes pose in front of the school building in 1882. At the time of Watertown's incorporation in 1869, the school system consisted of 9 schools, 25 teachers, and 1,903 pupils. The population of the city at that time was about 9,000. (Photograph courtesy of JCHS.)

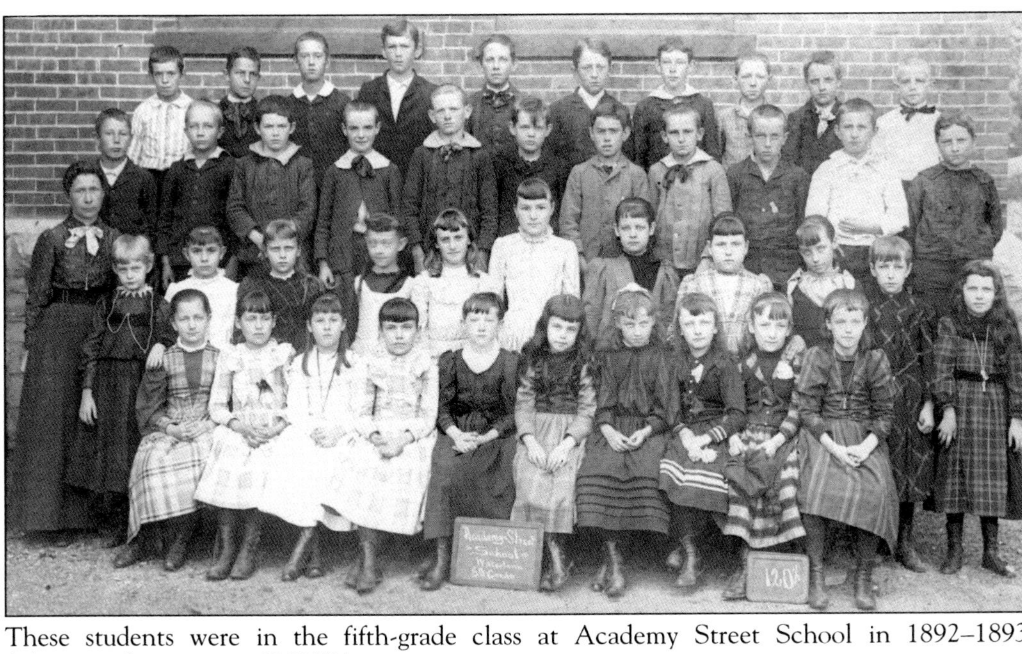

These students were in the fifth-grade class at Academy Street School in 1892–1893. (Photograph courtesy of JCHS.)

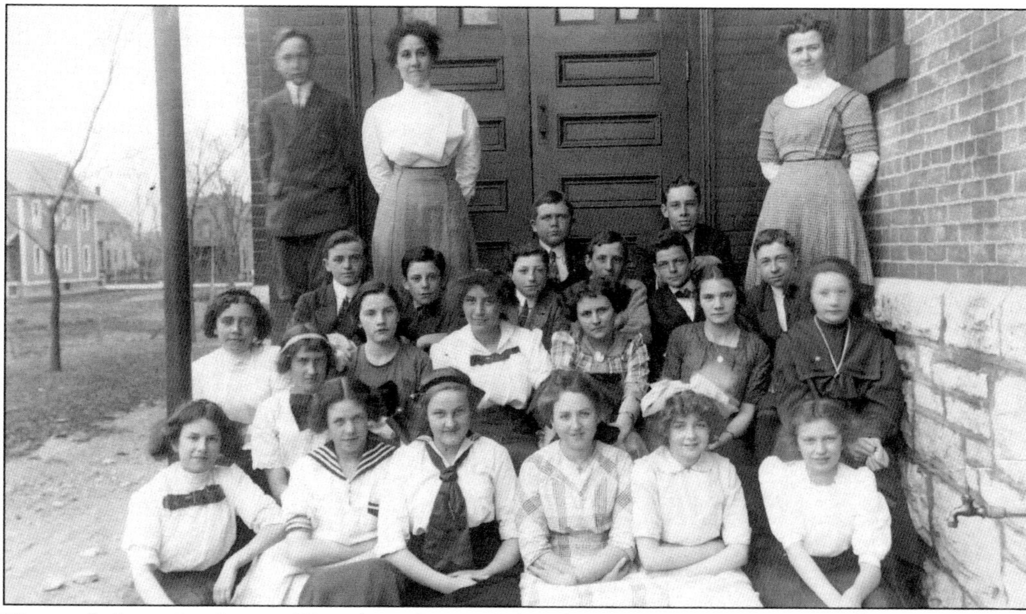

The eighth-grade class at Hamilton Street School poses in 1912. From left to right are the following: (first row) Mary Worthen, Bertha Sweeny, Korleen Henderson, Margaret McNamee, Evangeline McNamee, and Katherine Fisher; (second row) Bessie Moran, Lucie Lawrence, Mary Keegan, Bernice Parsons, Mabel Zeswitz, Louis Goodrich, and Viola Mierke; (third row) Vaughn Wheeler, Evan L. Sweeny, Emanuel Fink, Wayne Parsons, Harold Burchard, and William Hinds; (fourth row) Bernard Cook and Floyd Flansburg; (fifth row) Stuart Thompson, principal Florence Baker, and teacher Grace Terry. (Photograph courtesy of JCHS.)

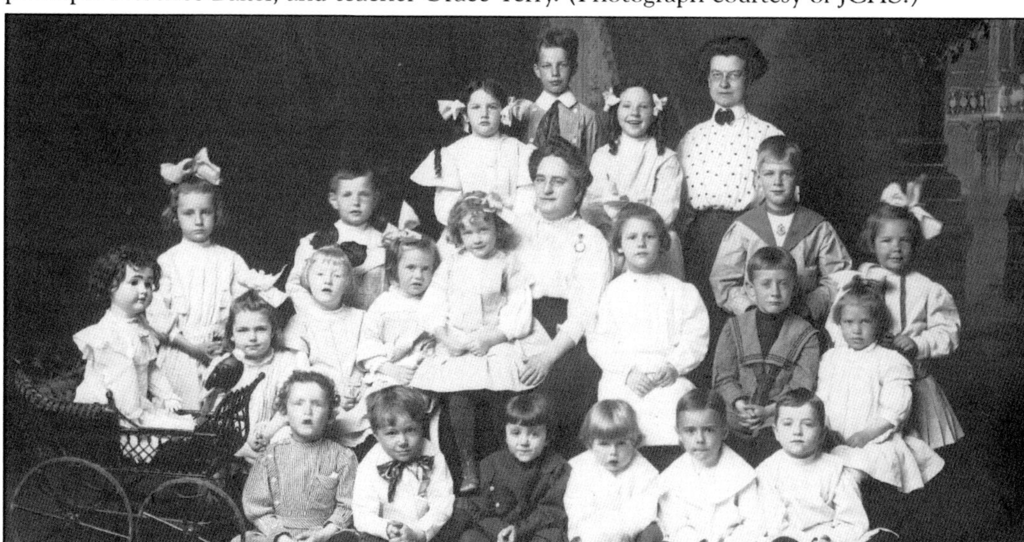

These beautiful children attended Antoinette Rogers's kindergarten in 1909. Classes were for three and four year olds as well as five and six year olds. The school also accepted six- and seven-year-old students who were then prepared to enter the second grade in the Watertown Public Schools. The tuition was $10 per quarter in advance and $15 per quarter for two children from one family. A charge of 25¢ per quarter was made to each pupil for materials. Rogers, of 5 Jay Street, was the principal. (Photograph courtesy of JCHS.)

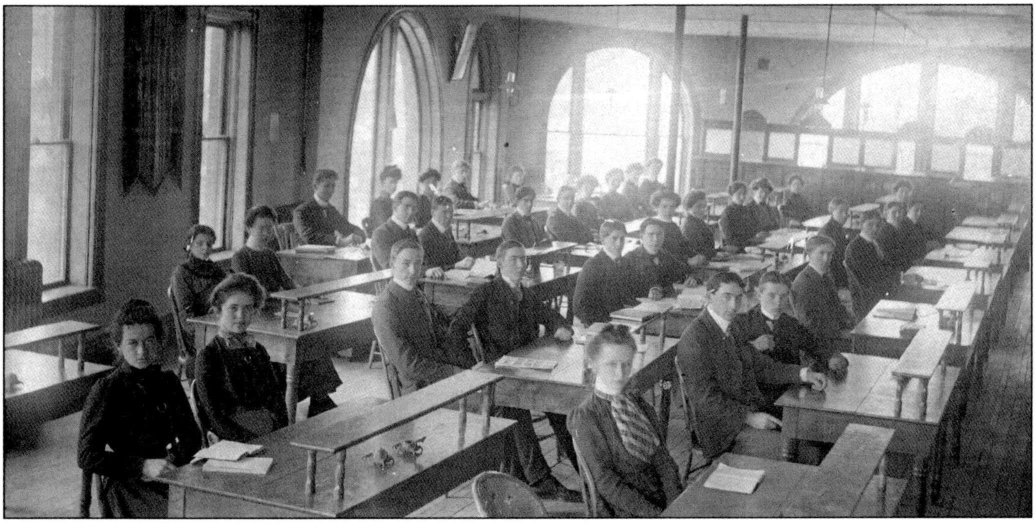

Students at the Northern Business College studied to be bookkeepers, stenographers, and office assistants. Located in the Mohican Building at the corner of State Street and Public Square, it later became known as the Watertown School of Commerce. (Photograph courtesy of JCHS.)

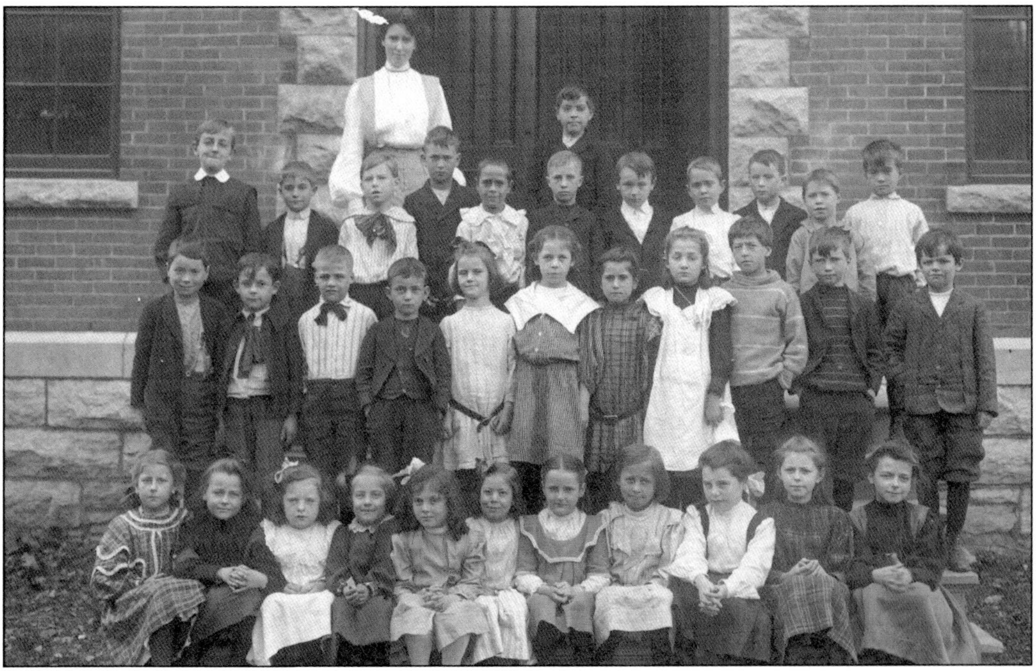

Second-grade class members at Mullin Street School pose in this *c.* 1904–1905 photograph. They are, from left to right, as follows: (first row) Clara Fuller, Lucy Burns, Mary Hughes, Mildred Dunbar, Mildred Brady, Ruth McIntosh, Greta Maxon, Minnie Burker, Ethel Hogan, Mary Doyle, and Anna Burns; (second row) Alfred Brislan, Evan Sweeney, James Smith, Francis Laverty, Harriet Gabourie, Bertha Sweeny, Lena LaRock, unidentified, Melvin Huntley, Roswell Leonard, and Sheldon Marion; (third row) Oscar Martin, unidentified, John Duggan, Lawrence McNulty, Pearl Morehouse, unidentified, Lloyd Van Duzee, Harvey Hyde, Edward McCorrie, Fred Lamphear, and Alfred Gilligan; (fourth row) teacher Marcia Phillips and Clifford Plummer. (Photograph courtesy of JCHS.)

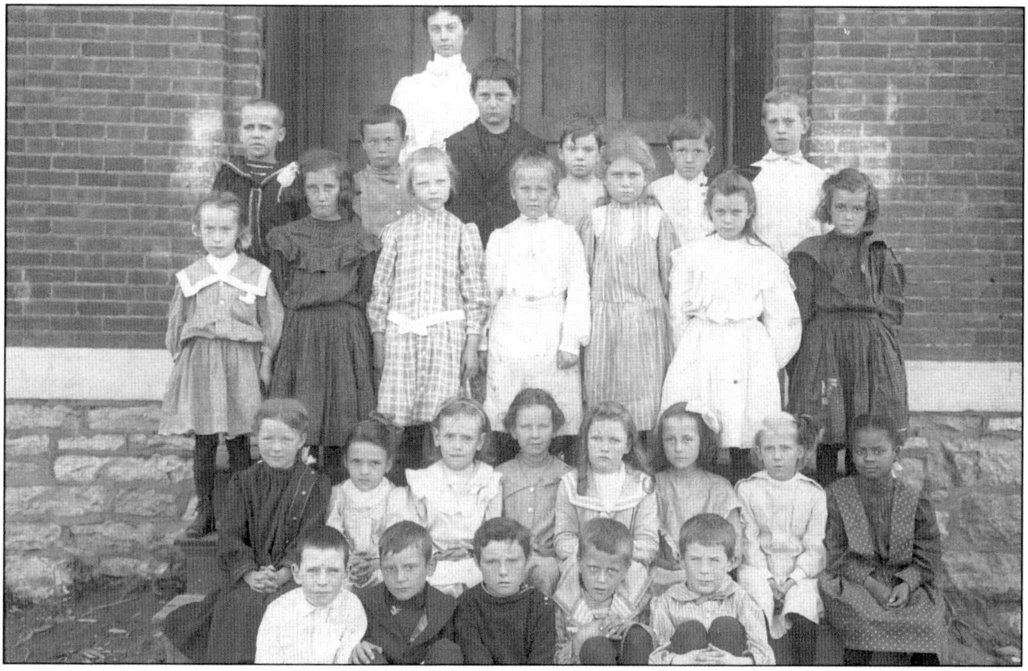

This 1905 Pearl Street School elementary class photograph shows 26 students whose expressions seem to indicate that they wished they were someplace else at the time. They are, from left to right, as follows: (first row) Willie Parnell, Robbie Dyer, Lyle Nellis, Andrew Tylka, and George Whitehill; (second row) Lillie Thomas, Leita Warren, Alice Root, Stella Jackson, Bessie Pearson, Bernice McLaughlin, Vanessa Moore, and Rose Lee; (third row) Isabelle Kerr, Delia Van Dusen, Louisa Paige, Josie Jozowski, Mary Minkler, Hattie LaFave, and Irene Van Dusen; (fourth row) Clarence Strader, Harold Townsend, Leonard Darby, George Darby, George Carron, and Leo Proctor. (Photograph courtesy of JCHS.)

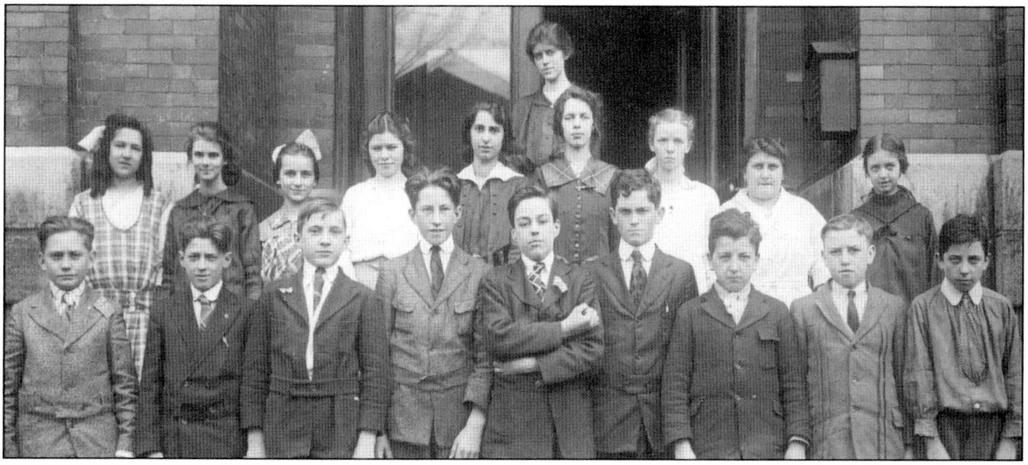

State Street School students had this photograph taken on April 3, 1917. They are, from left to right, as follows: (front row) Leo Valley, Oral Wisner, Paul Trahan, Gerald Danforth, Oscar Robbins, Bernard Kitts, Alonzo Hall, Elbert Burringham, and John Coughlin; (back row) Lillian Gagnon, Hilda Jarvis, Charlotte Kafka, Helen Valin, Ada Gowan, Mildred Rugar, Mae Murrock, Helen Farley, and Ruth Getman. The teacher was Rebecca Brett. (Photograph courtesy of JCHS.)

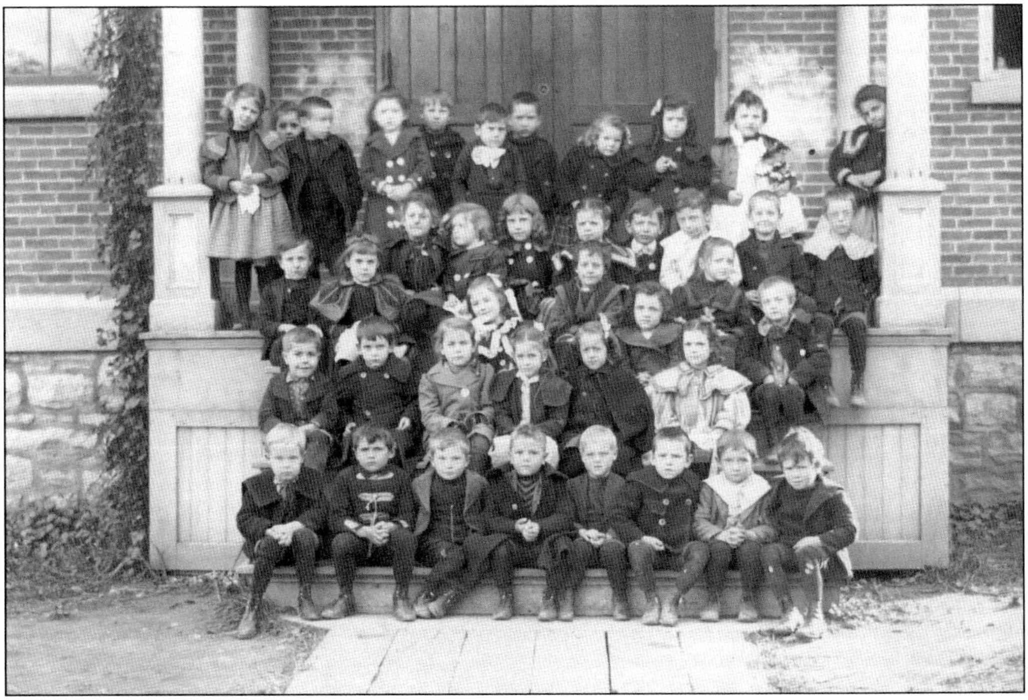

These students attended the Flower Avenue School. Behind them is evidence of where they cleaned the chalkboard erasers. (Photograph courtesy of JCHS.)

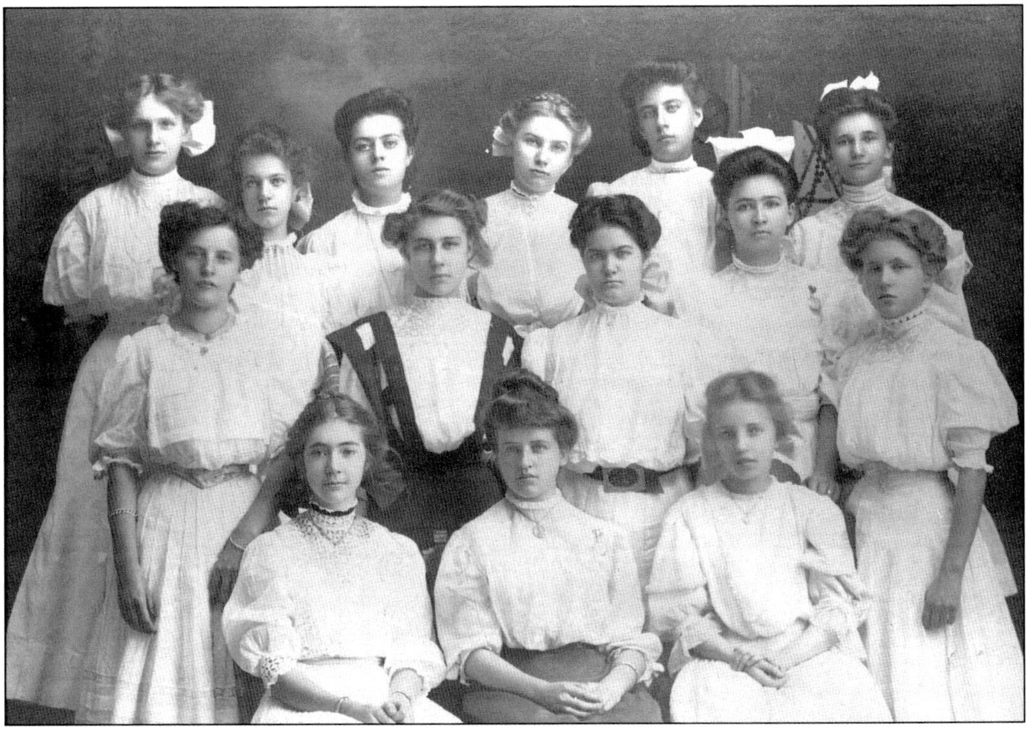

The young women posing for this picture in 1907 were members of the Watertown High School class. (Photograph courtesy of JCHS.)

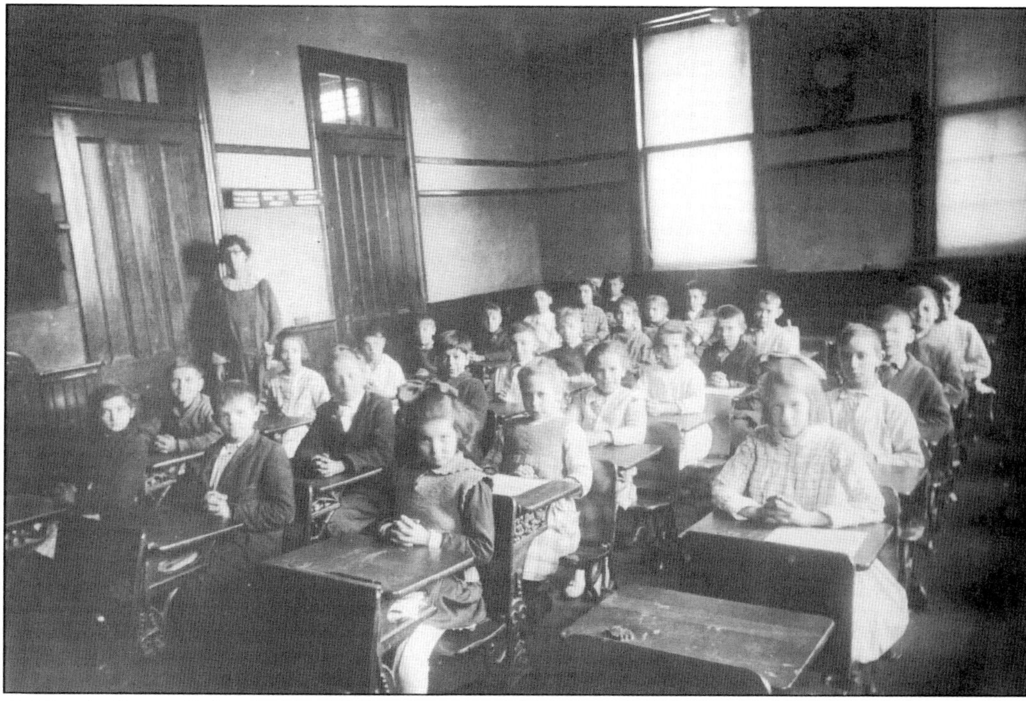

A Meade Street School class looks attentively at the photographer in this early 1900s picture. (Photograph courtesy of JCHS.)

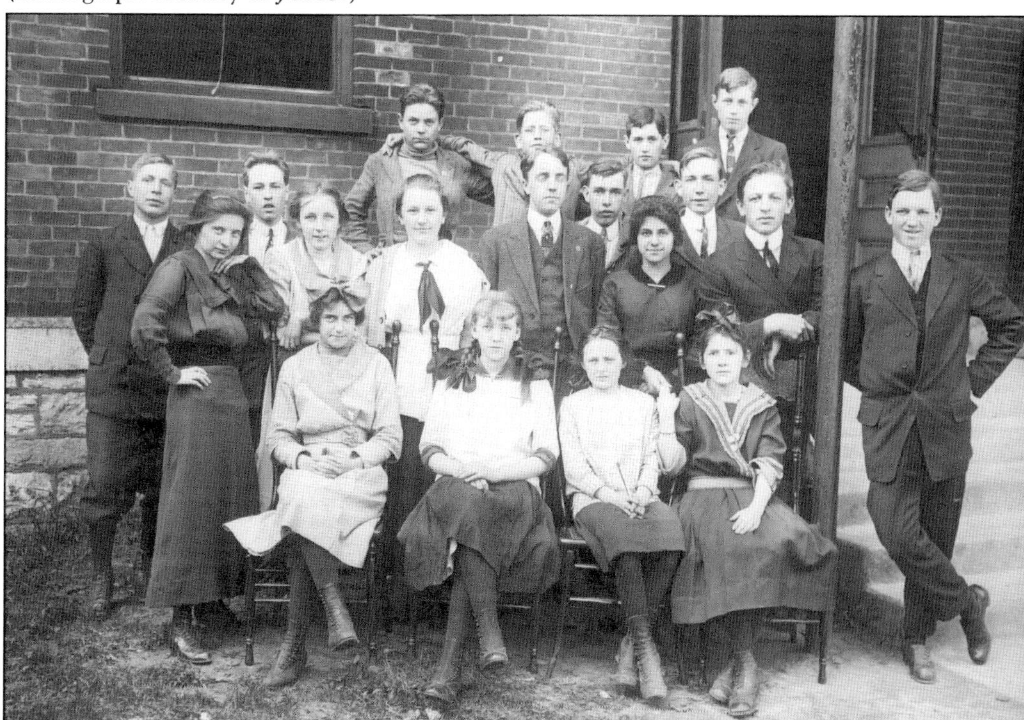

The members of this Cooper Street School class certainly look very stylish. (Photograph courtesy of JCHS.)

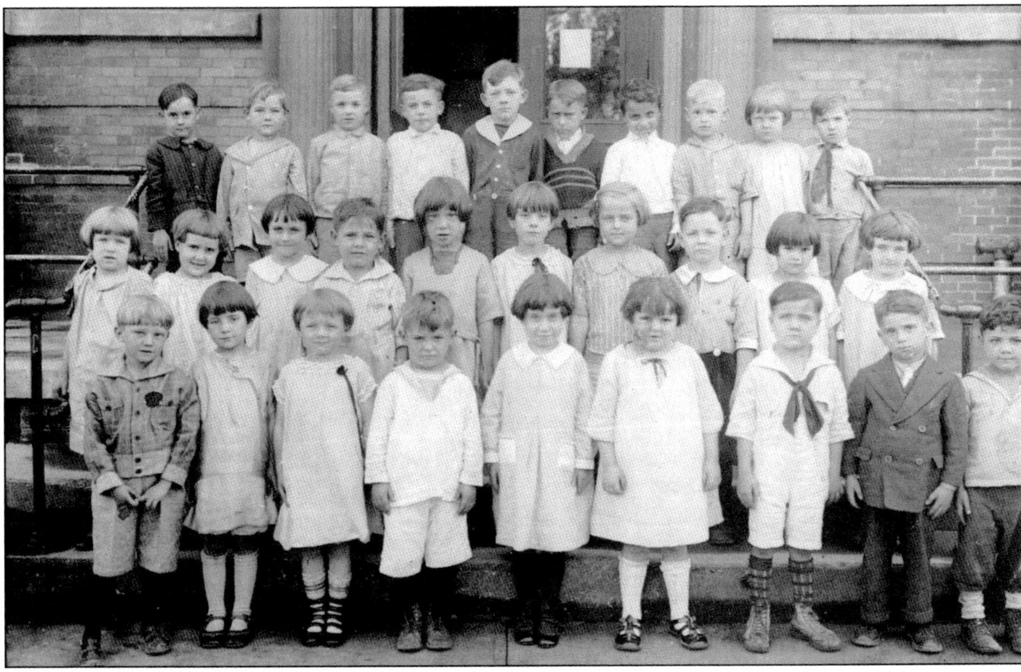

Mrs. Holland was the teacher for the first-grade class in 1926 at Lansing Street School.

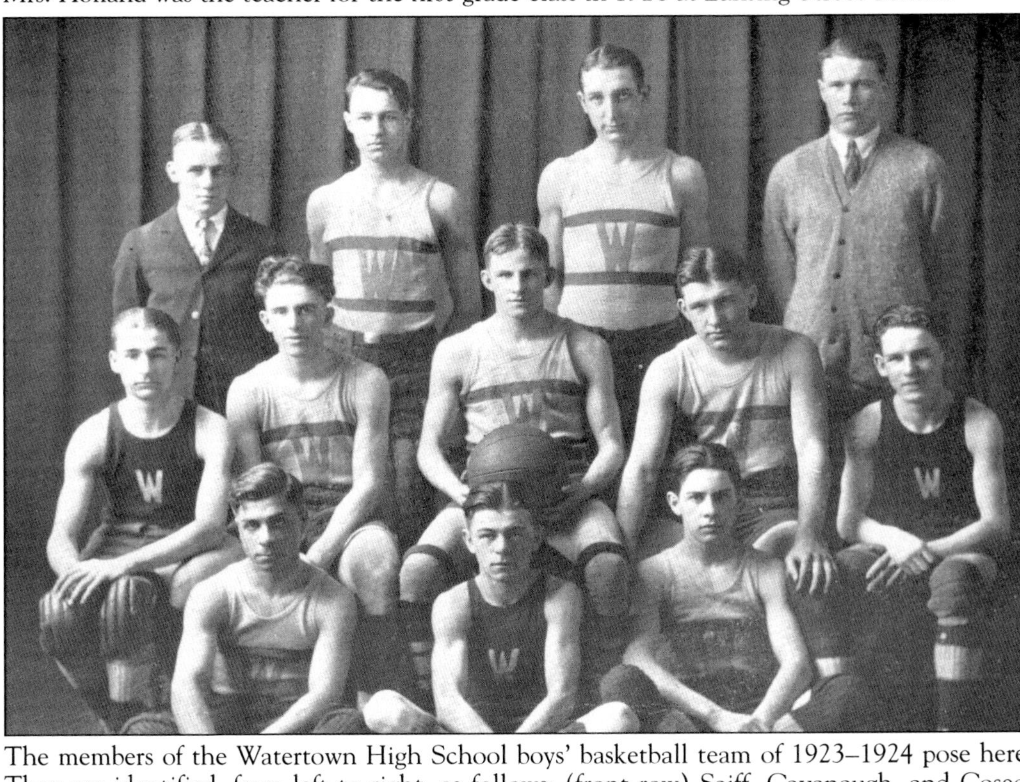

The members of the Watertown High School boys' basketball team of 1923–1924 pose here. They are identified, from left to right, as follows: (front row) Saiff, Cavanaugh, and Coseo; (middle row) Cholette, Whalen, Hodge (captain), Exley, and O'Reilly; (back row) Hank Hodge (coach), Renson, Hale, and Adams (manager).

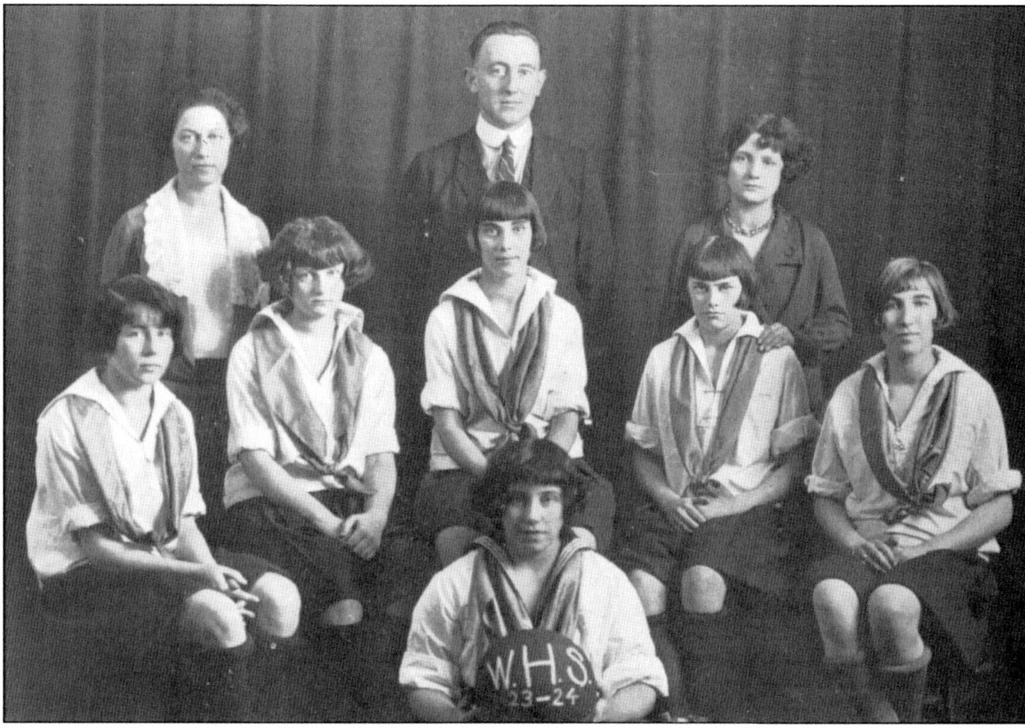

The Watertown High School girls' basketball team for 1923–1924 is shown here. From left to right are the following: (front row) Grace MacMillan (captain); (middle row) Isobell Carroll, Ruth Lorimer, Elizabeth Brenna, Dot Loucks, and Sylvia Felman; (back row) ? Flint (coach), Reed Spaulding (coach), and Dot Colburn (manager).

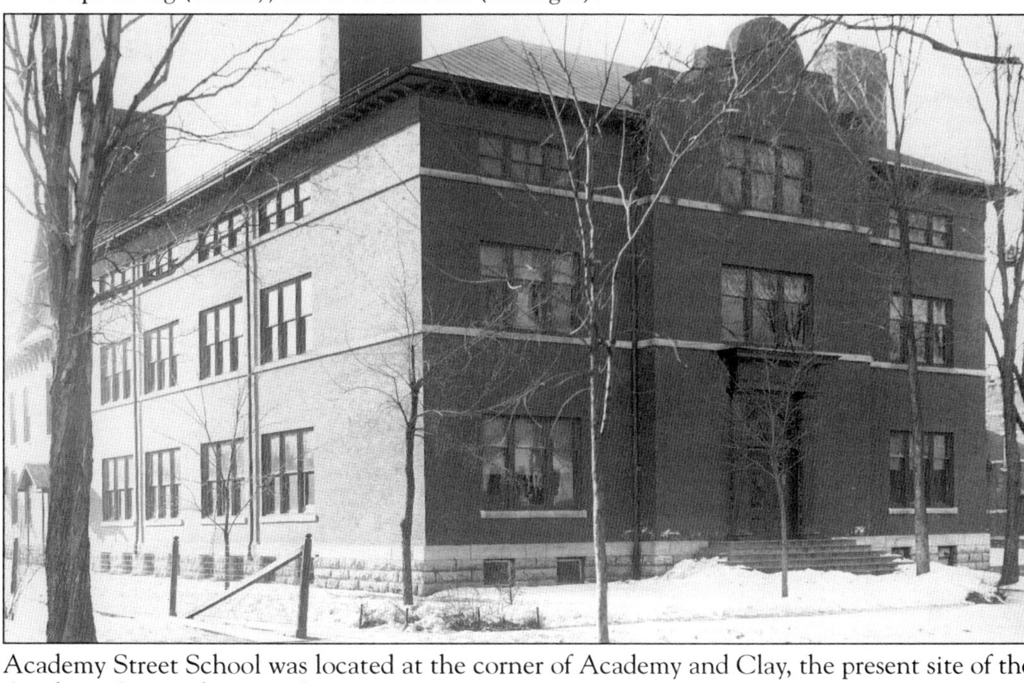

Academy Street School was located at the corner of Academy and Clay, the present site of the Academy Street playground.

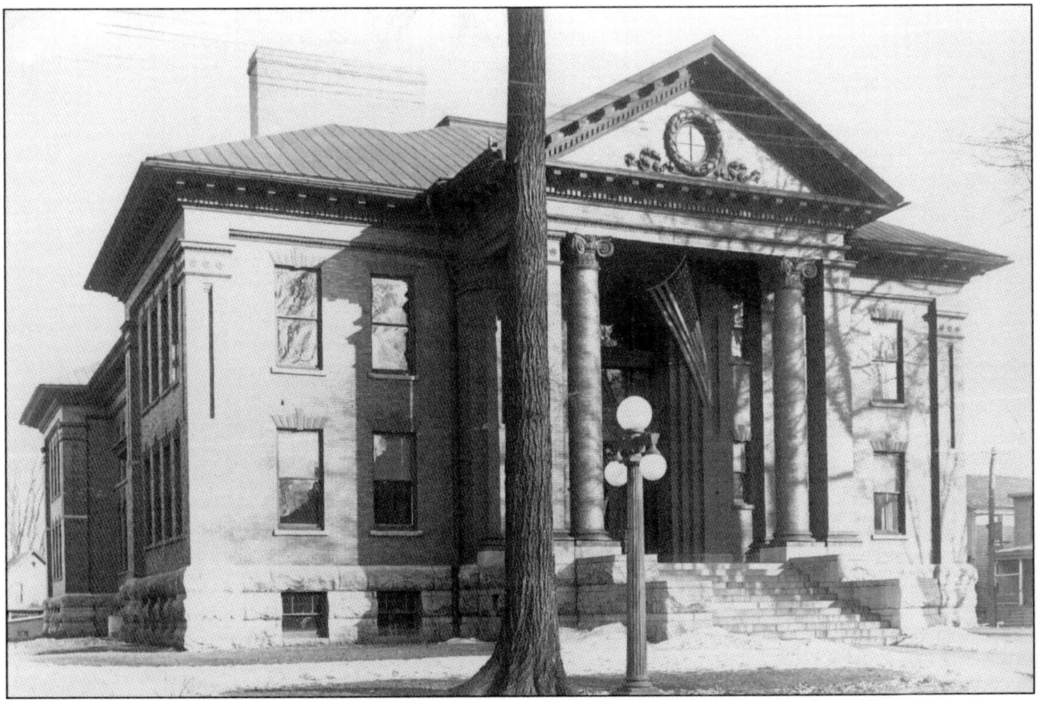

From 1865 to 1904, the Watertown High School was located at the corner of State and Mechanic Streets. This building was originally the Black River Literary and Religious Institute.

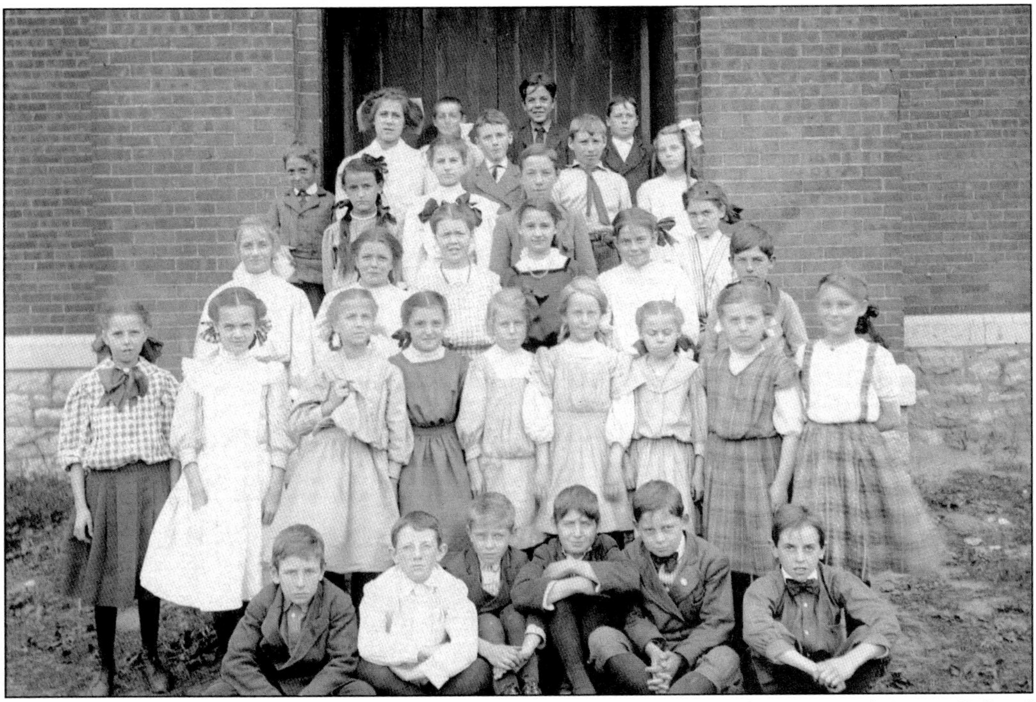

Pigtails and bows make a fashion statement for the young women of an Arsenal Street School class. Not to be outdone, most of the young men are wearing ties. (Photograph courtesy of JCHS.)

Six

Urban Renewal

There was probably no other federal program that had such a dramatic effect on downtown areas as the urban renewal program of the 1960s. While urban renewal was aimed at cleaning up blight and improving living conditions for lower-income families, in many cases the realities were quite different. With the leveling of buildings, businesses had to move to other locations until new buildings were constructed. Since there were so many delays, many of the businesses moved from their previous locations and stayed in the new locations or closed completely. In the case of Watertown, several developers pulled out from the program after the sites were ready for construction. When all was said and done, many of Watertown's grand old buildings came under the wrecking ball, and much of the architectural history of the city was lost forever.

At the time of the urban renewal project, its proponents were looking toward the future with many plans for futuristic-type buildings which, they felt, could only help the economy of downtown Watertown. Those who opposed the project felt that a building should not be taken down until there was something definite to put in its place. This was during a time when rehabilitation of a structurally sound building was not something to be considered. Cities wanted a sleek new look in an effort to entice development. Now, we have come full circle and realize the value of what our ancestors have left in our care.

The following pages show buildings on Arsenal and Court Streets before urban renewal. Some of these were taken down during the project and only remain vivid in our minds. Others are still standing and are home to downtown businesses.

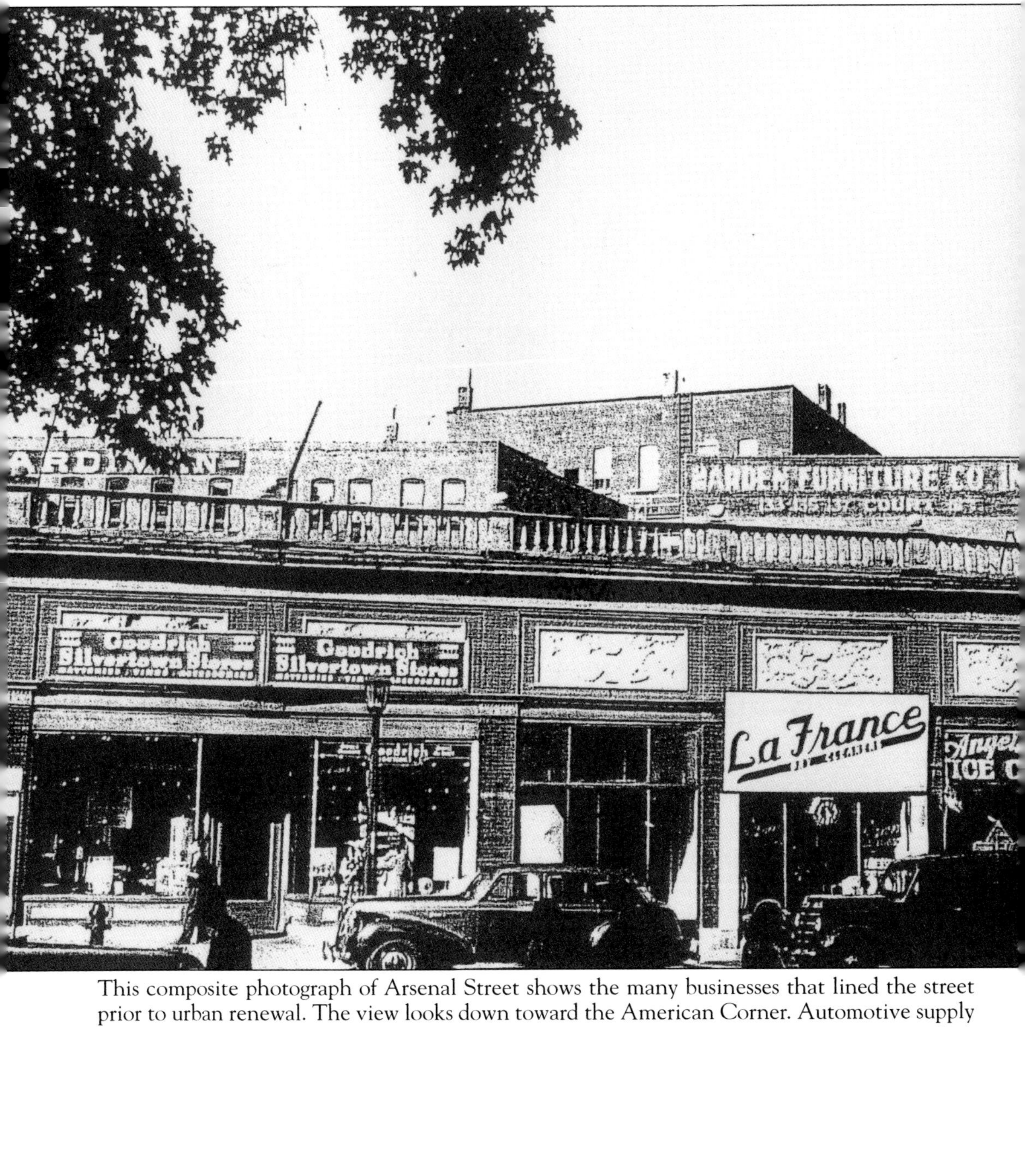

This composite photograph of Arsenal Street shows the many businesses that lined the street prior to urban renewal. The view looks down toward the American Corner. Automotive supply

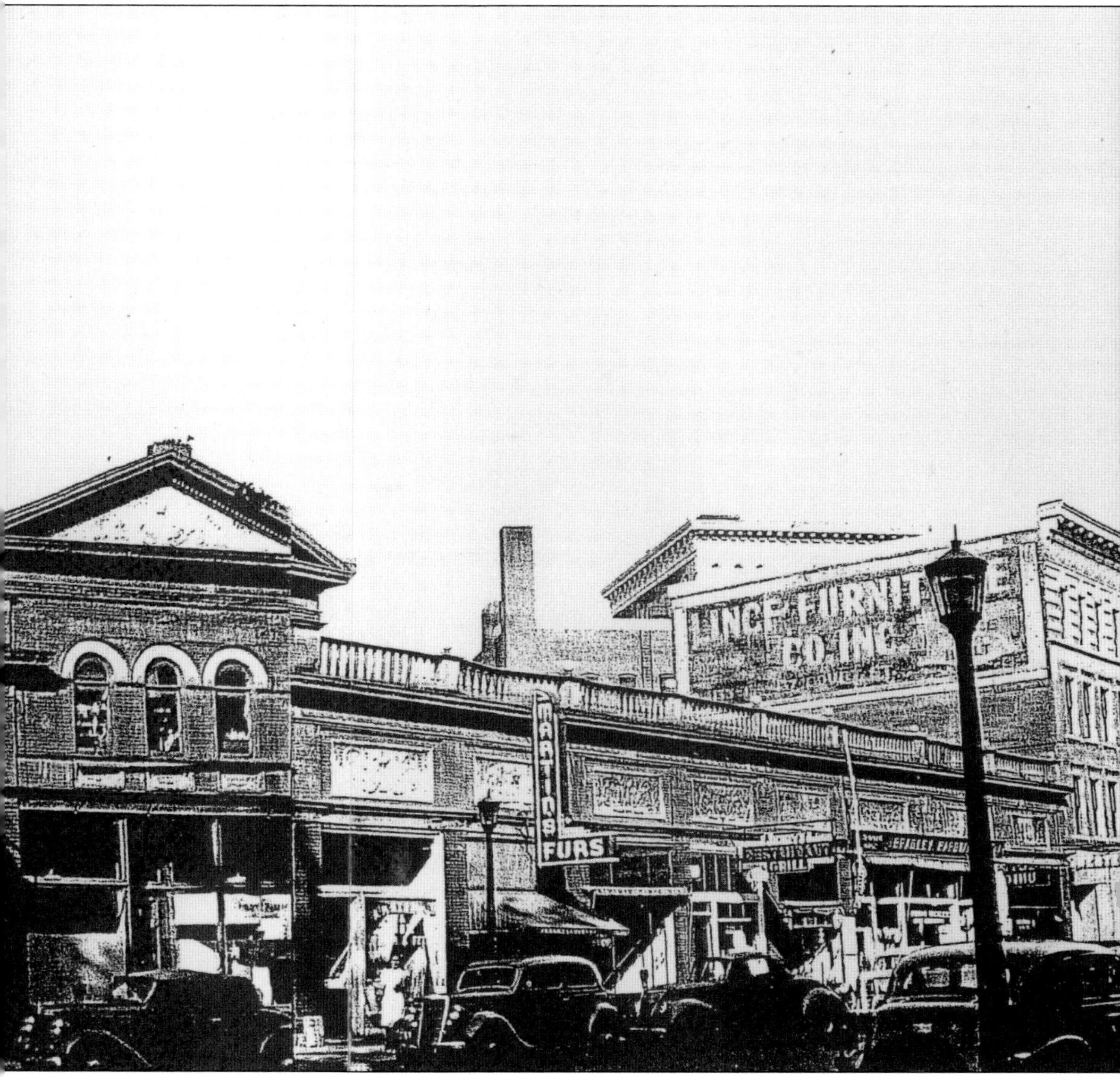

stores, furniture stores, dry cleaners, restaurants, clothing stores, and specialty shops such as hat shops and fur stores helped to make the downtown a busy and prosperous economic area.

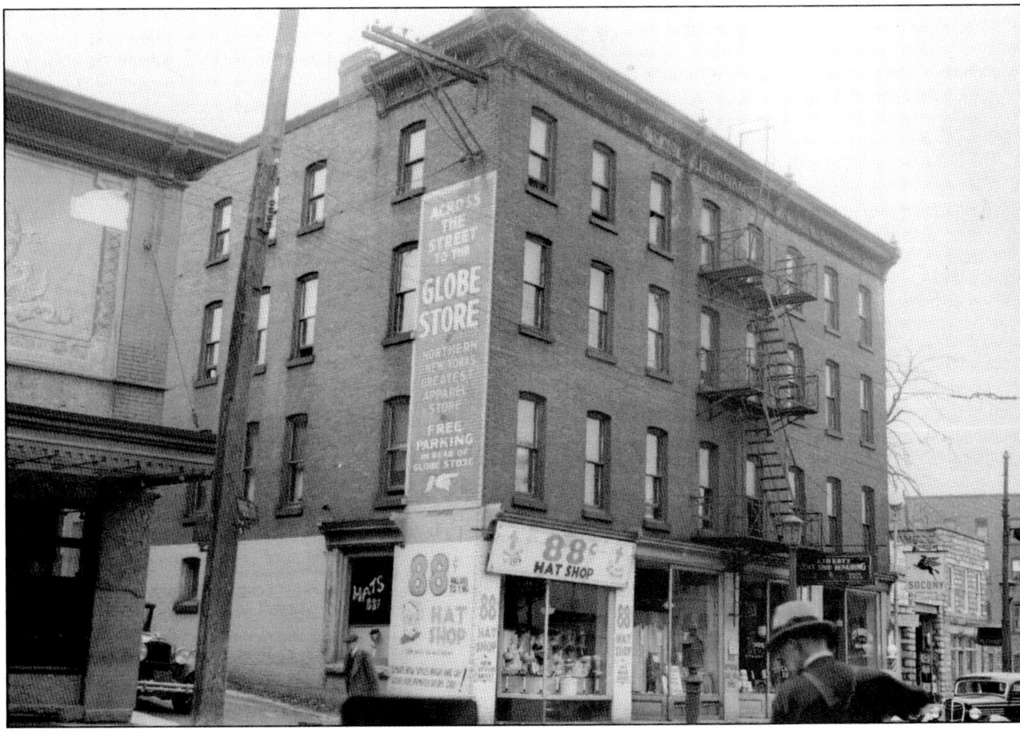

The 88¢ Hat Shop was located at 301 Court Street in 1936. Their slogan was "Smart New Styles Bright and Gay Arrive Here Promptly Every Day!" All hats were 88¢ with values to $1.95.

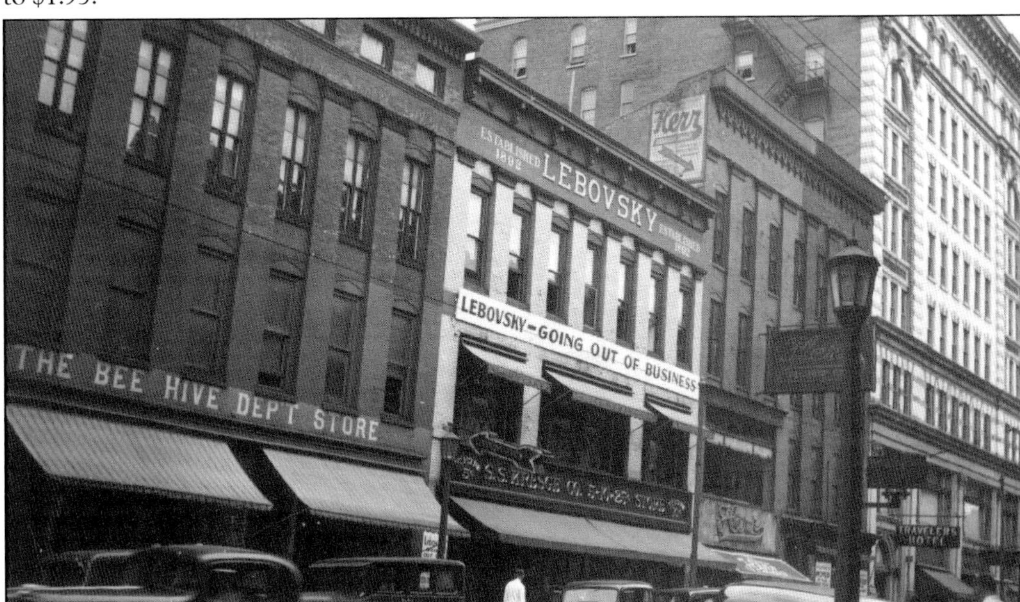

The Bee Hive Department Store is shown in this view of Court Street. This store still brings back memories to many shoppers who went in to buy the perfect gift. The LeBovsky Company, started in 1892, specialized in clothing, men's furnishings, and tailoring. Herr's Fashion Shop was located next to Kresge Company—"the best for 5¢"

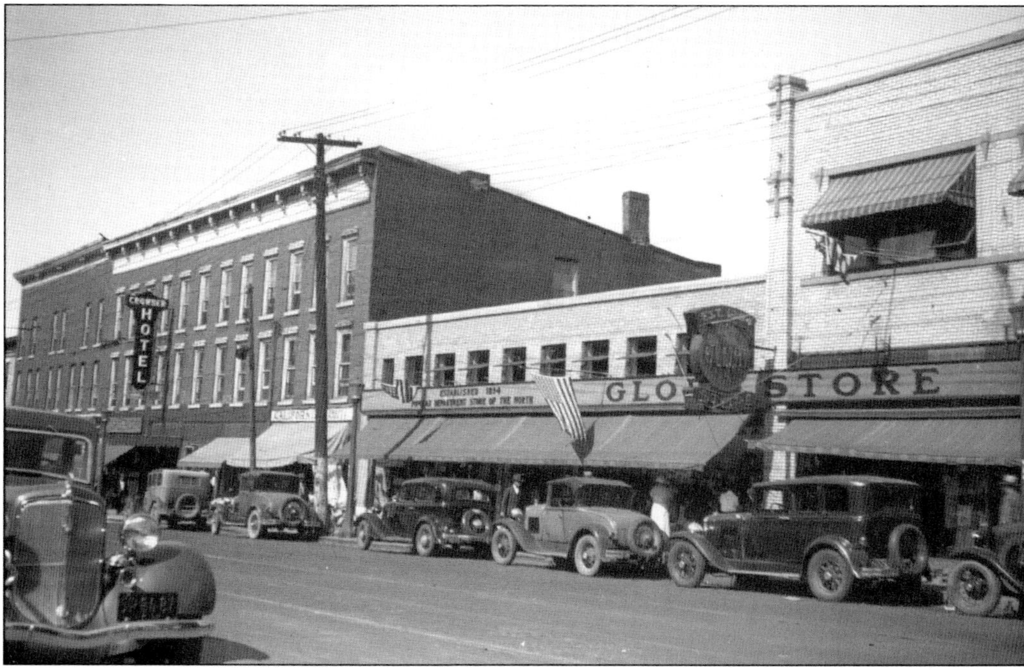

The Globe Store was a mainstay in the economy of Watertown for many years. Located in the 300 block of Court Street, it was a prosperous department store, which spanned many generations. The building now houses specialty stores and antique shops.

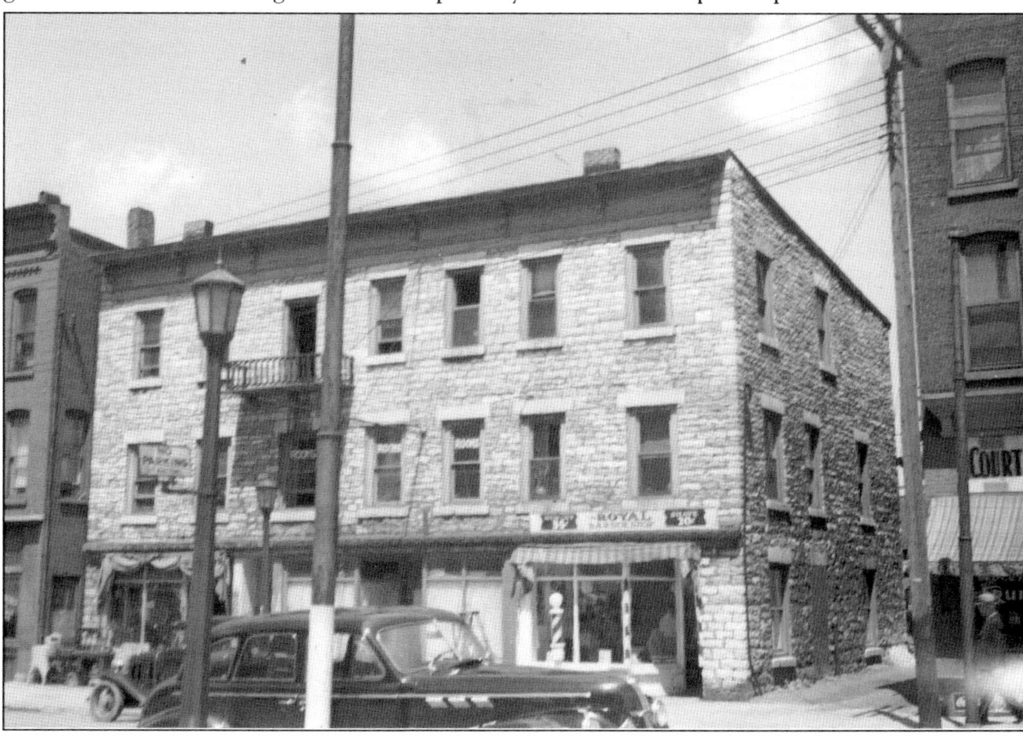

In 1942, the Royal Barber Shop at 342 Court Street offered a haircut for 35¢ and a shave for 20¢.

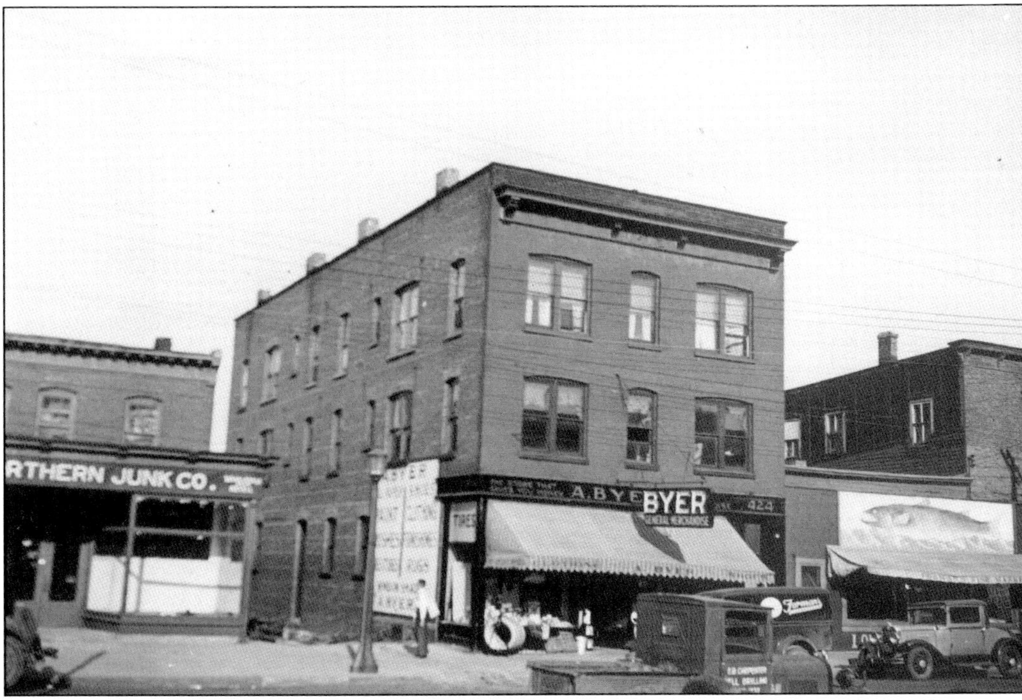

A. Byer General Merchandise, "the Store That Saves You Money," was located next to Forman's Fish Market.

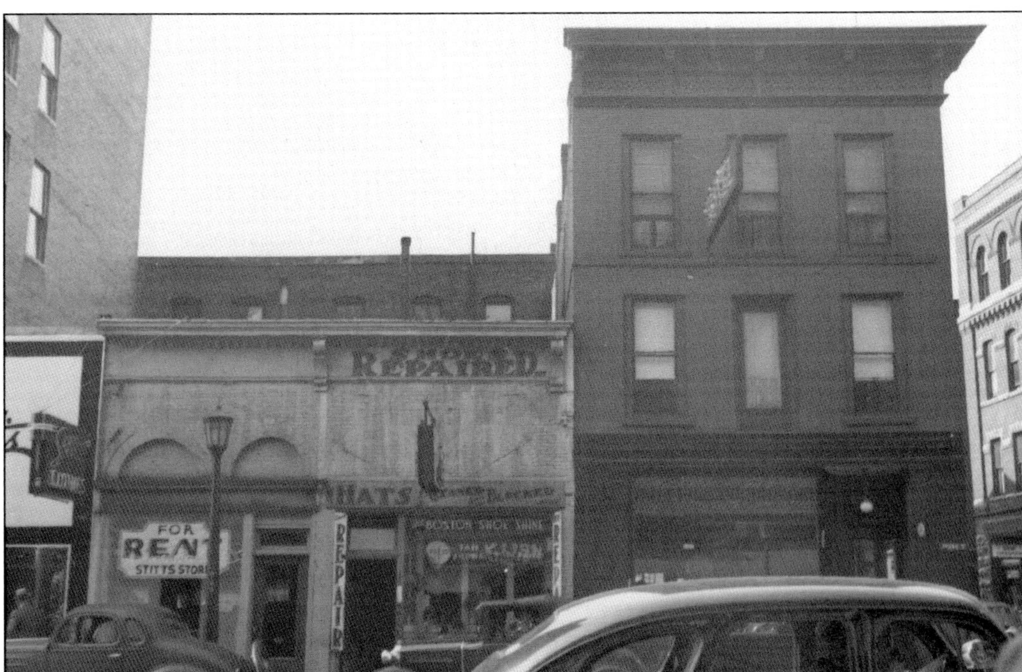

The American Hotel is pictured in this 1940 photograph. At the beginning of the 21st century, this building was waiting for a developer. The buildings next to it that housed the Stitts Store and the Boston Shoe Shine business have been demolished.

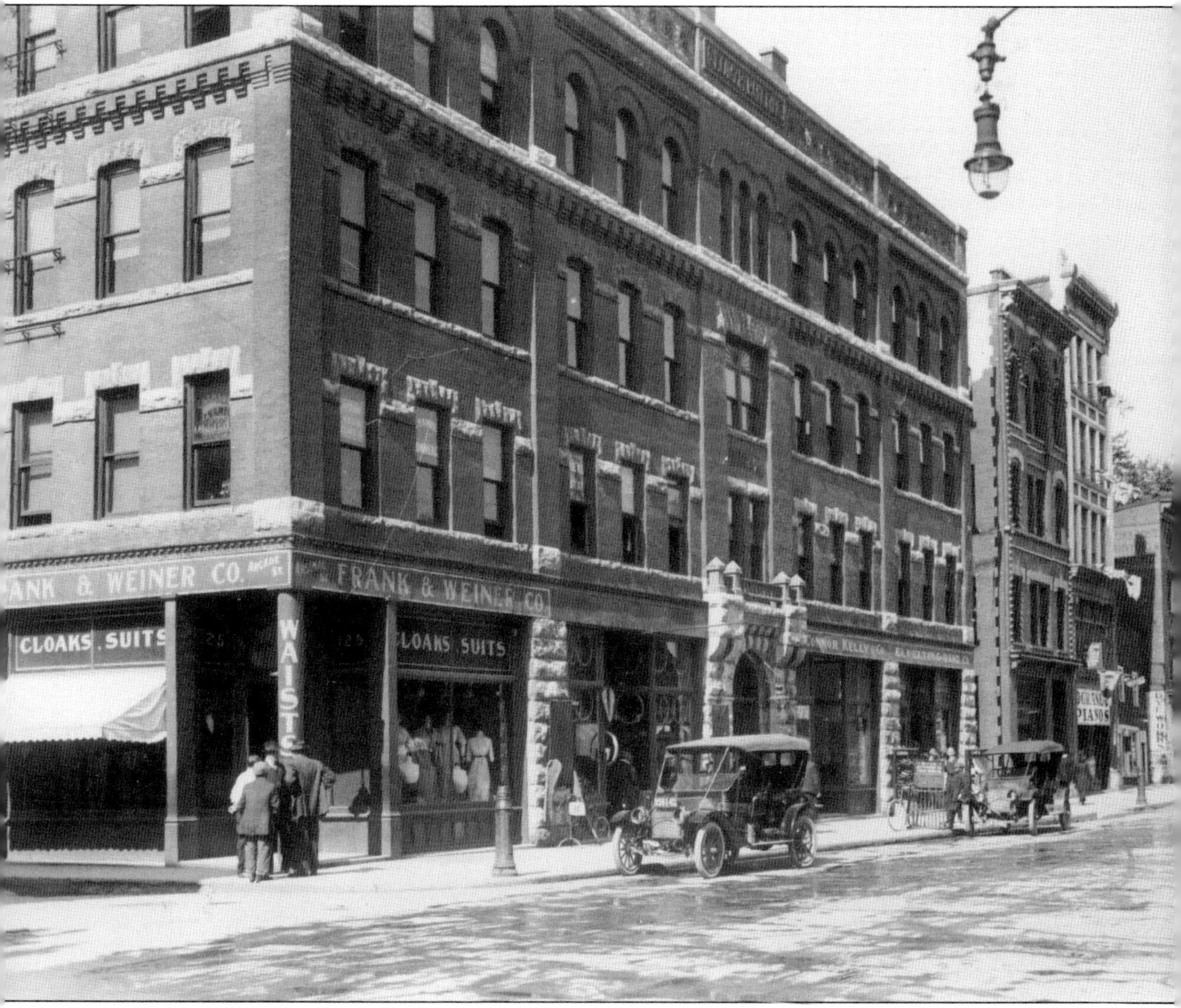

The Flower Building was located on the corner of Arsenal and Arcade Streets and housed offices as well as retail establishments such as Frank & Weiner Company, which sold men's and women's clothing. The location of the building is now a parking lot.

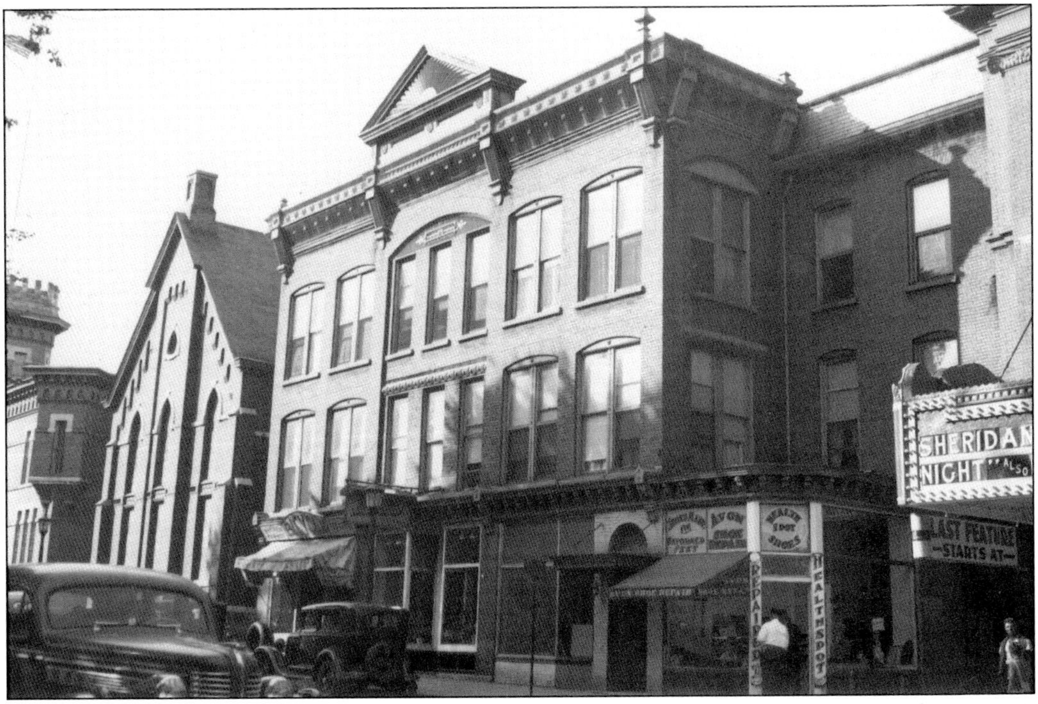

The Bradley Building was located on Arsenal Street. The Arcade Shoe Store and Bennett's Florist were located on the first-floor level. To the right of the building was the Avon Theater, and to the left were the New York State Armory and the First United Methodist Church.

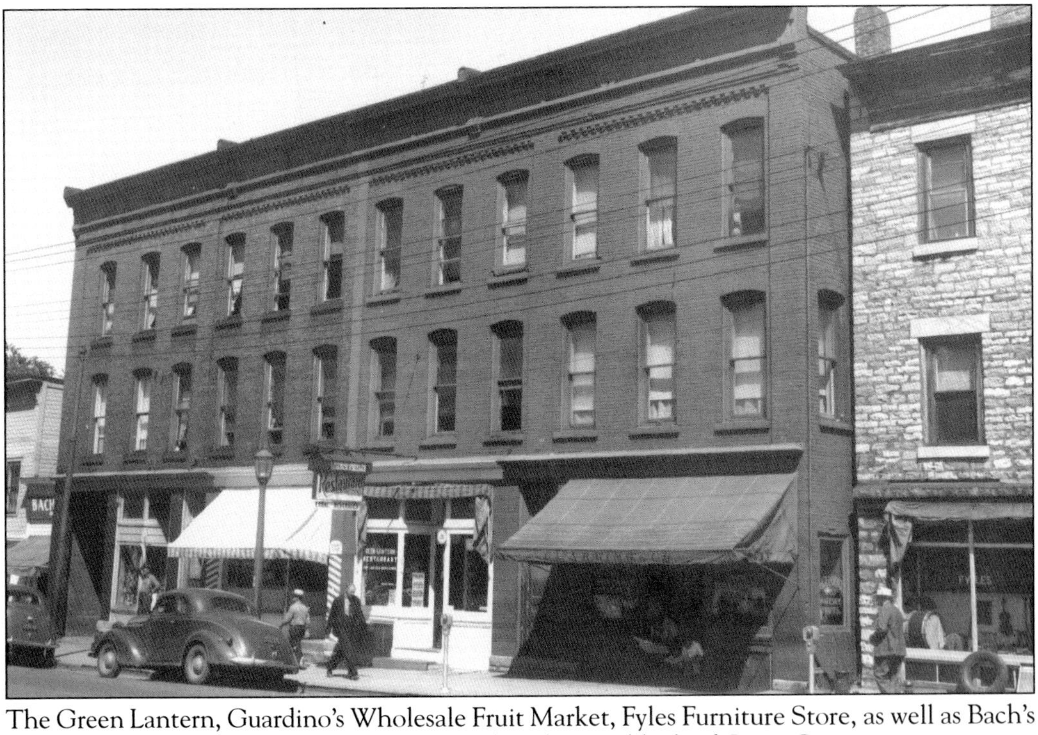

The Green Lantern, Guardino's Wholesale Fruit Market, Fyles Furniture Store, as well as Bach's Market and Brouse Barber Shop were located in the 300 block of Court Street.

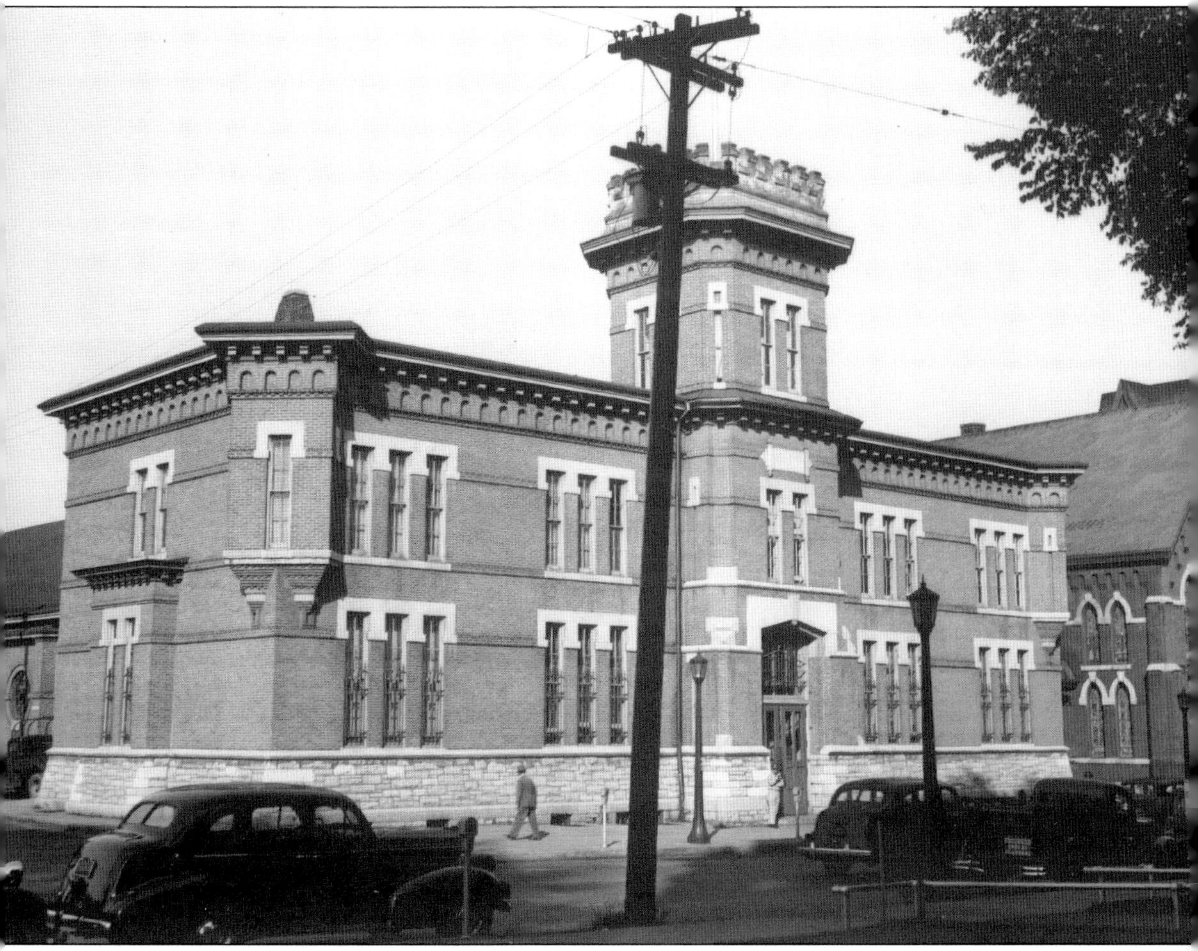

This stately building is the New York State Armory. Located at 190 Arsenal Street, it was built in 1879. George W. Flower and Patrick Phillips were the builders. N. Dillenbeck was the local architect. The unit that was originally quartered in the armory was "C" Company of the 25th Battalion and consisted of 3 officers and 56 enlisted men. The building was leveled in April 1967 as part of the final major urban renewal development building leveling.

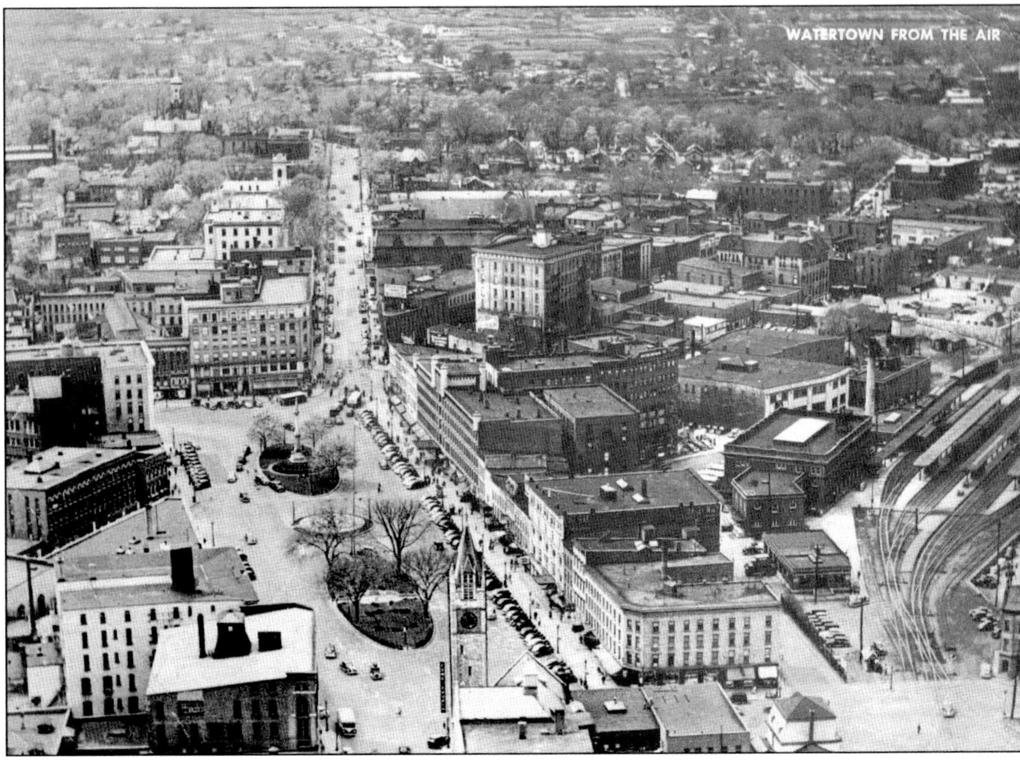

An aerial view of downtown Watertown shows the railroad depot to the right. Looking down Arsenal Street, one can see farmland that later became home to the Salmon Run Mall. Many of the buildings in this photograph were demolished during the urban renewal project.

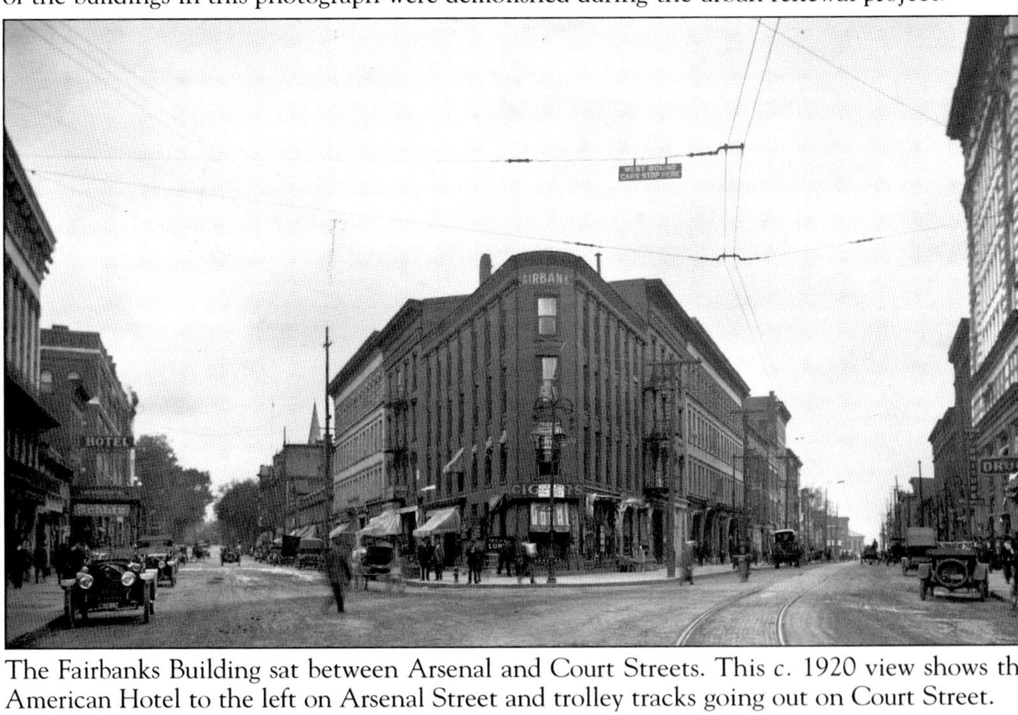

The Fairbanks Building sat between Arsenal and Court Streets. This *c.* 1920 view shows the American Hotel to the left on Arsenal Street and trolley tracks going out on Court Street.

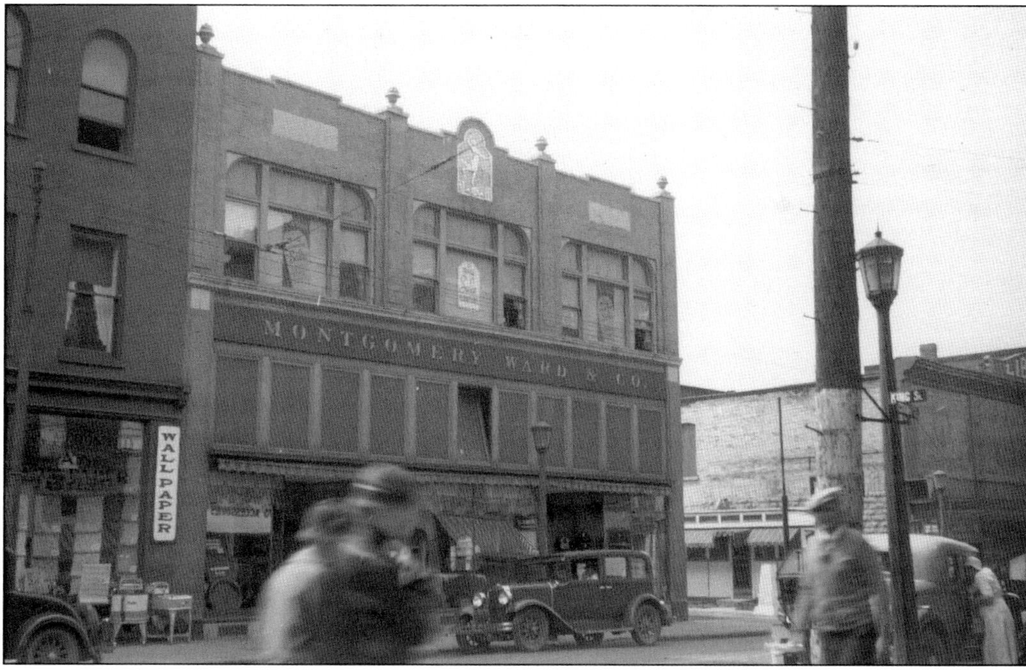

The Montgomery Ward & Company store was located on Court Street for many years. McDonald's Paint and Wallpaper, which was next door, is advertising wringer washing machines in this 1934 photograph.

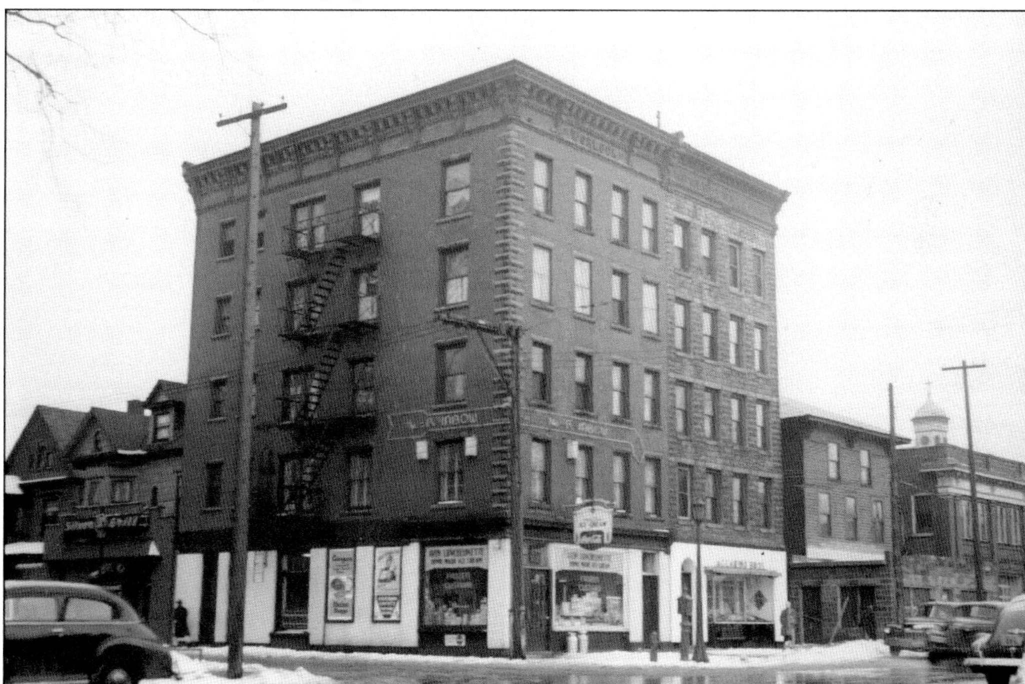

The building shown here was located on the corner of Sherman and Arsenal Streets. It housed apartments as well as the Avon Luncheonette, Accarino Brothers Meat Market, and the Rainbow Restaurant. To the far right is what was the Arsenal Street Fire Station.

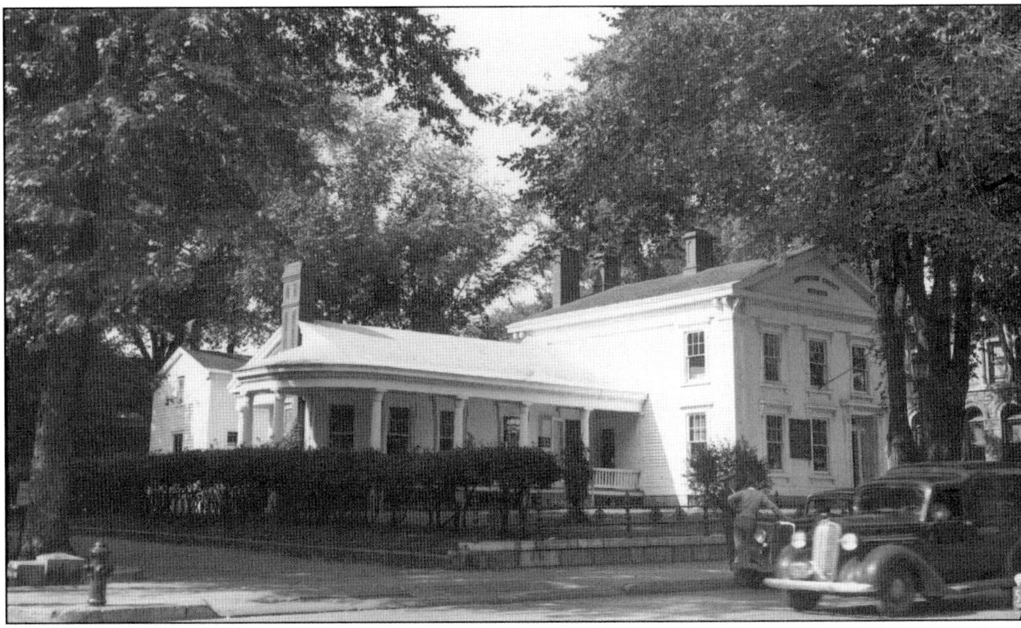

The stately home of Gov. Roswell P. Flower later housed some county offices. It has since been replaced with the Jefferson County office building.

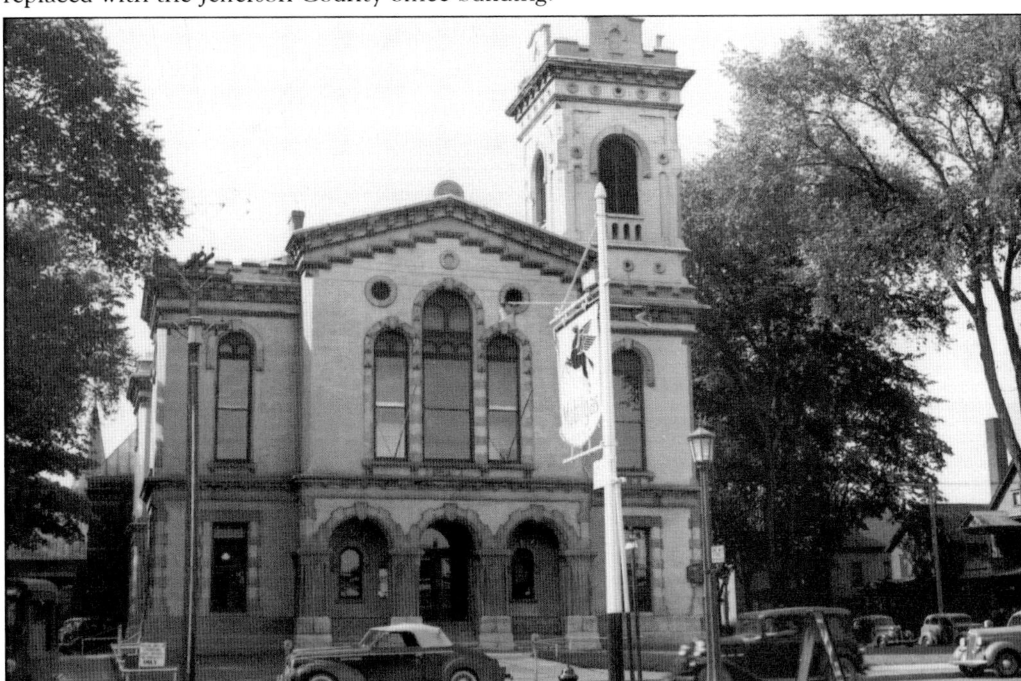

This 1940 view of the Jefferson County Court House was taken from the Mobil station across the street that was removed during urban renewal. While the goal of the project was to relocate businesses back into the area after reconstruction of new buildings, federal regulations prohibited a gas station from being constructed in the area. Although there was support for the station, the urban renewal officials would not allow it to rebuild.

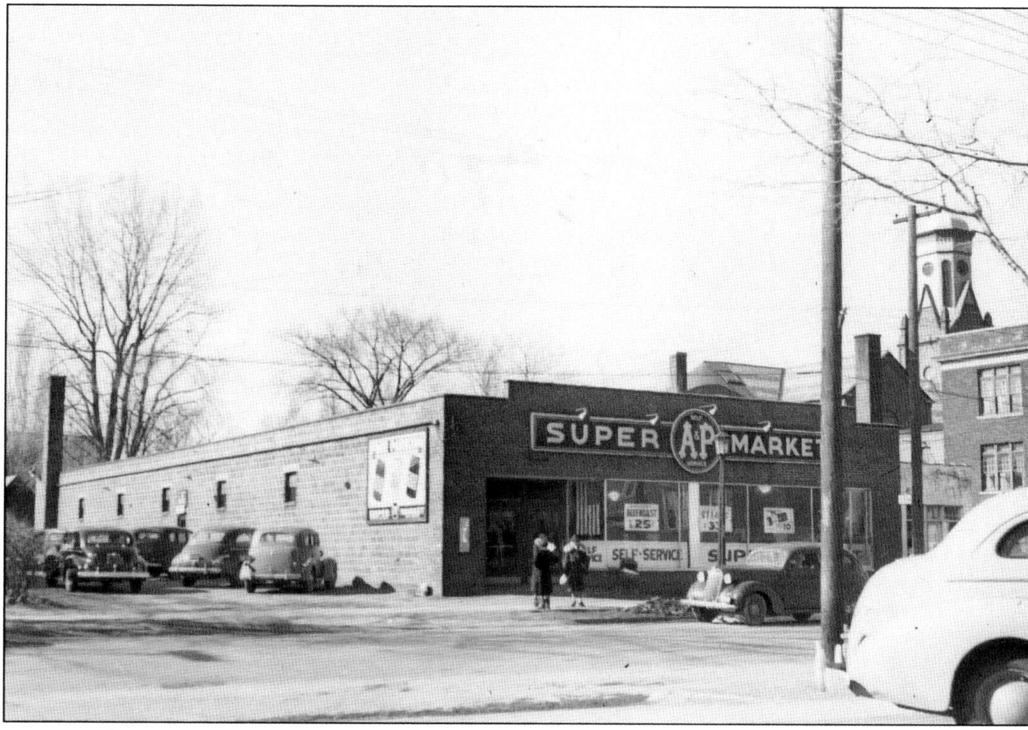

Supermarkets were located in the downtown area for many years. The A & P was across from the Grand Union on Arsenal Street.

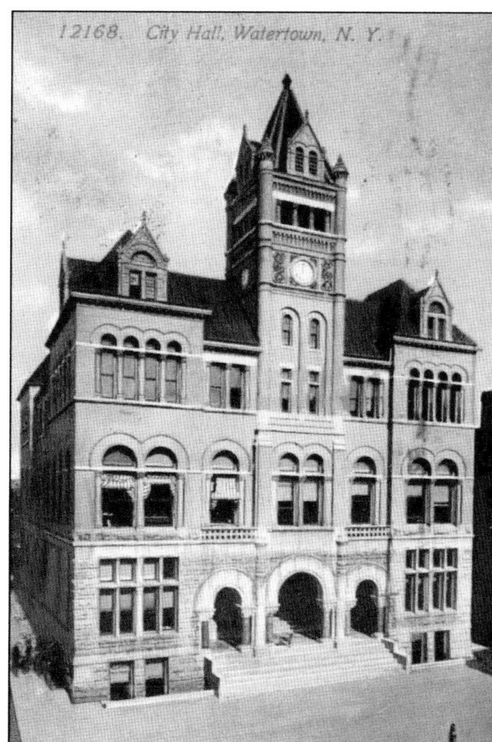

The majestic city hall building was built during the term of Mayor J.B. Wise. Architecturally impressive, this building served the community until the early 1960s.

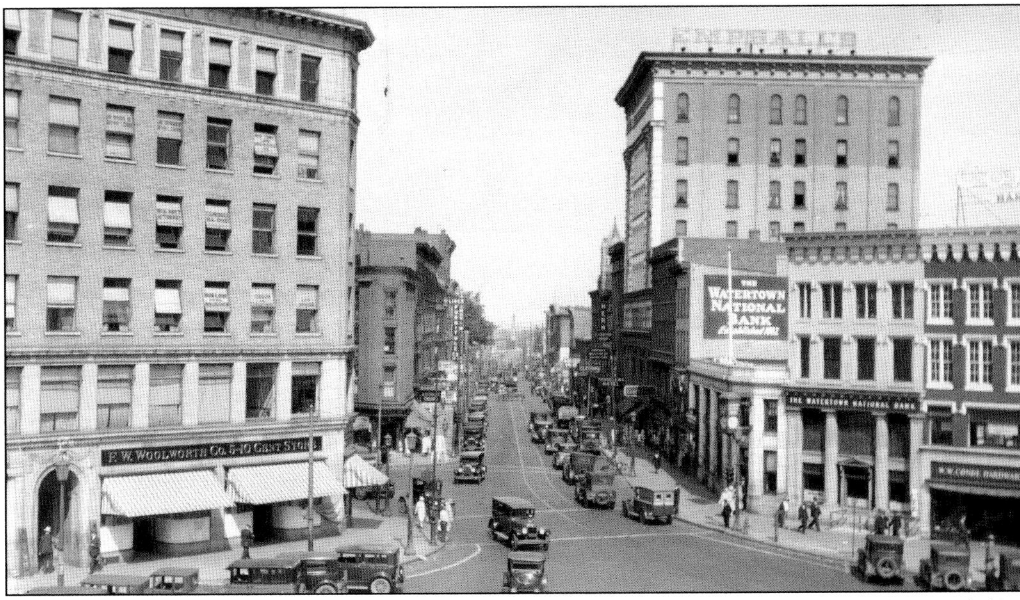

The Woolworth Building on the American Corner was not only home to the five-and-dime store but also housed many offices. The façade of the Watertown National Bank building was impressive with its marble columns. The Brighton stands tall in the skyline. Farther down Court Street, one can see the tip of the city hall tower.

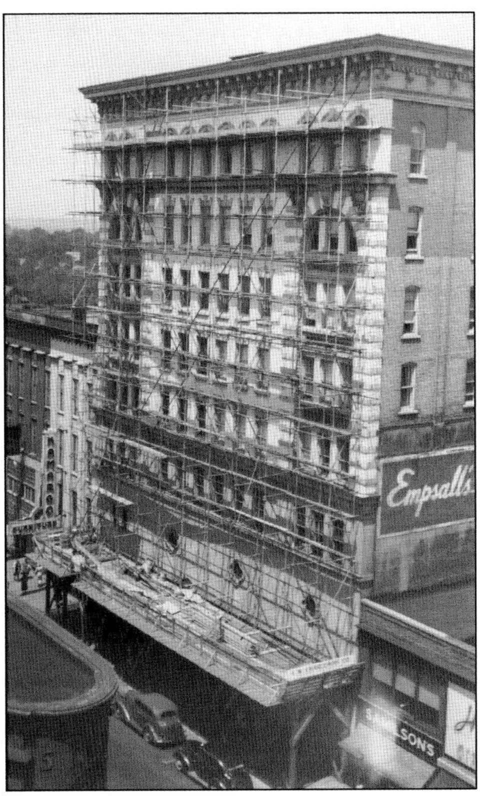

The Brighton Building and Empsall's Department Store get a face-lift in this 1949 photograph, which was taken from the Woolworth Building roof.

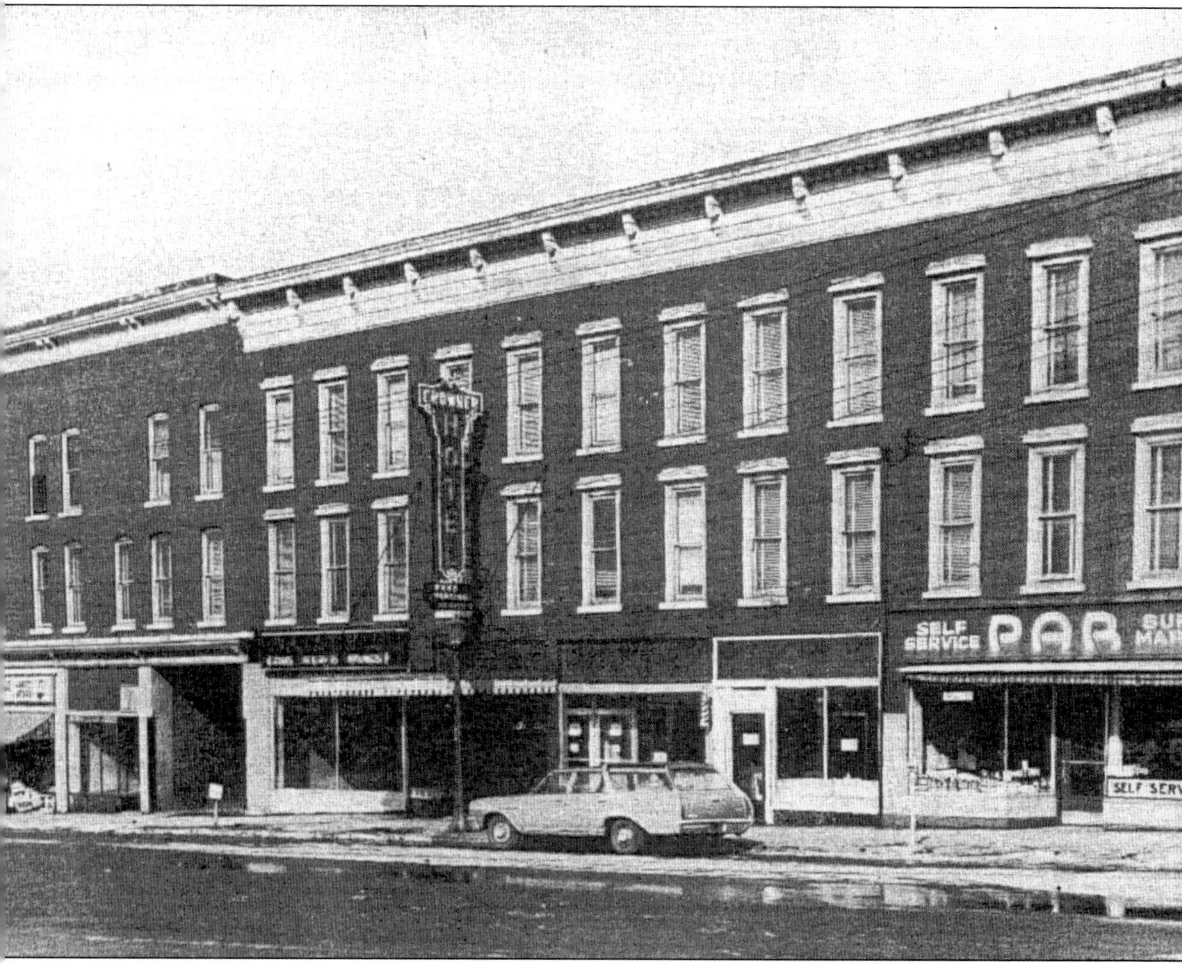

The historic Crowner Hotel was located on lower Court Street. The block was torn down in January 1966. John Crowner started the hotel when he took over the building in 1843. Fire destroyed the original wooden building in 1854. A new, two-story hotel was begun in 1855 and opened to the public on New Year's Eve 1856.

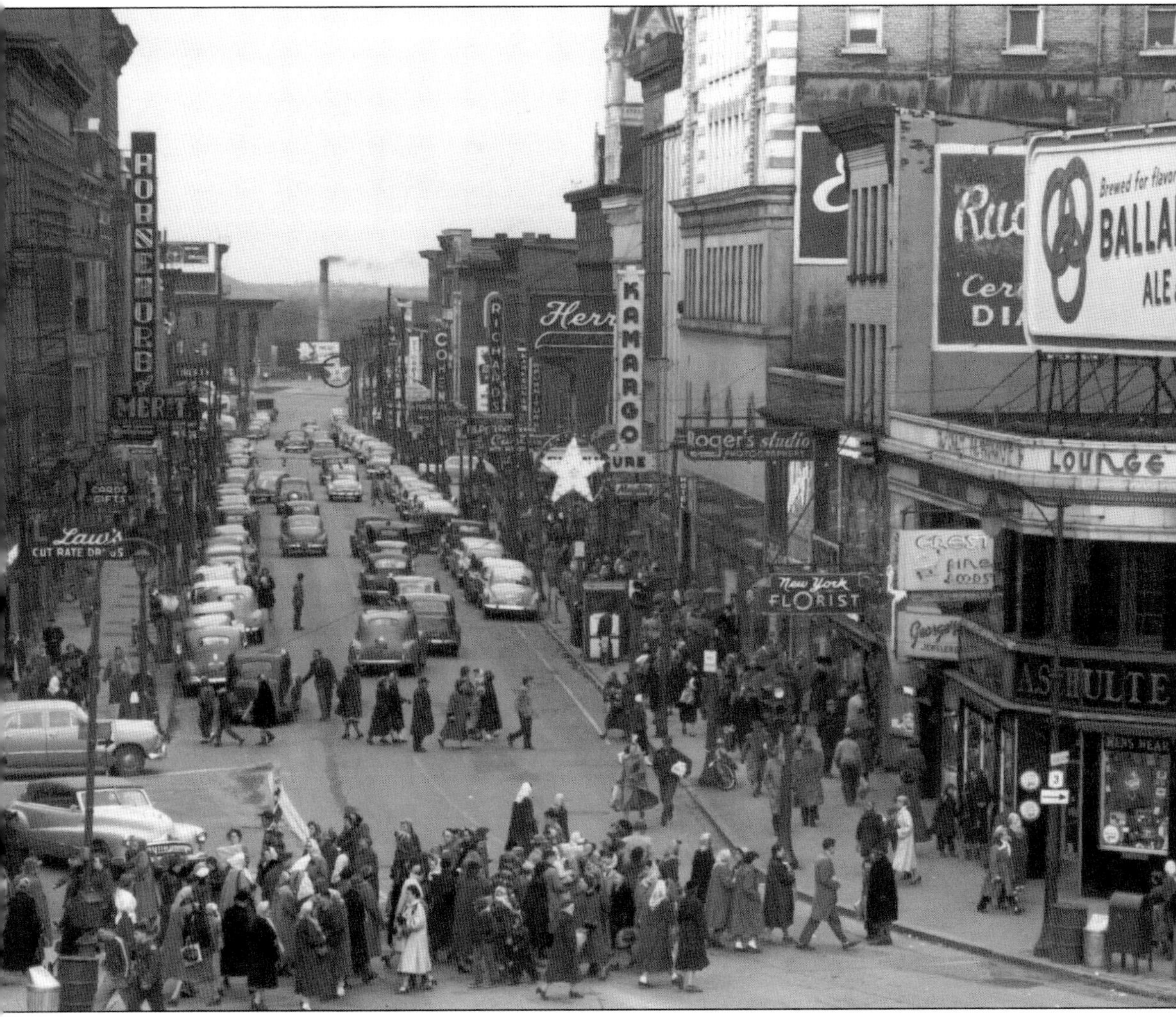

Christmas shoppers cross at the American Corner on December 13, 1952. The hustle and bustle of shoppers can be viewed all the way down Court Street. A bus stop was located in front of Empsall's, and cars frequently stopped to allow pedestrians to cross the street.

Seven

Industry and Business

Many of the first settlers were men skilled in mechanics and construction. Their background of experience and their willingness to venture into new enterprises helped to give direction to Watertown as an industrial center. The waterpower capabilities of the Black River attracted the early settlers who envisioned the settlement as an industrial and trading community.

Jonathan Cowan secured land along the south shore of the Black River opposite Beebee Island, as well as the island itself, which consisted of about five acres. For 30 years, it was known as Cowan's Island. He constructed a dam between the south bank and the island in 1802 and was the first to harness the waters of the Black River to turn the wheels of industry. At about the same time, he built a sawmill and a gristmill on the island.

For quite some time, goods were transported to the area by oxcart or team from down state or by boat from Oswego. Therefore, the first industries to be started were those that supplied the greatest needs of the settlers. Trees needed to be sawed into lumber. Grinding mills converted the grain into flour. Cooper shops made barrels to hold potash, which for several years was the principal source of cash money for this region. Potash, a by-product of ashes from burning down trees, was shipped abroad, where it was used in the glassmaking industry.

Census records indicate the following industries and business in Watertown in 1827: 3 tanneries, 7 shoe shops, 3 saddle and harness shops, 8 taverns, 3 flour mills, a foundry, a nail factory, a paint shop, 2 machine shops, 8 blacksmith shops, 4 wagon shops, 2 jewelers, 2 leather shops, 2 chair factories, a sash mill, 2 druggists, 4 cabinet shops, a hat factory, a woolen mill, 2 hat shops, a cotton factory, 4 tailor shops, 3 paper mills, 2 bookstores, 2 printing shops, 15 dry good stores, 2 hardware stores, and 2 pail shops.

Few of these industries depended upon distant markets. They were small concerns, each employing only a few people and requiring only a small amount of capital investment in machinery and equipment. During the next 100 years, Watertown was prominently identified with textiles, paper, and carriage making. In the case of each, changing economic conditions intervened.

The growth of early Watertown was due, in part, to two different types of people coming together to help create a community. One group consisted of those who knew how to use tools, such as the carpenters, millwrights, masons, metal works, cabinetmakers, and engineers. The other group consisted of individuals, such as Bronson, TenEyck, Keyes, and Hungerford, who were willing to risk their capital to enable these others to develop their ideas. Both groups played a significant part in the development of the city of Watertown.

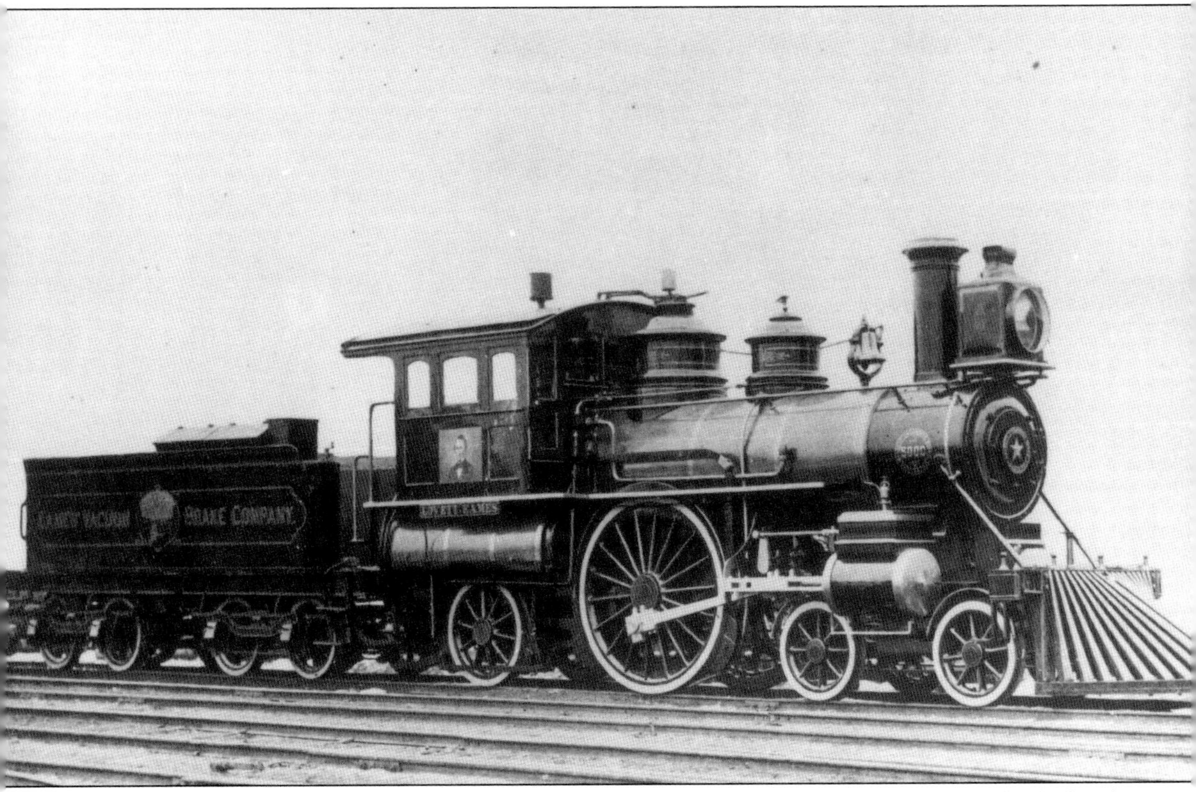

The *Lovett Eames*, a Baldwin 5,000 Special built in April 1880, was originally built for the Delaware and Bound Brook Railroad. The locomotive was later purchased by the Eames Vacuum Brake Company and used to demonstrate the action of the Eames brake on heavy trains. It made a number of trial runs in the United States hauling passenger-filled trains at express speed. In 1881, it was shipped to England to demonstrate the Eames vacuum brake.

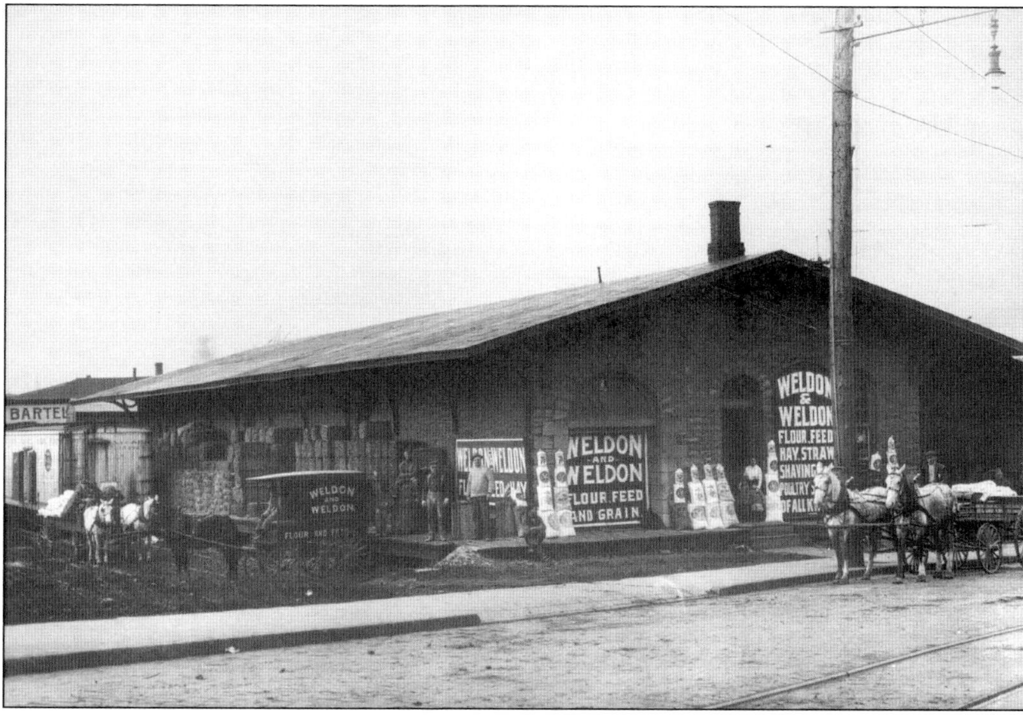

Bartel's Brewery and Jim Weldon's Feed Store were located on Newell Street, under the Court Street Bridge.

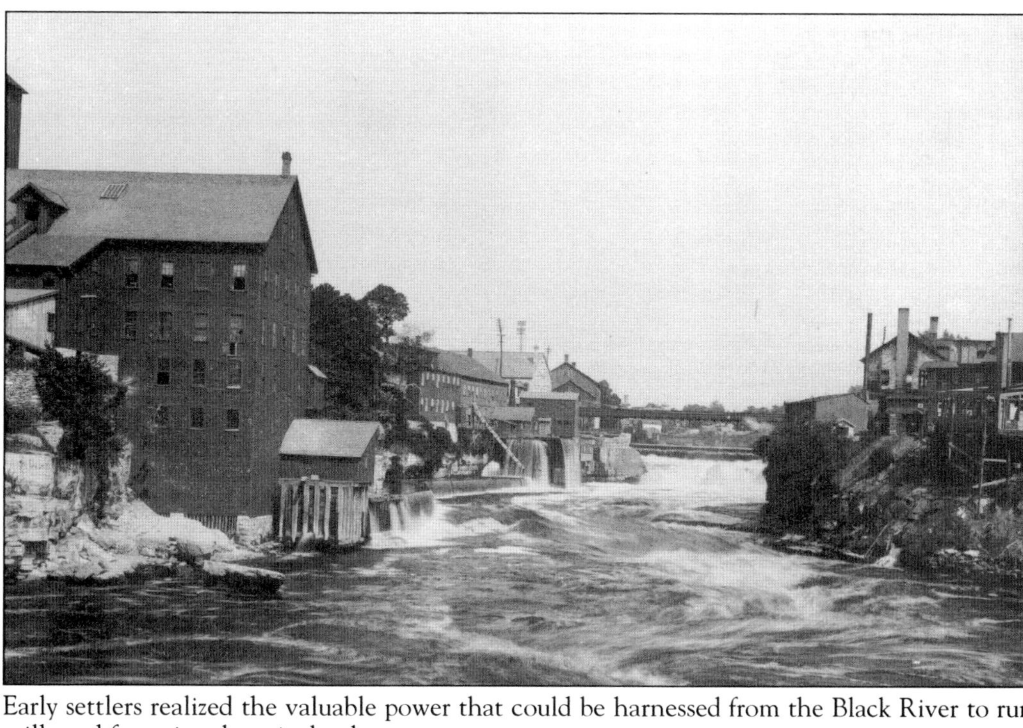
Early settlers realized the valuable power that could be harnessed from the Black River to run mills and factories along its banks.

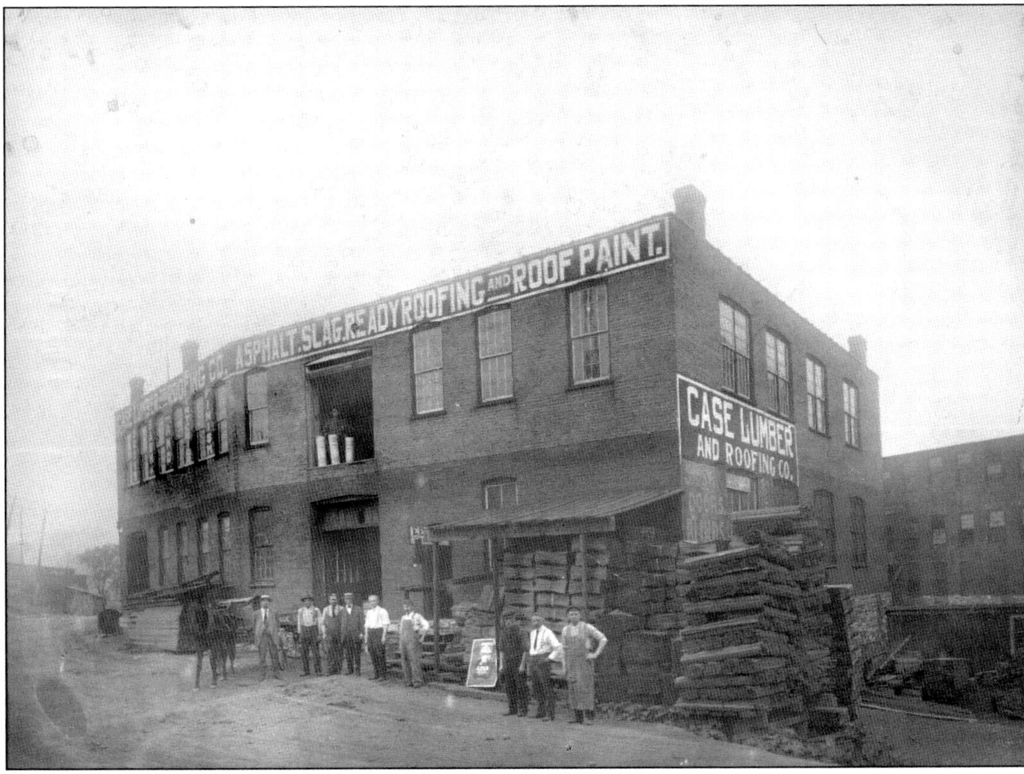

The Case Lumber & Roofing Company was located at 108–112 River Street. This photograph was taken *c.* 1910, when E.E. Case became president of the company.

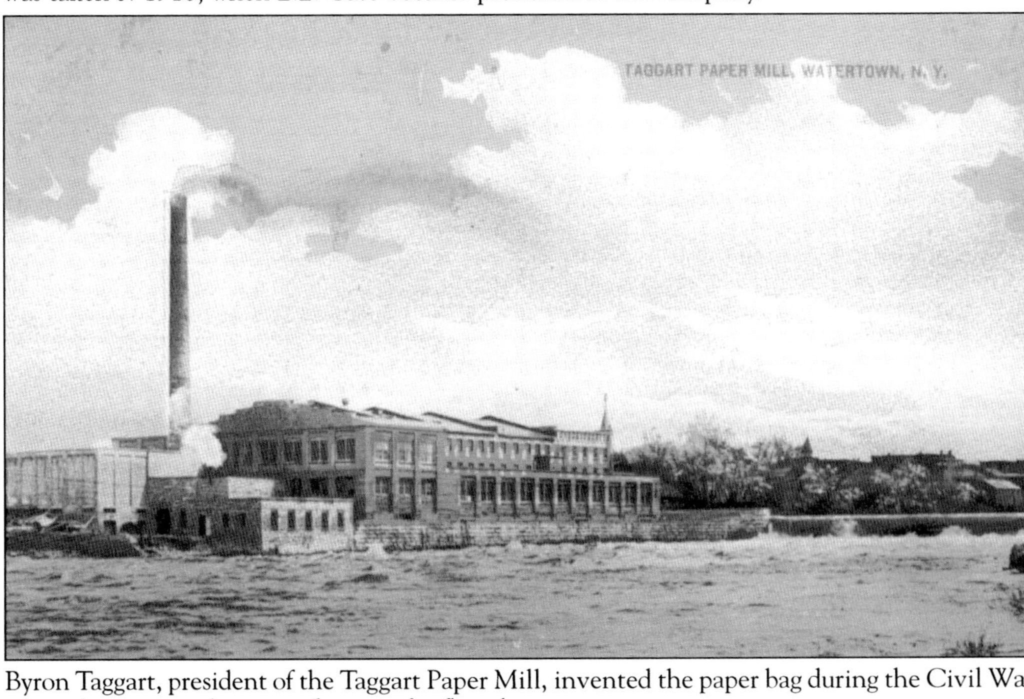

Byron Taggart, president of the Taggart Paper Mill, invented the paper bag during the Civil War when there was a shortage of cotton for flour bags.

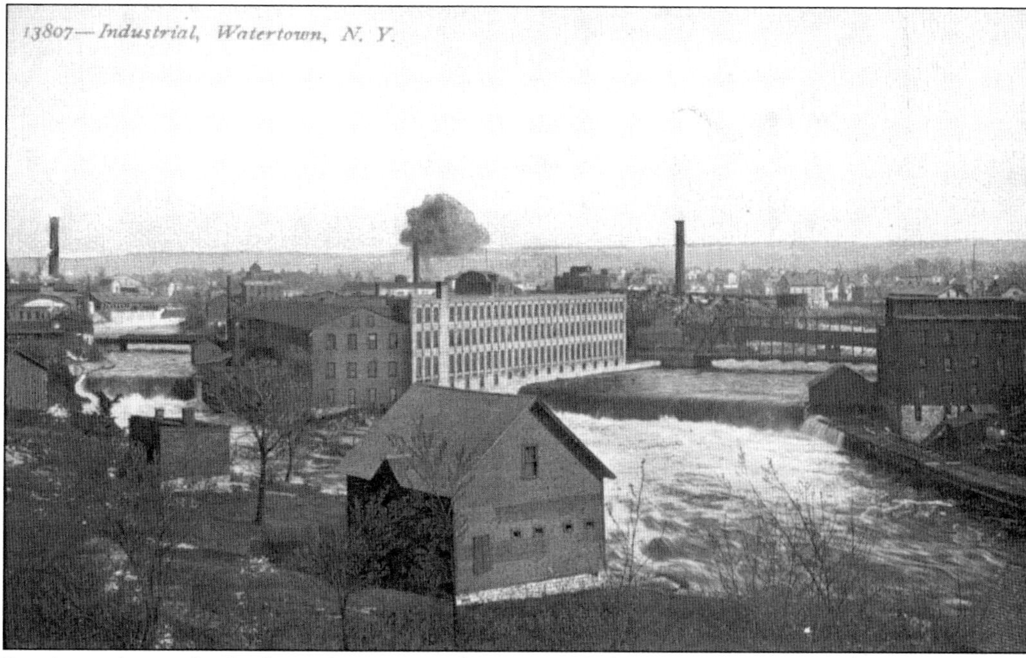

Smokestacks rise high above factories in this postcard showing "industrial Watertown."

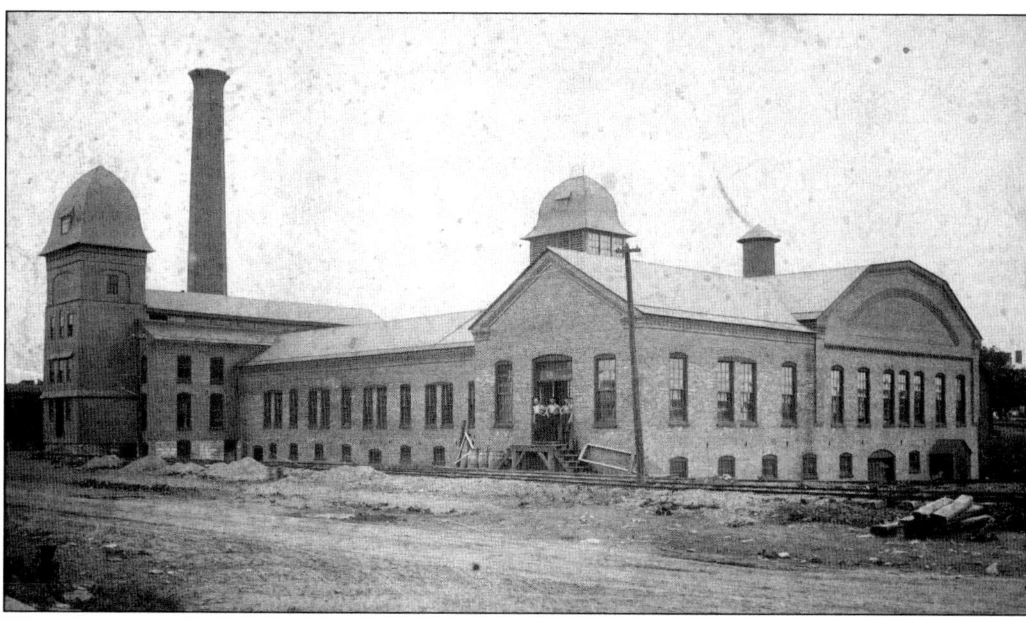

The Continental Paper Mill was located at the corner of Mill, Water, and Factory Streets. (Photograph courtesy of JCHS.)

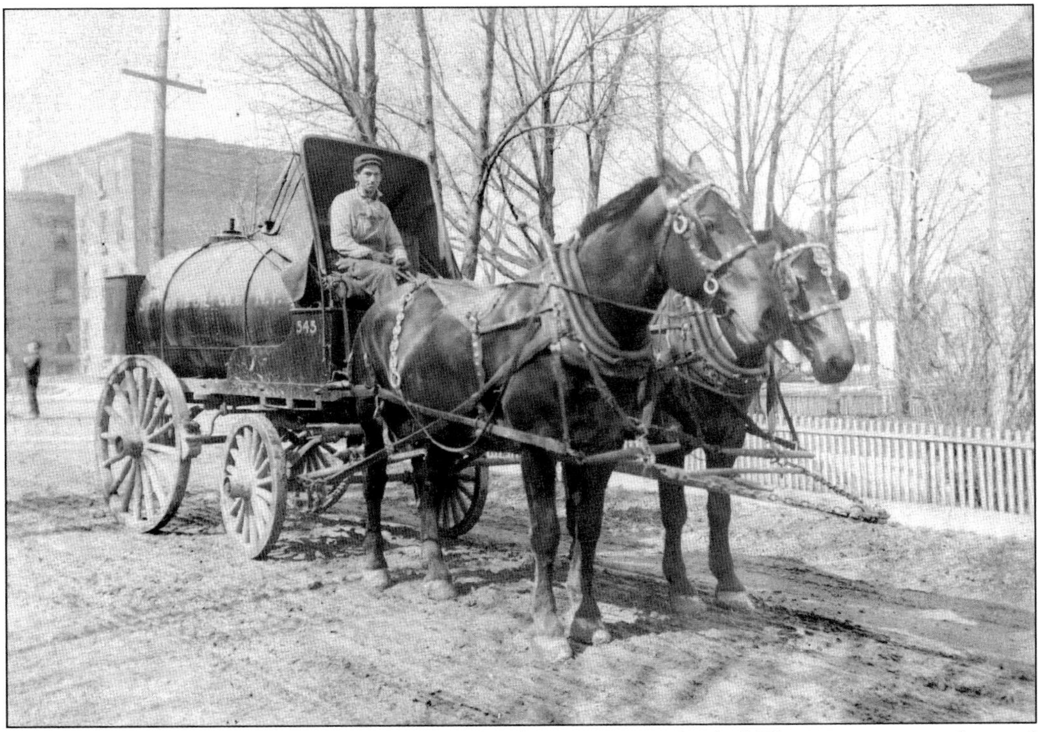

Bert Brownell is shown driving the Standard Oil Company "vehicle." The company was located on Coffeen Street. Brownell resided on Maple Avenue. (Photograph courtesy of JCHS.)

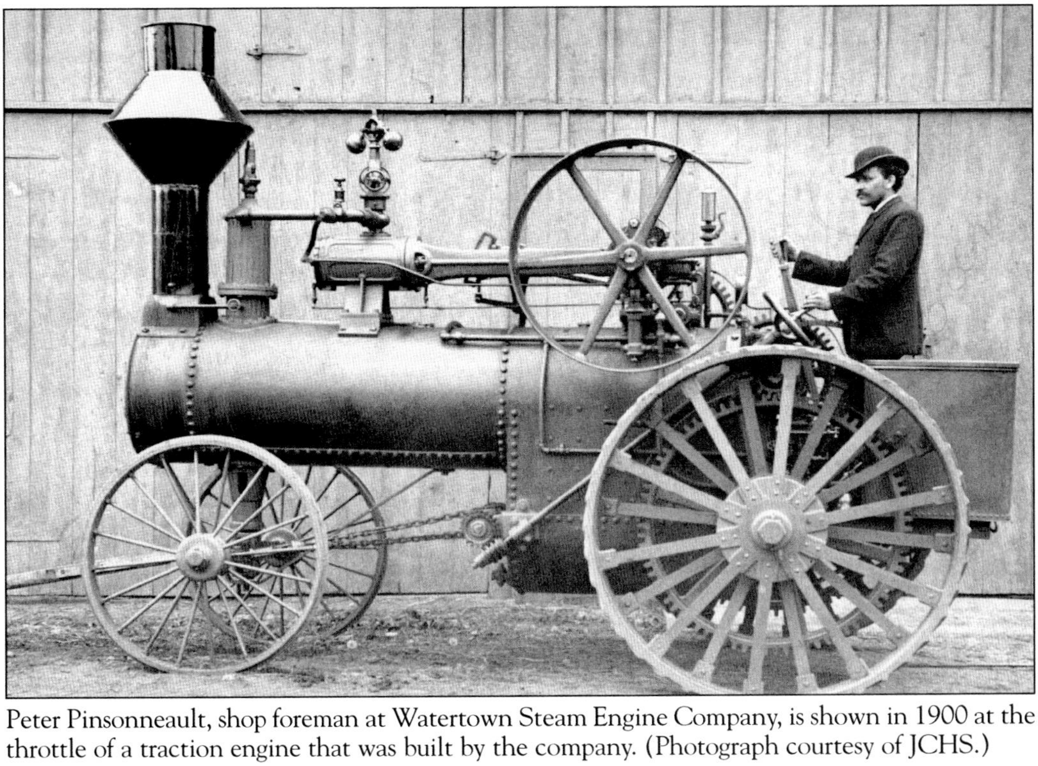

Peter Pinsonneault, shop foreman at Watertown Steam Engine Company, is shown in 1900 at the throttle of a traction engine that was built by the company. (Photograph courtesy of JCHS.)

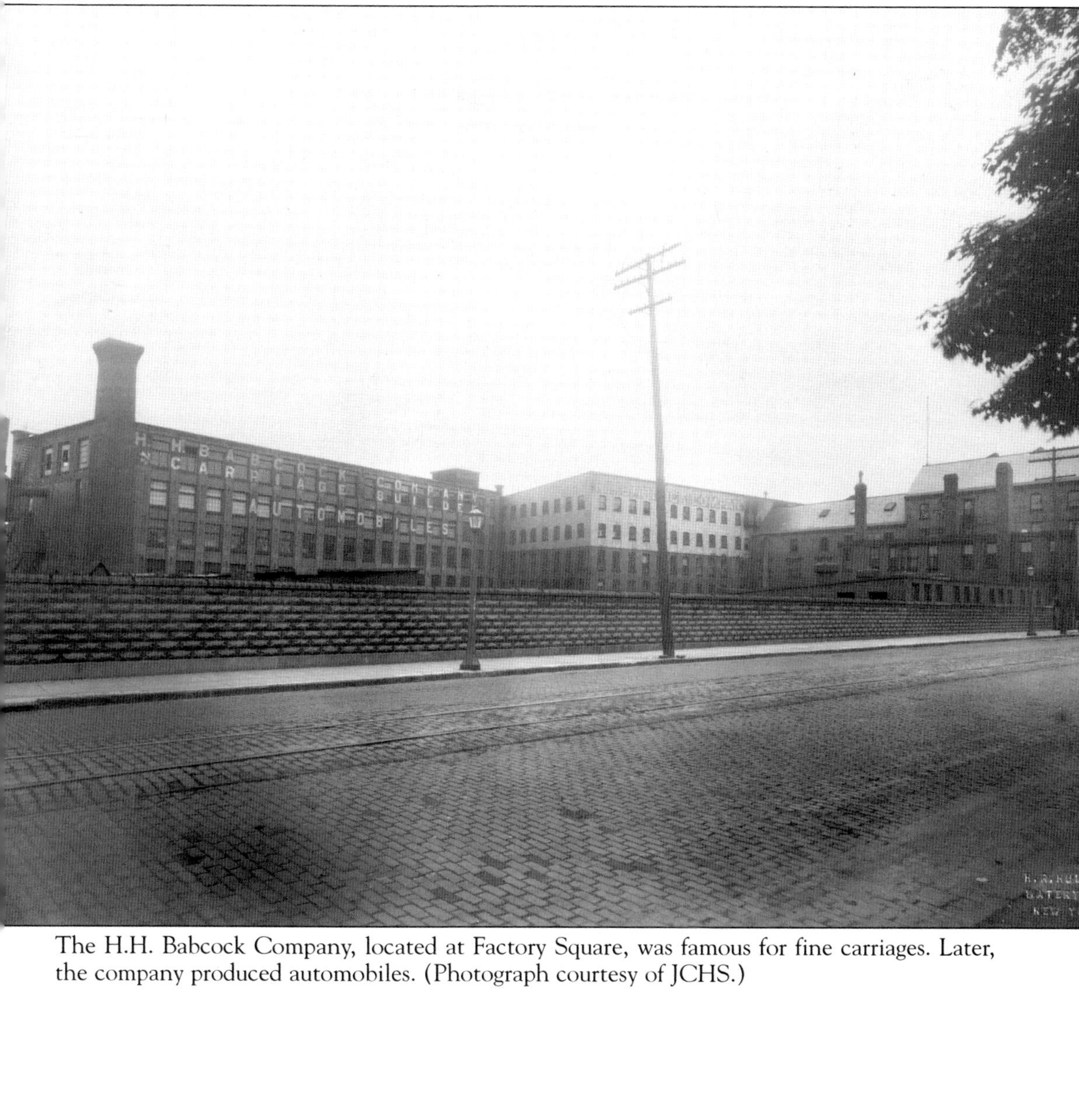

The H.H. Babcock Company, located at Factory Square, was famous for fine carriages. Later, the company produced automobiles. (Photograph courtesy of JCHS.)

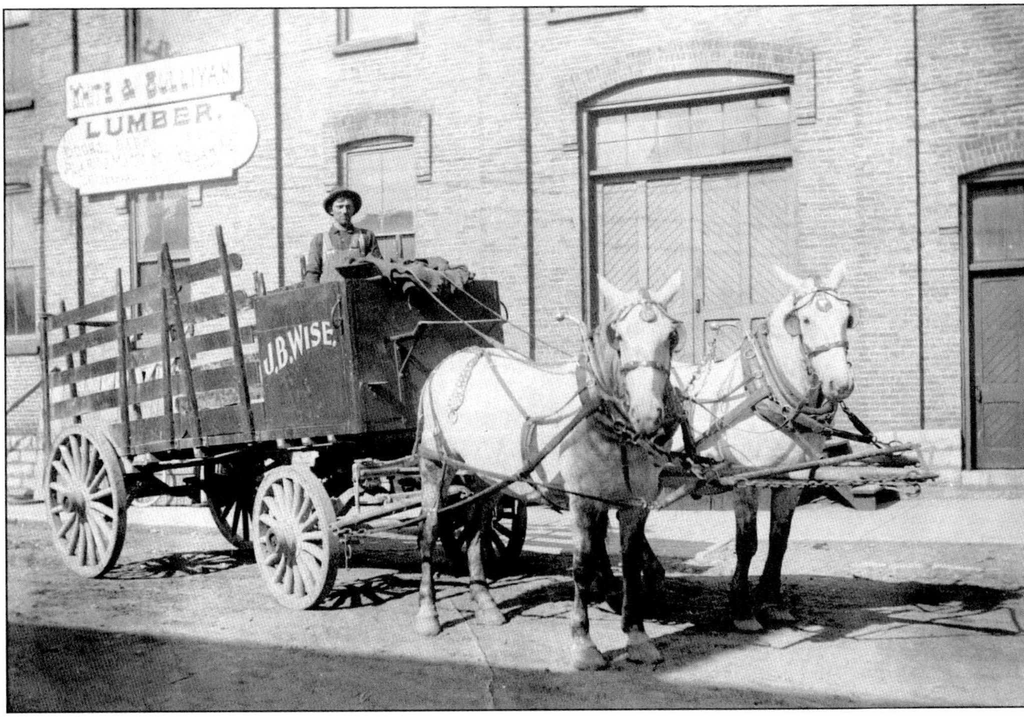

A J.B. Wise employee drives a wagon and team past the White & Sullivan Lumber Company. White & Sullivan was located at 125 Moulton Street and was the predecessor to G.W. White & Sons.

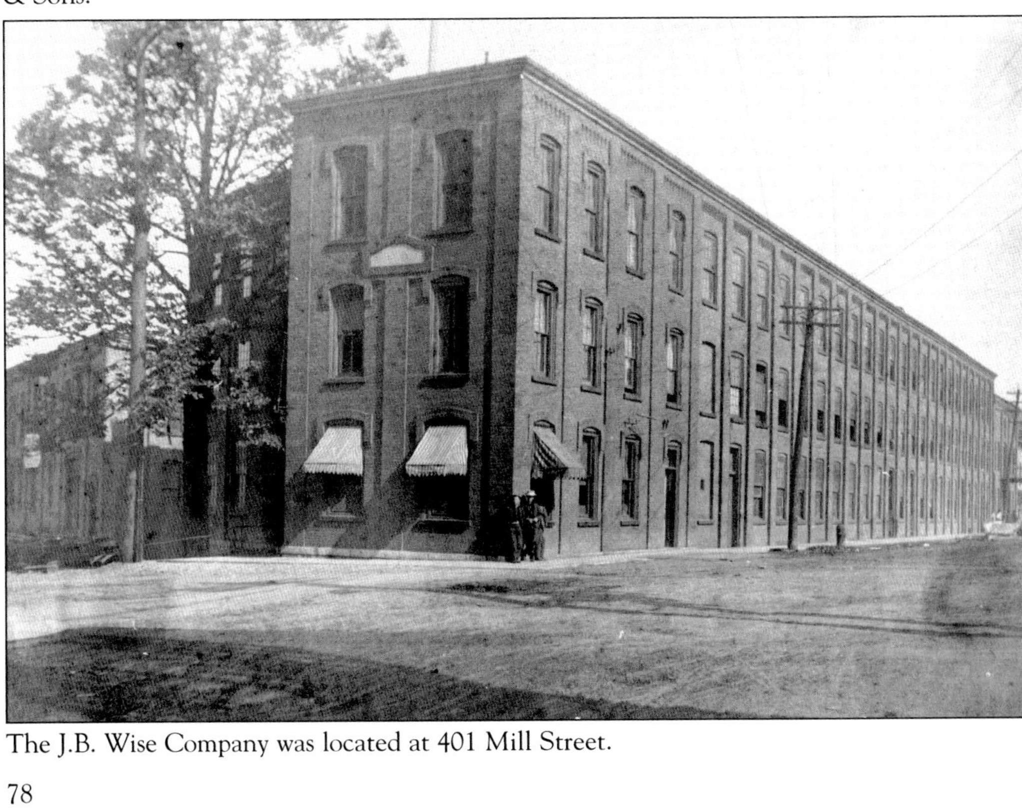

The J.B. Wise Company was located at 401 Mill Street.

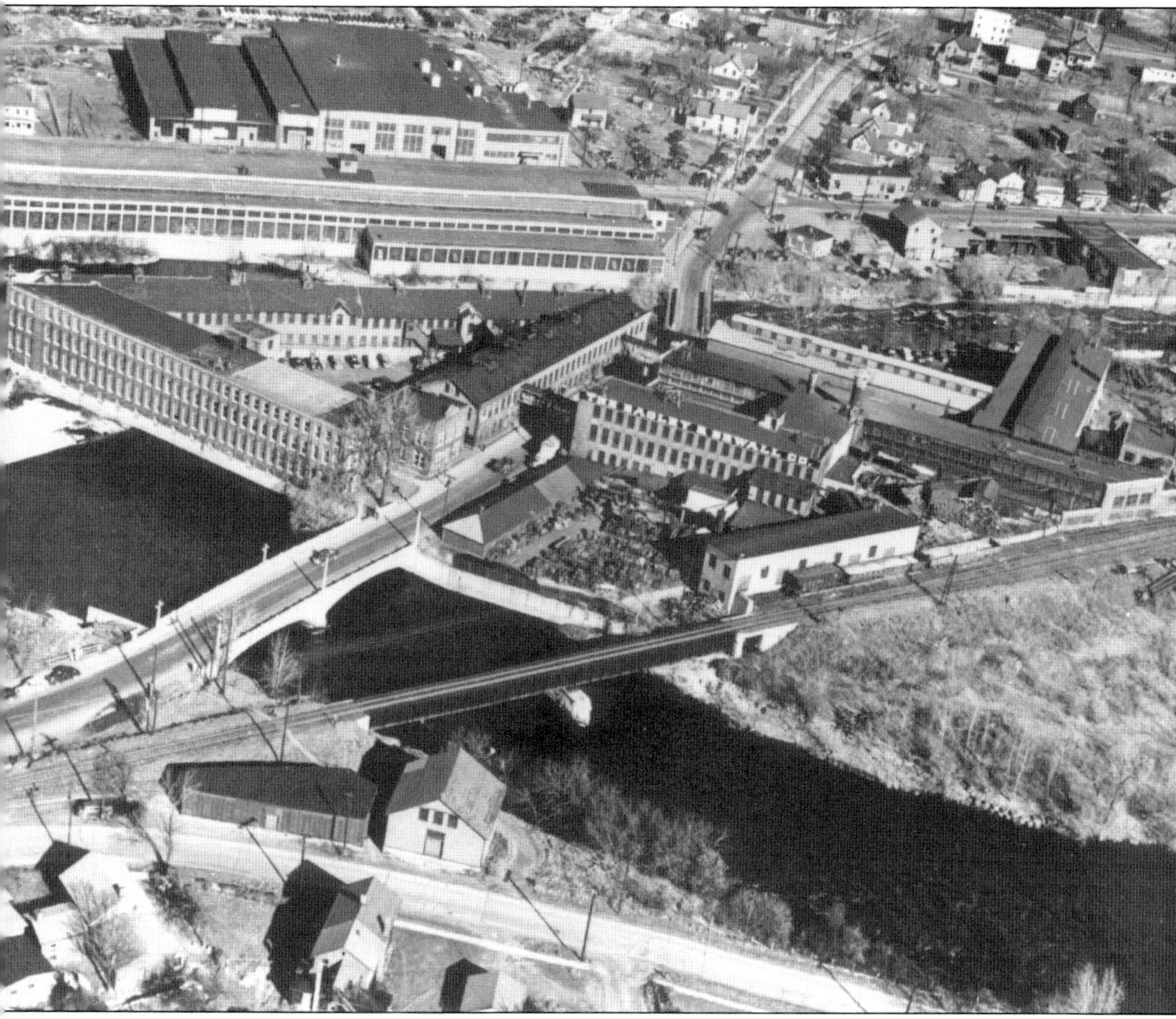

The Bagley & Sewall Company plant was located partly on Sewall's Island and partly on the north bank of the Black River at the intersection of Pearl and Moulton Streets. The company was founded in 1853 by George Bagley, George Goulding, and Edmund Sewall. It manufactured central discharge waterwheels, boilers, engines, and did general foundry work. Goulding retired from the firm in 1862.

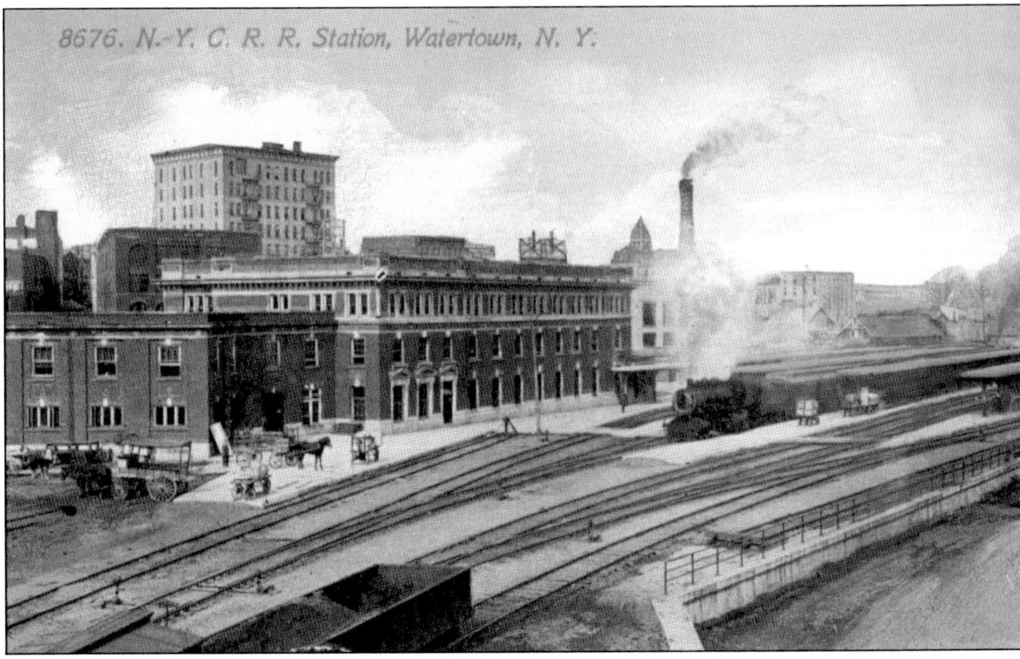

The New York City Railroad Station was located behind the Woodruff Hotel in the present area of the J.B. Wise parking lot.

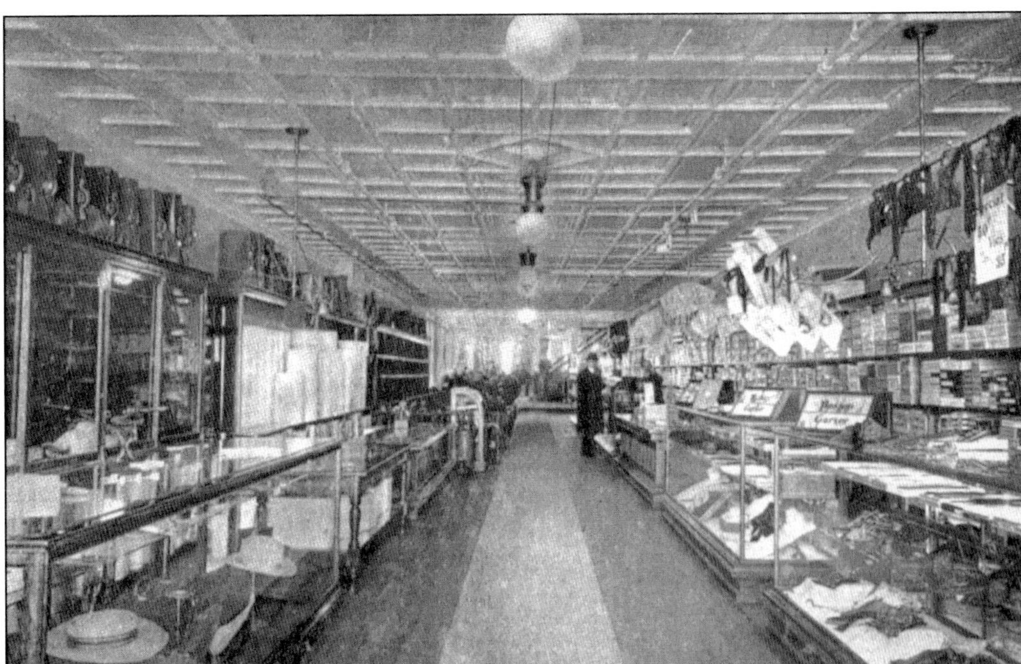

The James R. Miller Company had a sale on Boston Garters and 50¢ ties. The clothing store was located at 26 Public Square.

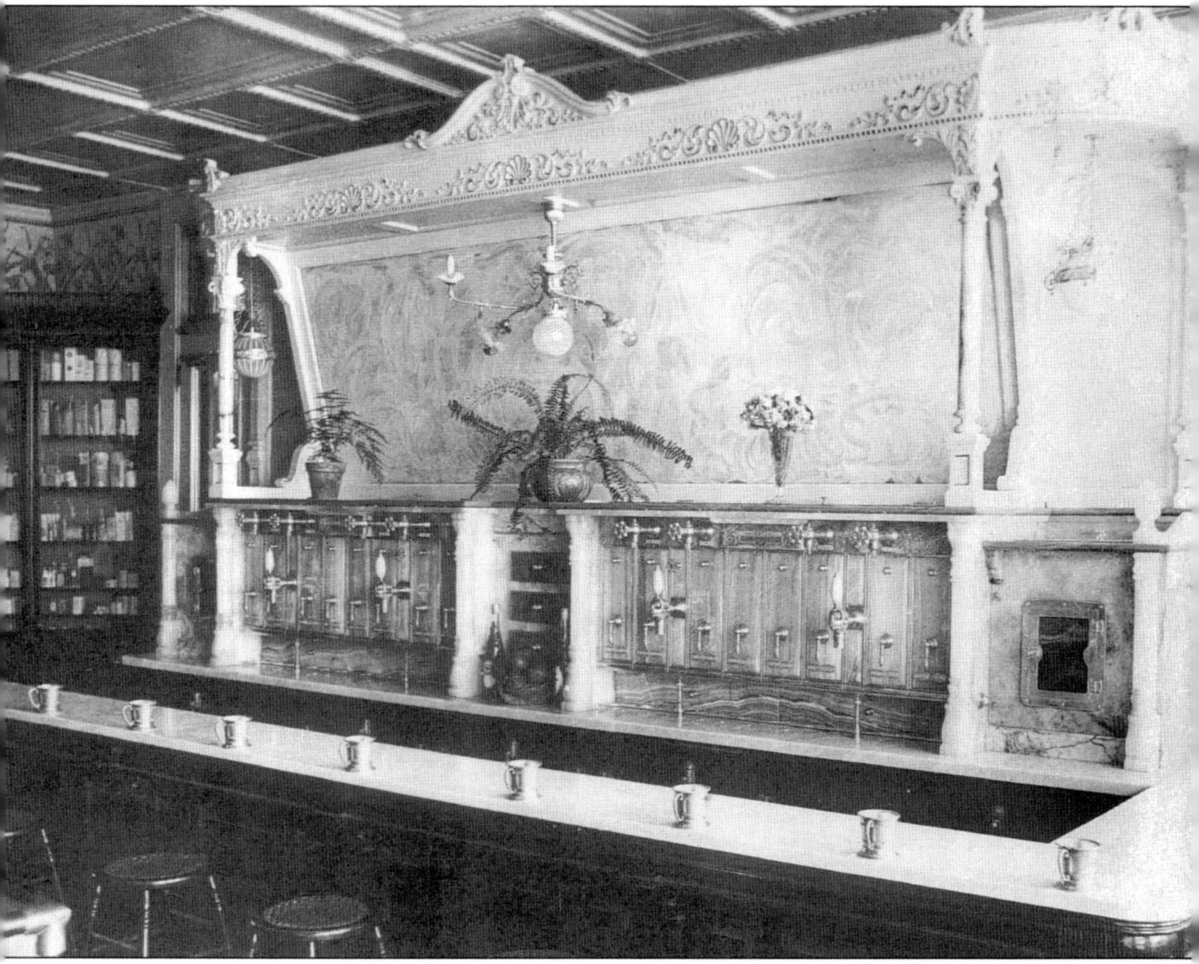

Nill & Jess Confectionary & Manufacturers of Fine Cigars was located at 9 Court Street in the 1880s. This soda fountain was at the Court Street store. They also owned a bakery on Factory Street.

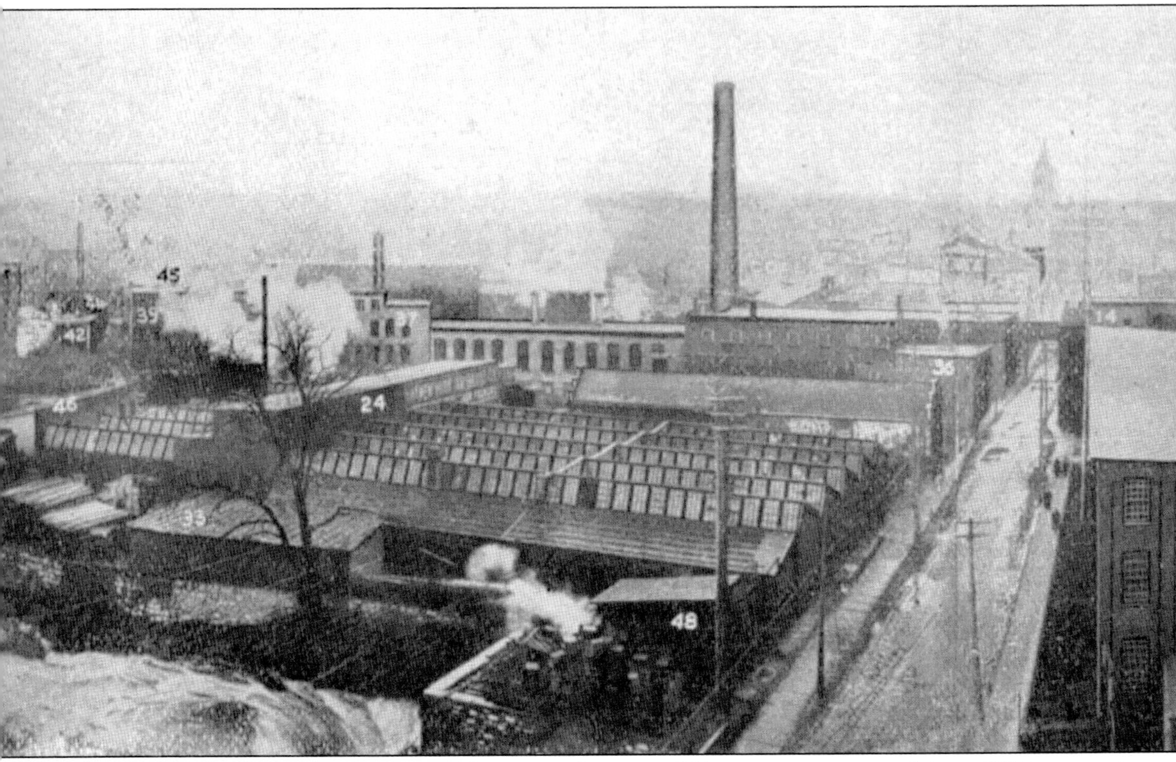

This bird's-eye view of the manufacturing district of Watertown appeared in a 1911 souvenir

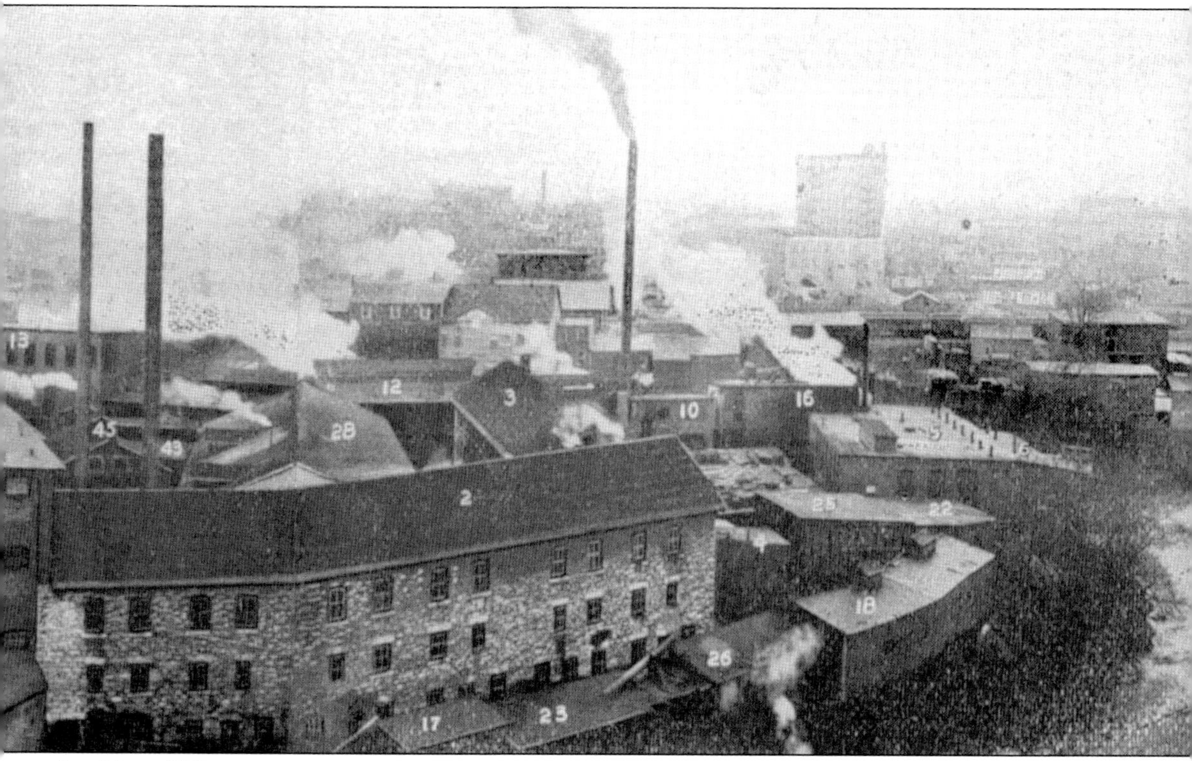

booklet of Watertown.

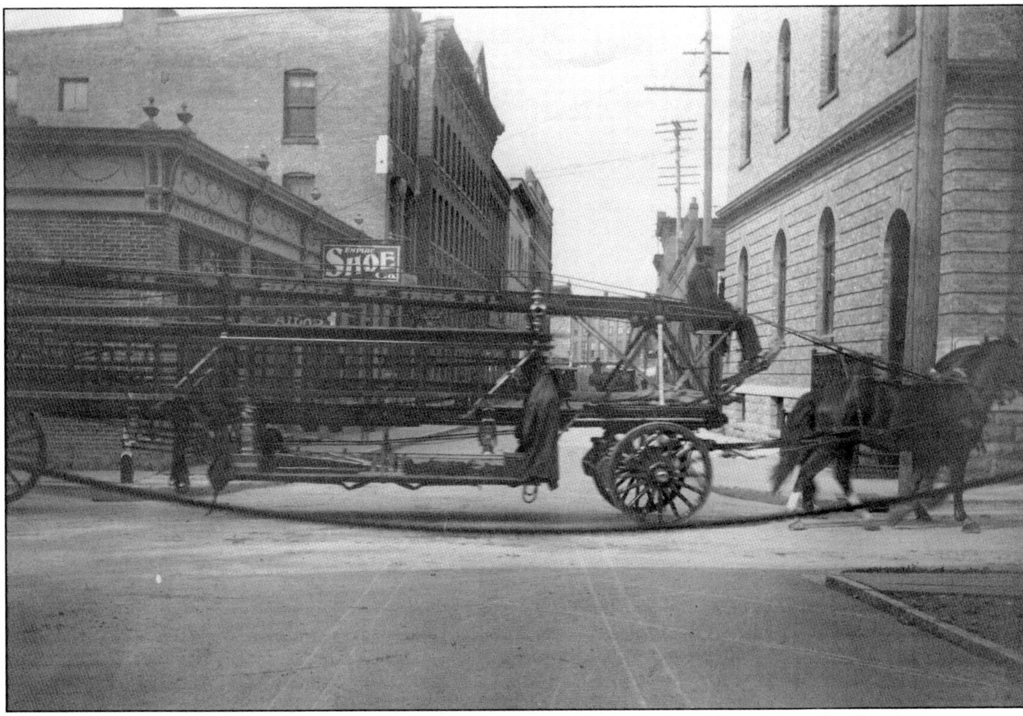

A piece of fire equipment is shown crossing Franklin Street. This view looks down toward Public Square. Many businesses were on this street, including the Empire Shoe Company.

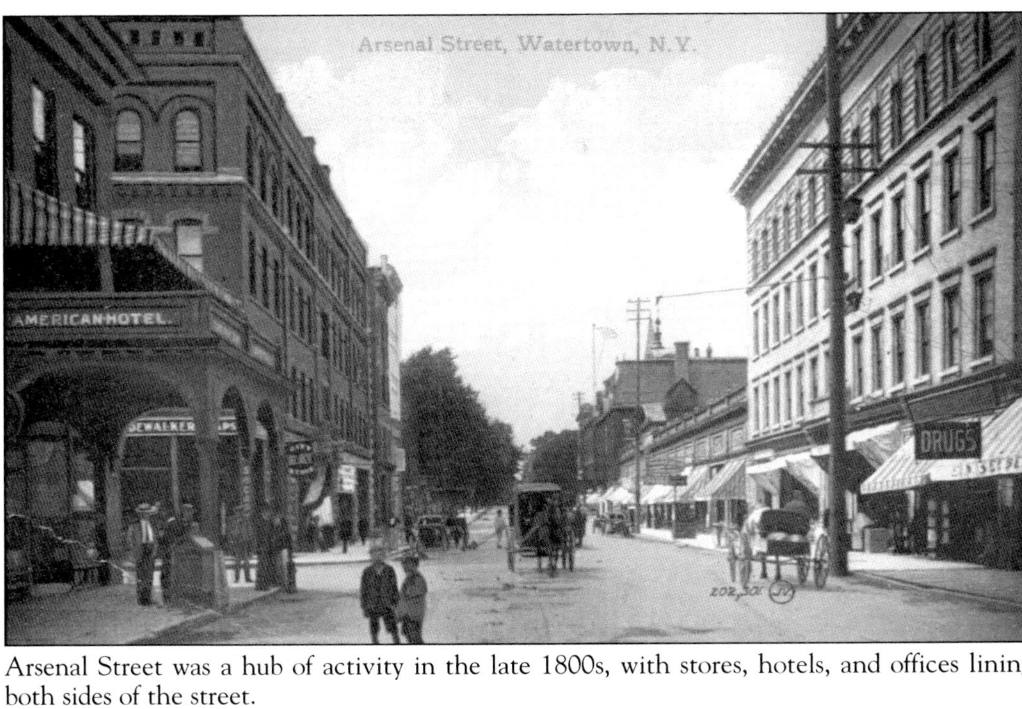

Arsenal Street was a hub of activity in the late 1800s, with stores, hotels, and offices lining both sides of the street.

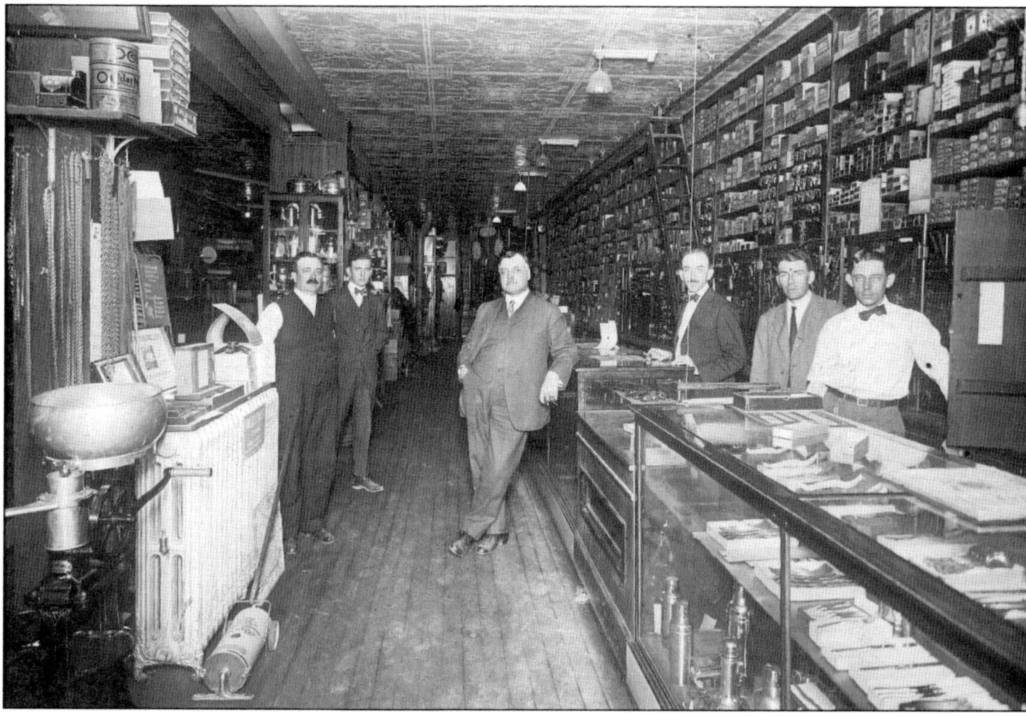

The staff of W.W. Conde Hardware Store is ready to serve the public in this August 19, 1915 photograph. The store was located at 29 Public Square.

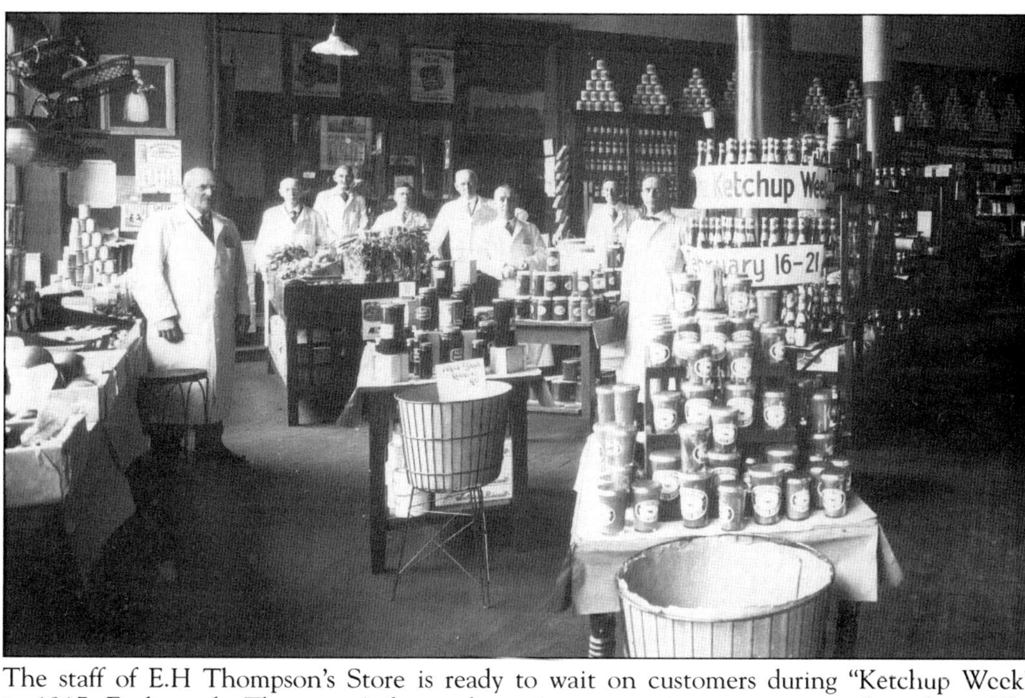

The staff of E.H Thompson's Store is ready to wait on customers during "Ketchup Week" in 1917. Each week, Thompson's featured one item to entice customers to shop there. The previous week, the store had "magnificent oranges" on sale for 25¢.

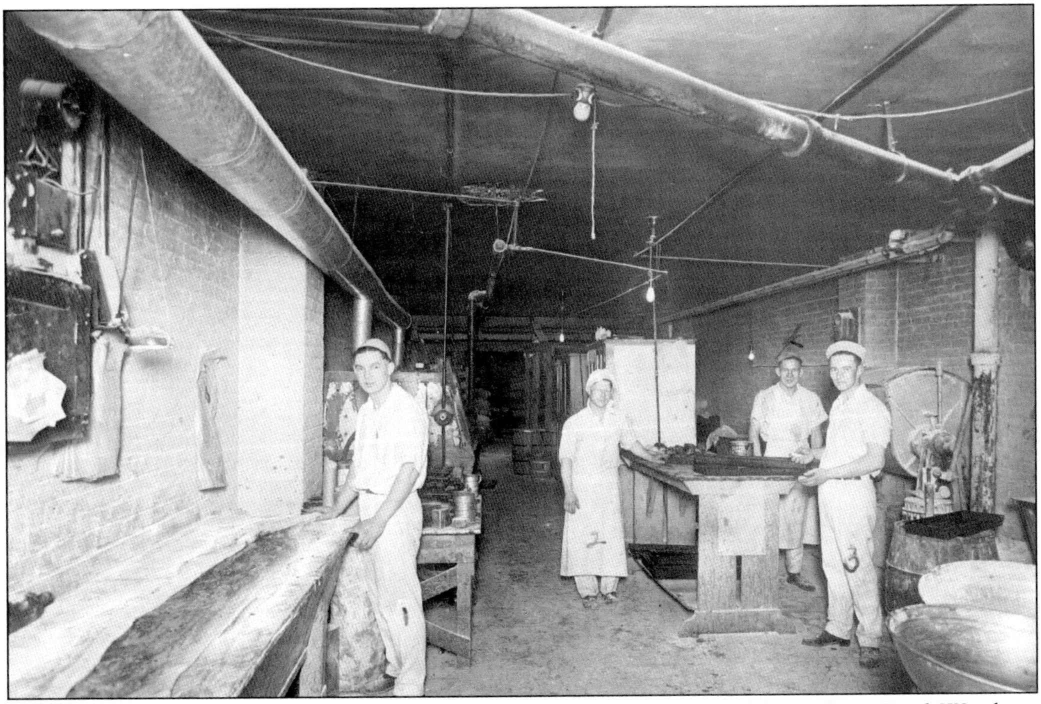

These Perfection Cake Shoppe bakers are, from left to right, Harold Gardner, Fred Woolsey, Maurice O'Connor, and Carlton Lephart.

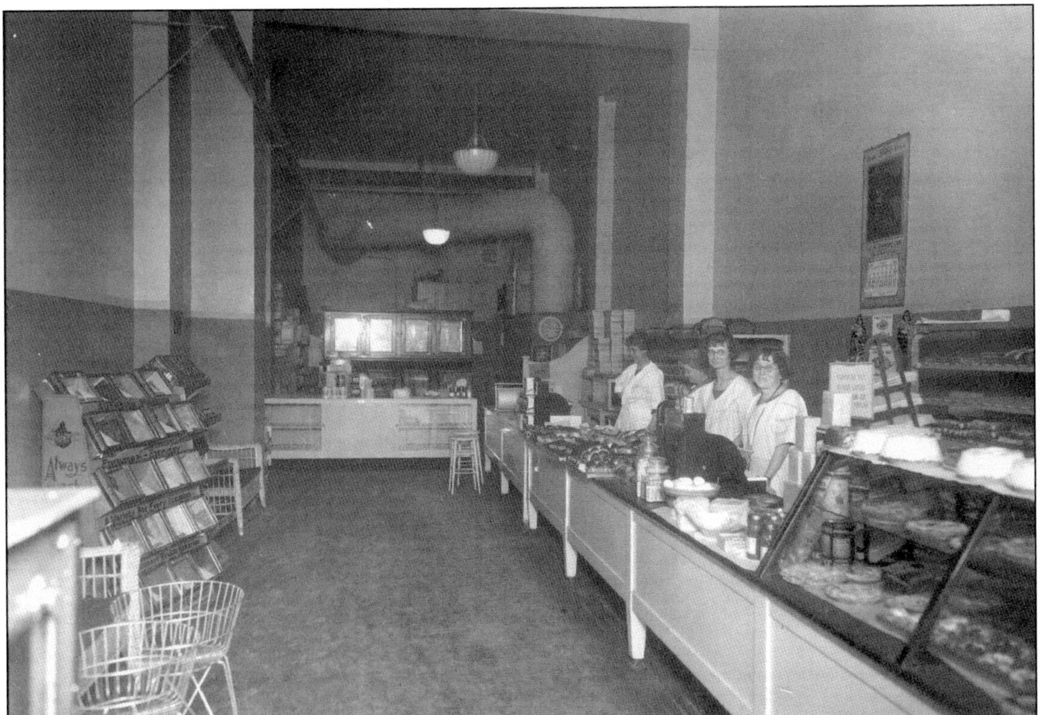

The Perfection Cake Shoppe was located at 6 Public Square. Counter help included, from left to right, Harriet Tooley, Lucy Hambley, Emma Hagan, and Velma Strobeck.

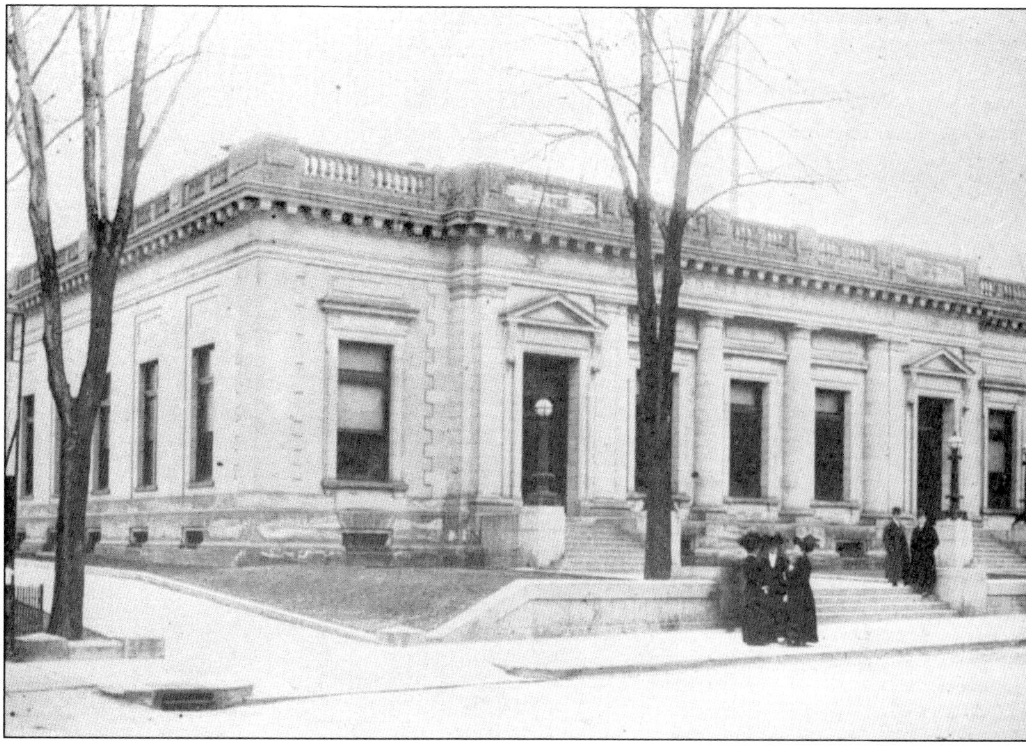

This 1912 view of the post office, which was located on Arsenal Street, shows the building before the construction of additional floors. This location is now the site of the Jefferson County Court Complex.

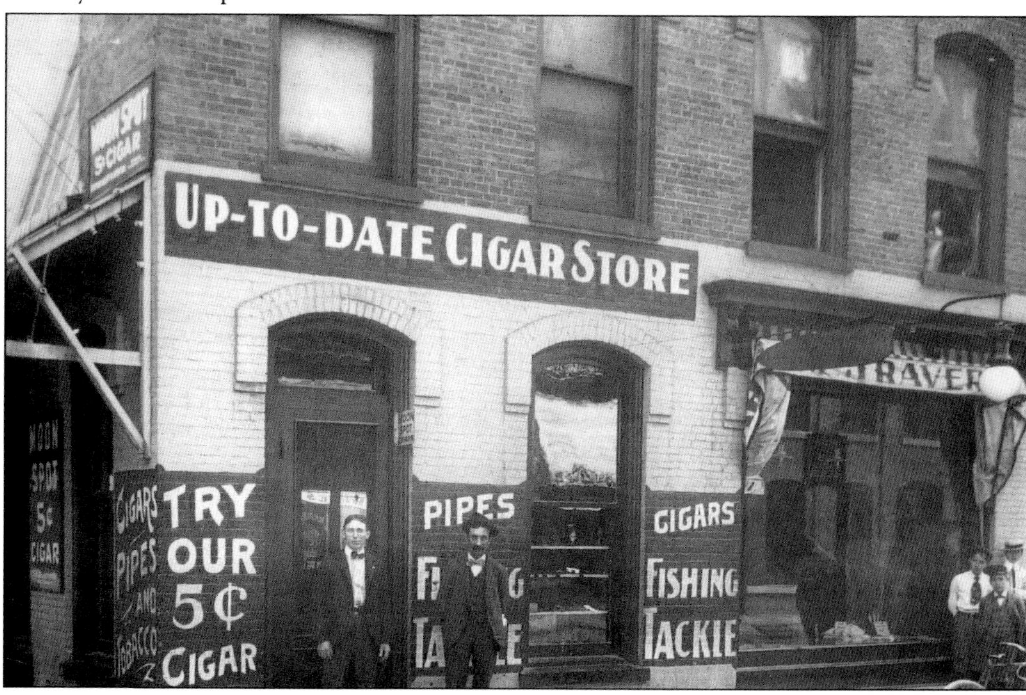

In 1898, G.L. Traver, a cigar and tobacco manufacturing dealer, was located at 9 Arcade Street.

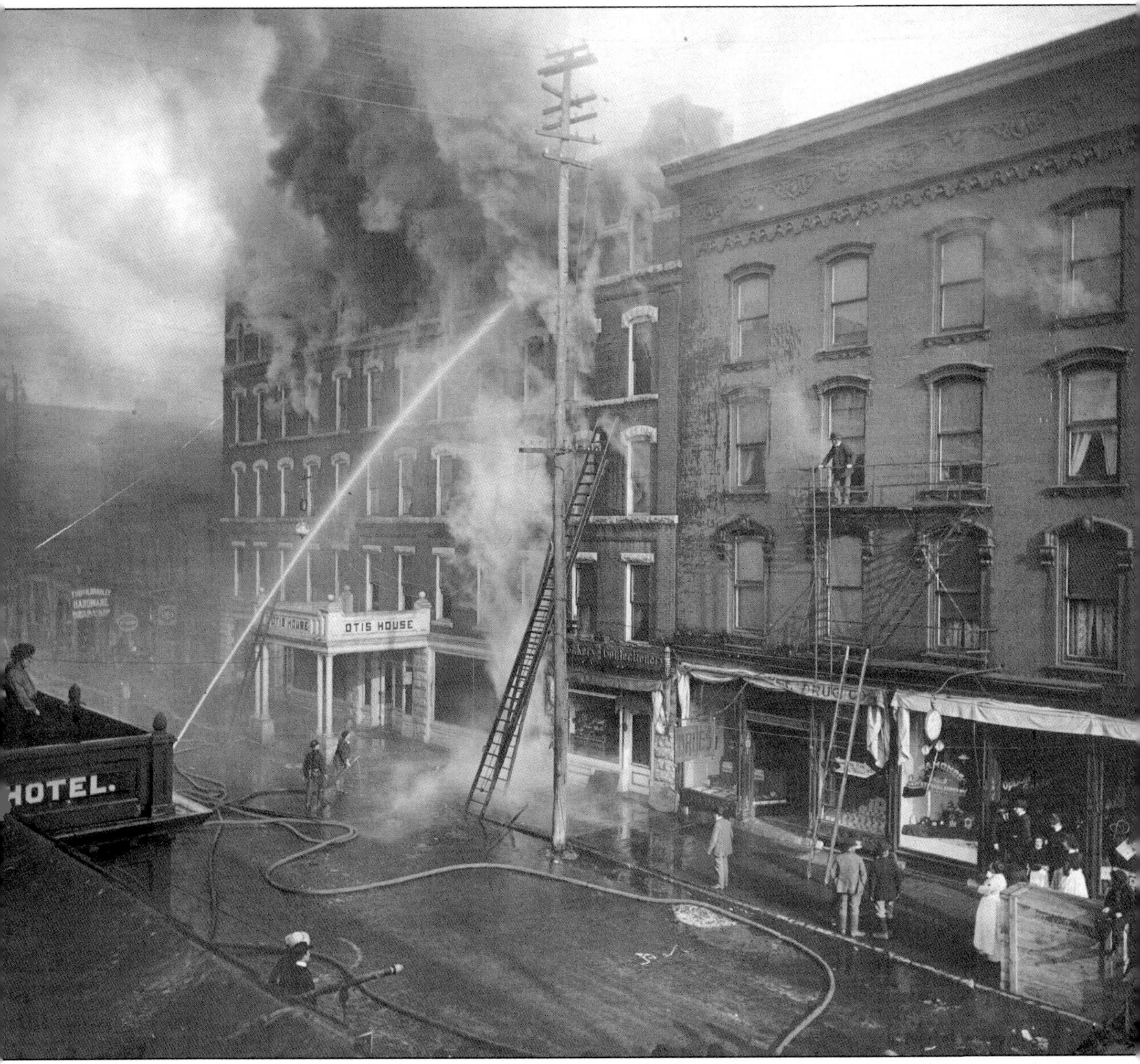

The Globe Hotel was originally built in 1850. It was renovated in 1891 and renamed the Otis House. It fronted both Arsenal and Court Streets and was owned by H. Fred Inglehart & Company. A fire destroyed the structure on March 6, 1903.

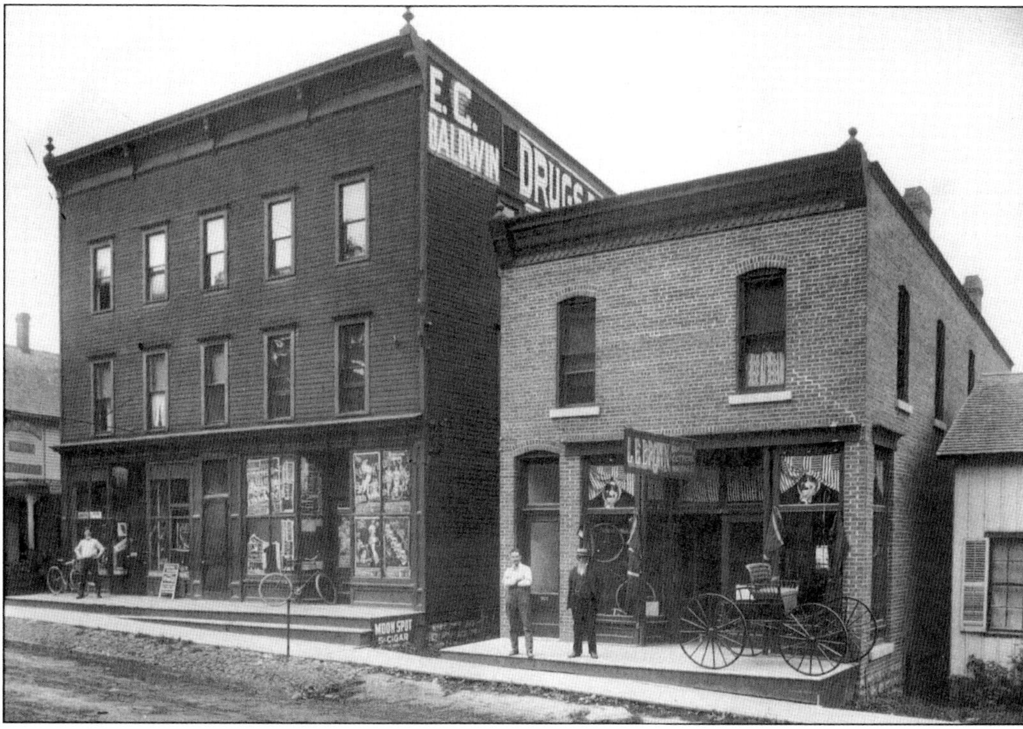

E.C. Baldwin Drugs and L.B. Brown Carriages were located on West Main Street.

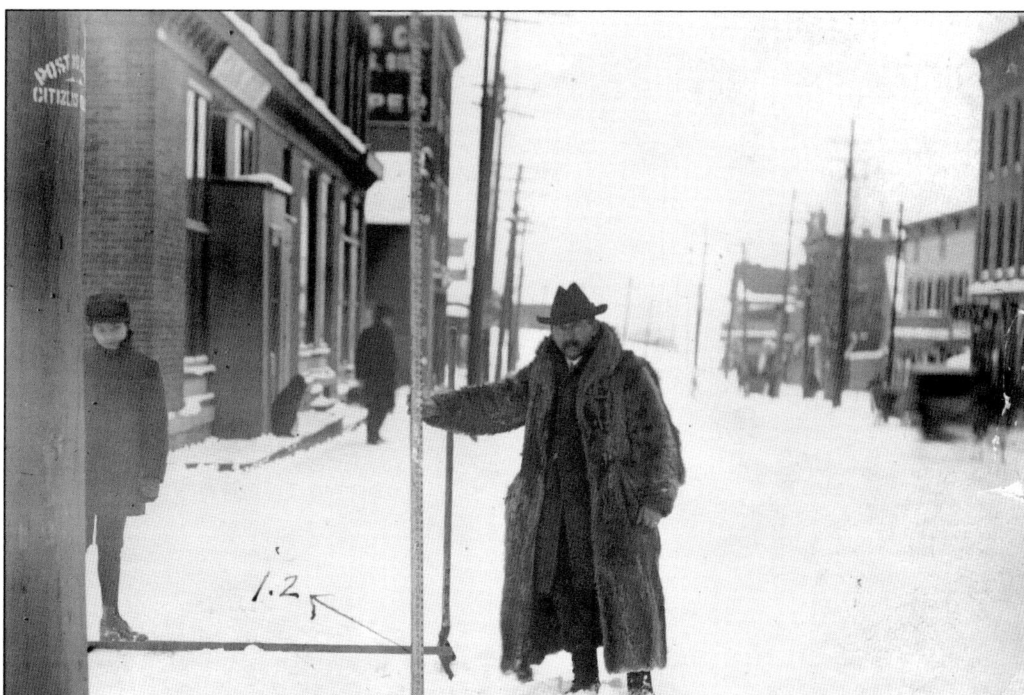

A young boy helps Simmons D. Taylor, proprietor of the Hotel Norman, measure from the sidewalk to the road on January 9, 1903. The Hotel Norman was located at 104 Court Street.

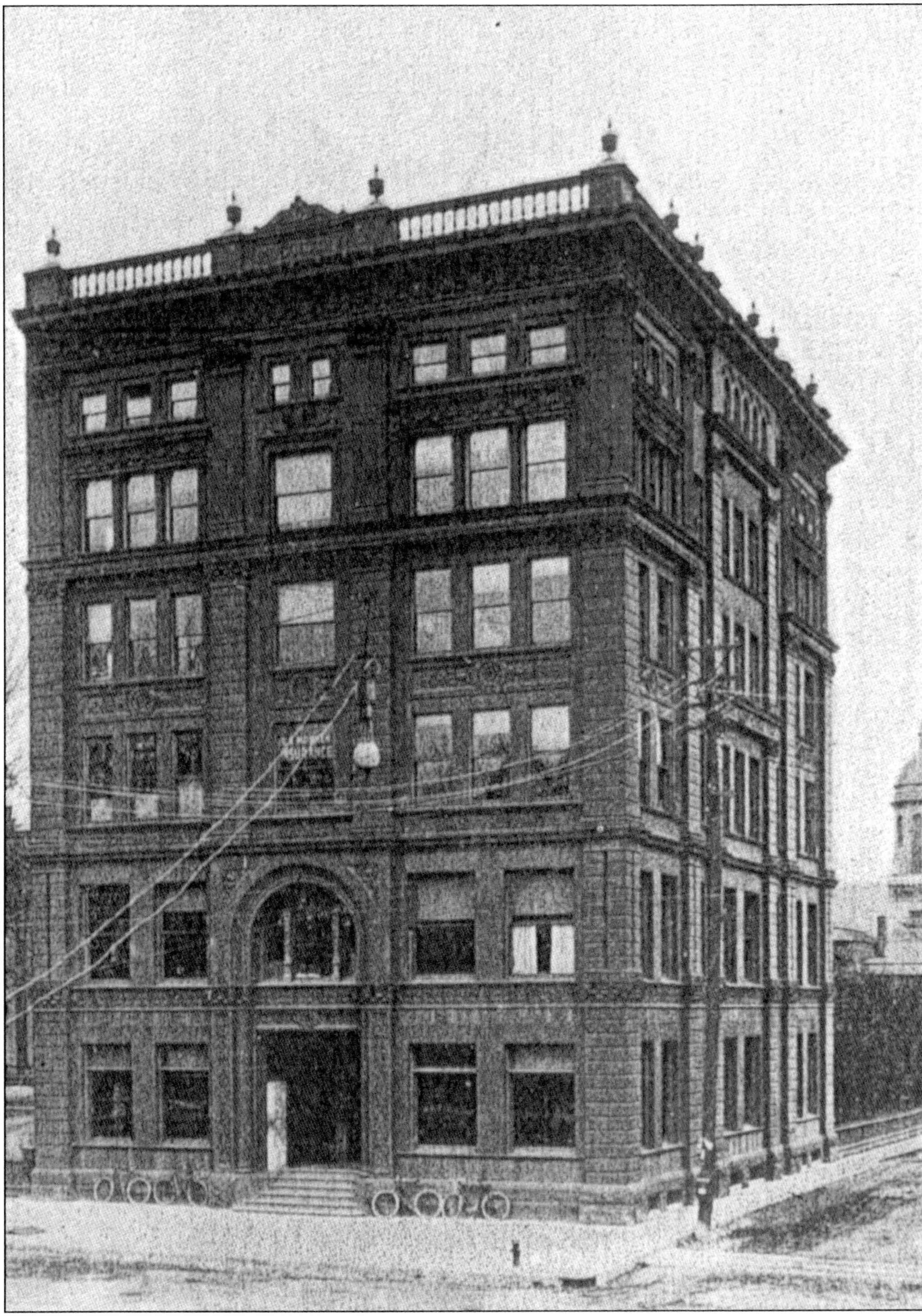

Jefferson County Savings Bank was located on the corner of Washington and Stone Streets.

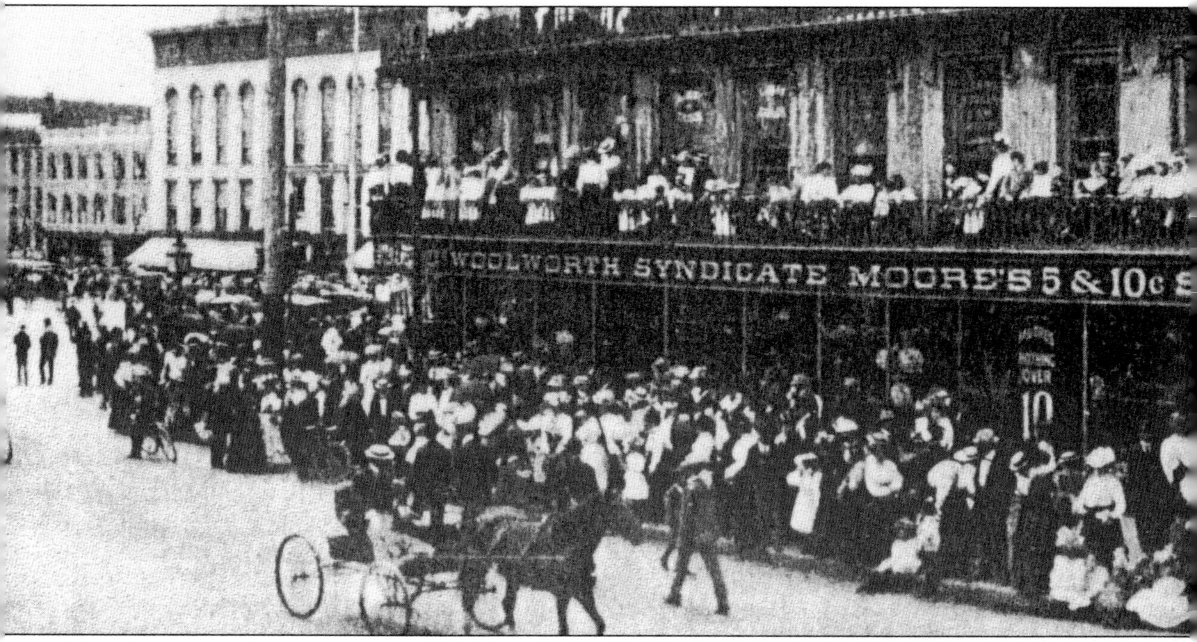

The American Corner was also home to William Moore's Corner Store, which launched Frank Woolworth's retailing career. Frank Woolworth wrote daily general letters advising his managers how to run their stores. Often he would send the same telegram to all the stores. One read: "Good morning. Did you say 'Good morning' to each customer this morning?"

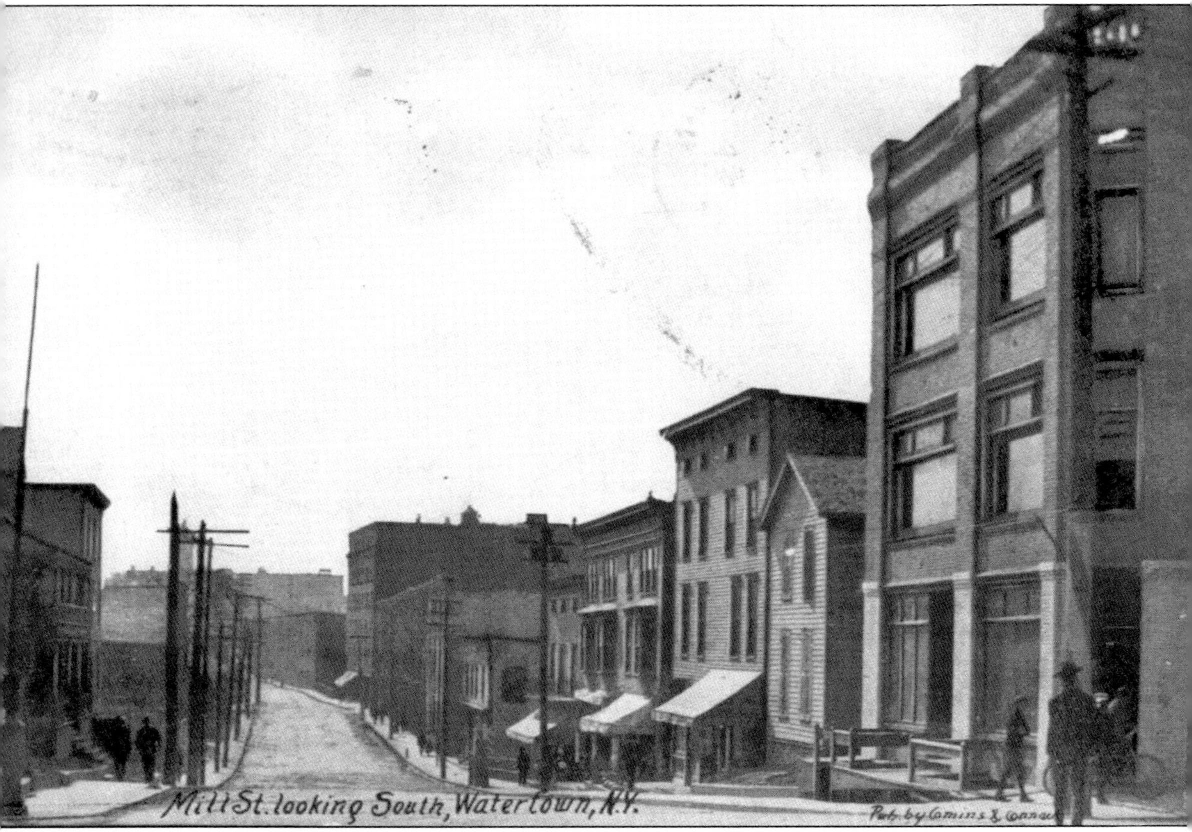

An early-1900s postcard shows the view on Mill Street looking south toward downtown. Mill Street was also a business area of the city. J. Frost & Son's lumber and coal yard was located there as well as the Marcy, Buck & Riley Coal Company. J.W. Nott was a druggist at 2 Mill Street. John Eckhoft had a blacksmith shop at 14 Mill Street. Several saloons were also located on Mill Street.

Eight

CHURCHES

Shortly after the settlement of Watertown at the beginning of the 19th century, missionaries began to visit this section. The story is told that when one of the missionaries was on his way to this area, he was asked where he was going. He replied that he was on his way to the Black River country to preach to the heathens. Such a statement makes an amusing story, but our early settlers were far from being heathens. In fact, history records that the first Sunday the Massey family spent in the settlement, the few others residing here gathered in the Massey home and held the first religious services ever enjoyed within the present city limits of Watertown.

These early settlers brought with them a heritage of a religious conviction and determined spirit that has had a lasting influence on the development of the city and the character of its people. For many years, the great forested wilderness of the area was thinly populated with scattered hamlets such as Watertown. Missionaries and circuit riders came into the area and conducted religious services in schoolhouses and private homes. Everyone in the neighborhood attended, regardless of denomination. Among the earliest of these preachers were Methodists, Congregationalists, and Baptists. Later came the Universalists, Episcopalians, and Roman Catholics. As the various sects grew, church societies were organized and, eventually, church buildings were constructed.

The churches that are featured in this chapter are those that were in existence in 1869, when Watertown became an incorporated city. Some of the buildings have been replaced with larger ones, and others have been substantially altered from the original. Still others moved to new locations since the 1800s.

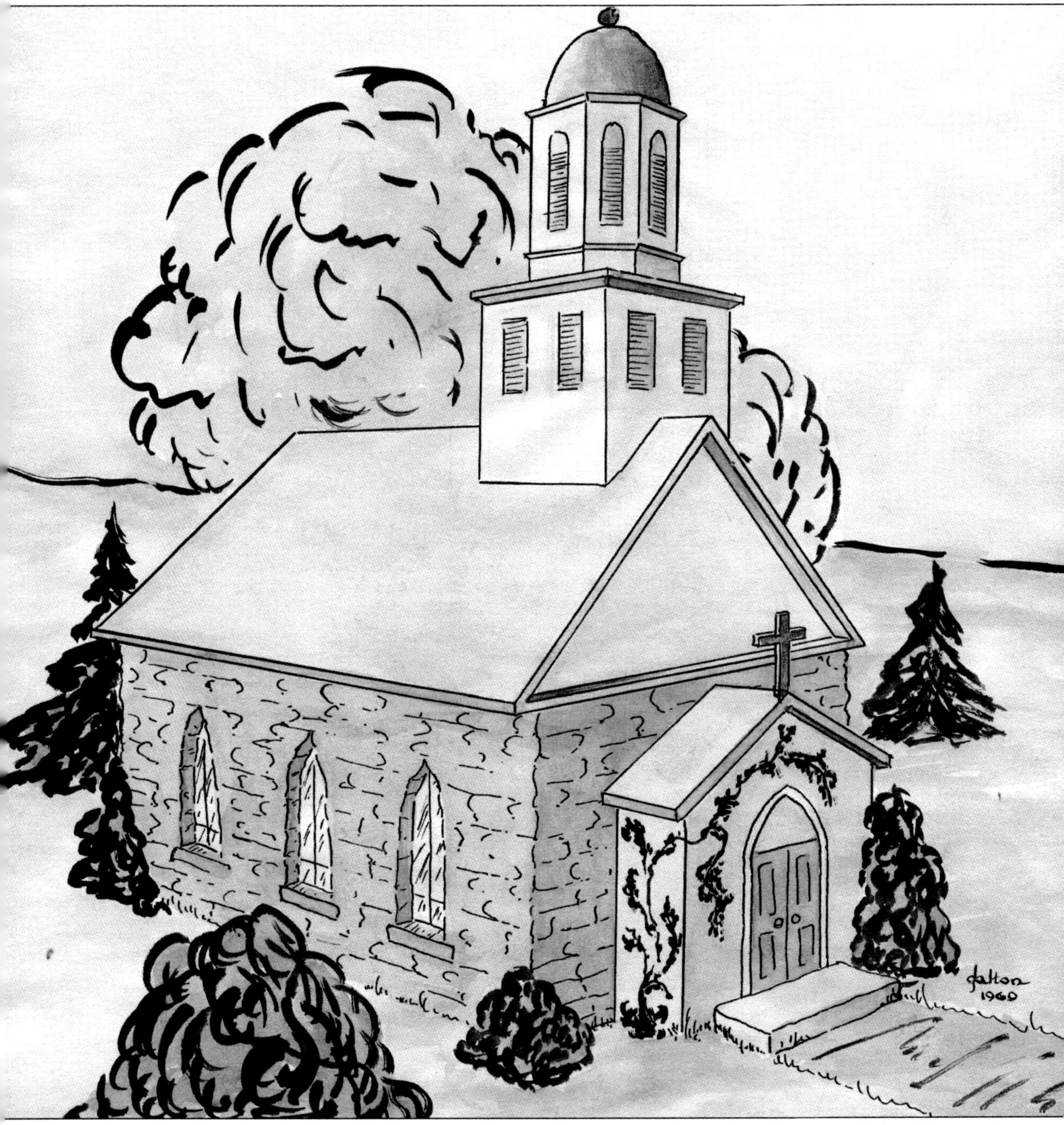

On May 29, 1823, "an Ecclesiastic Council" convened at the Factory Schoolhouse in Watertown to establish a Baptist church. In 1827, this organization was duly organized under the general statute as the Watertown Baptist Church and Society. In 1828, a meetinghouse was built on Factory Street (artist's rendition above). Prior to 1838, the Catholic population had no formal edifice in which to worship. The Baptist church building became available when the Baptists were building their new church on Public Square. The Catholics purchased the building and named it St. Mary's. It served this denomination until 1856, when St. Patrick's was opened for worship. The French population then purchased the Factory Street church for $2,000. As a French mission, the priests visited it from Cape Vincent until the first resident pastor was appointed in 1876.

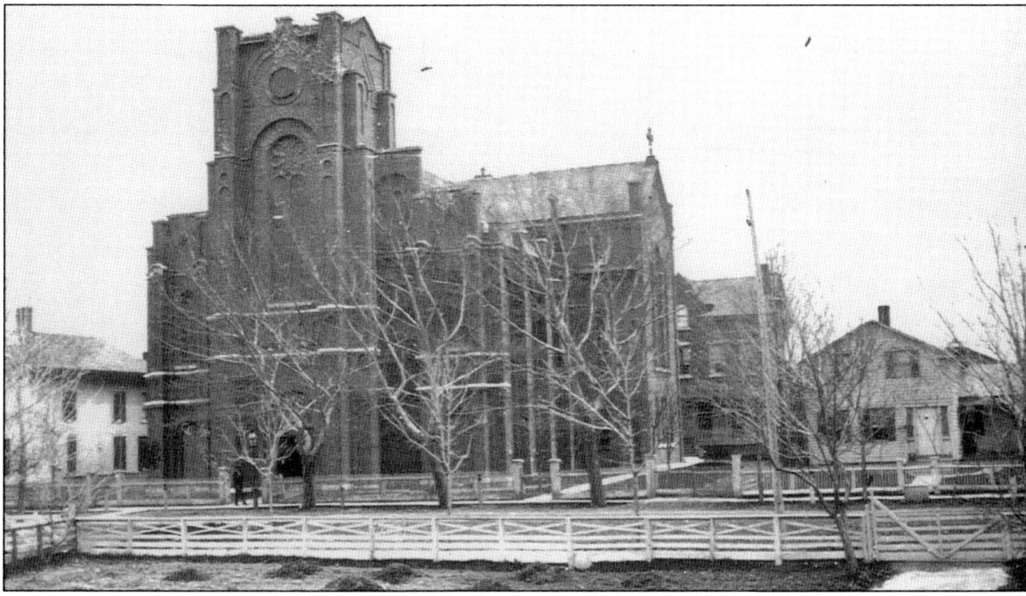

The Church of St. Patrick was built in 1856 by its Irish-American congregation after having worshiped at St. Mary's on Factory Street. The first mass was celebrated at St. Patrick's on Christmas Eve 1856. This photograph shows St. Patrick's before the bell tower was added in the late 1880s. (Photograph courtesy of the *Watertown Daily Times*.)

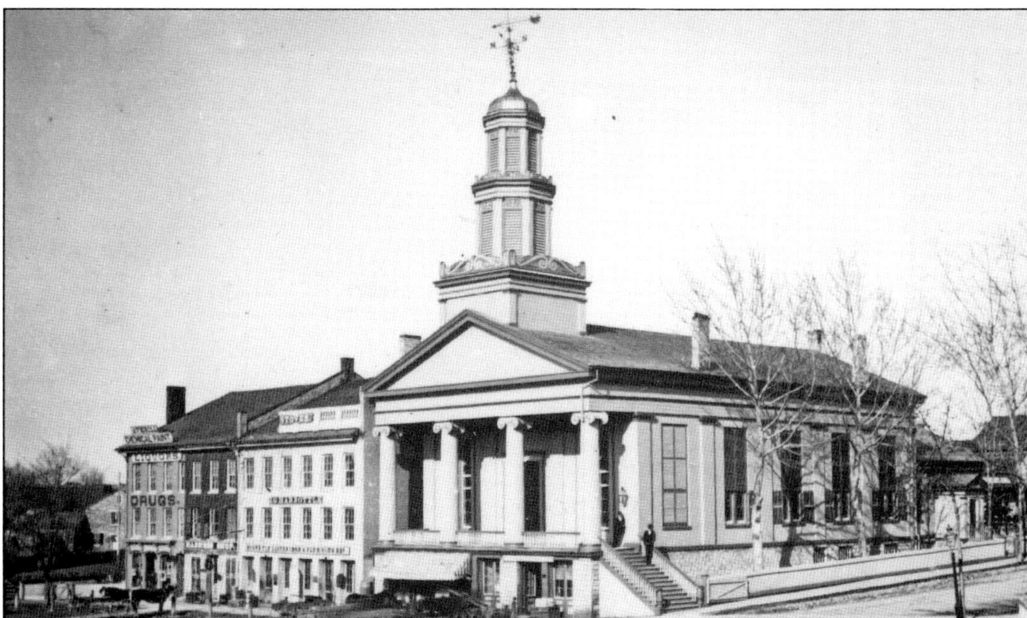

This Baptist church was the second church built on the site at Public Square. The first one was built in 1837 but was destroyed by fire in 1846. This photograph shows the church that was rebuilt in 1846 at a cost of $6,000. The building was an architecturally beautiful edifice and was used until it was torn down *c.* 1891 to make room for the present Watertown Baptist Church. Its carpeted aisles were woven by Harry Tyler, famous for his Tyler coverlets. (Photograph courtesy of the *Watertown Daily Times*.)

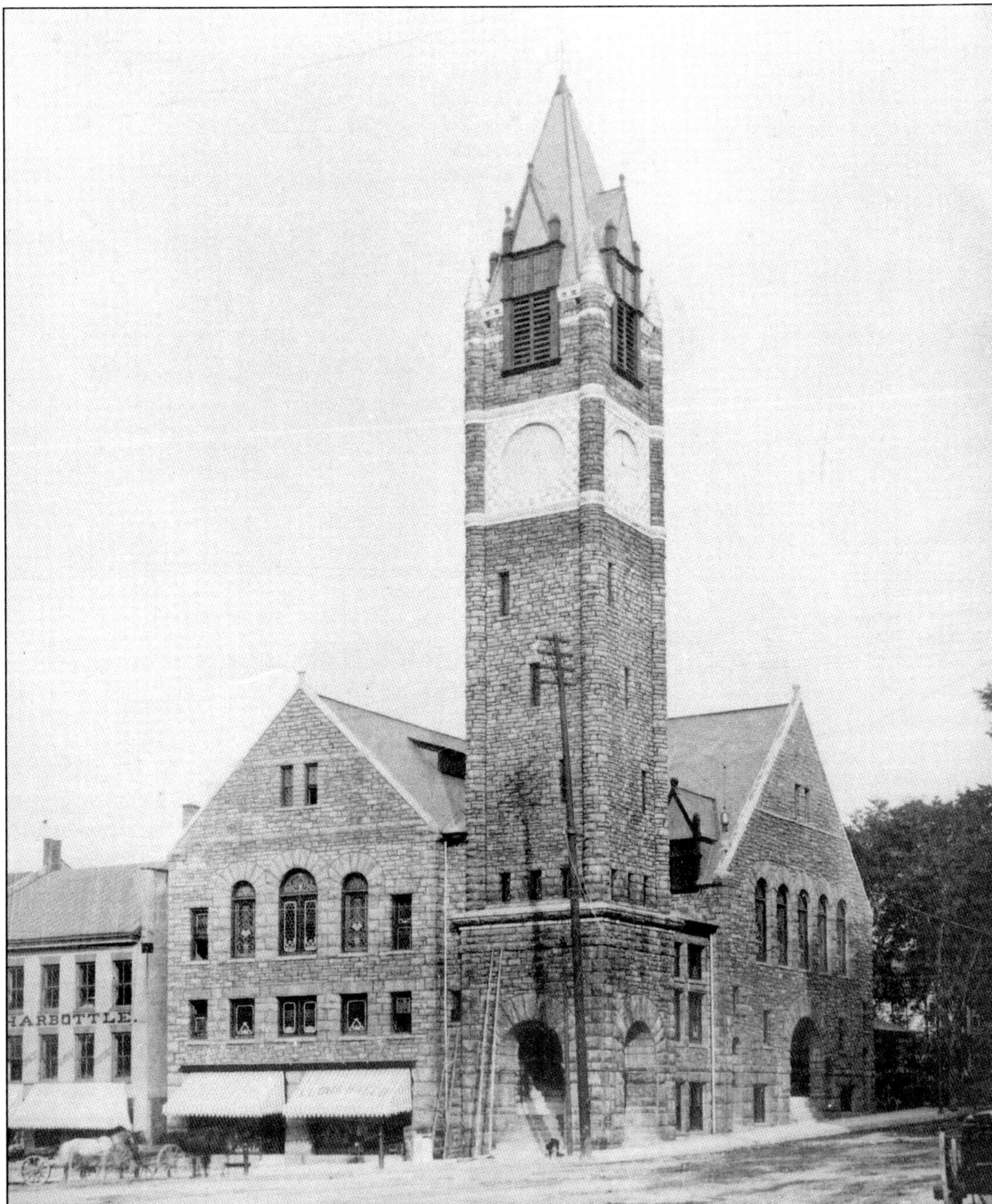

The Watertown Baptist Church built in 1891 was built of native limestone from quarries located near the city. Patrick Phillips was the contractor, and Charles H. Smith of New York City was the architect. The marble used in the building was brought in from Gouverneur. As far as possible, the timbers of the old building were used. The hewed pine beams were cut from the forest a short distance up the Black River. The north and east walls, with their respective foundations, are as they were made in 1846, save that a retaining wall was built inside. The pulpit furniture, including the chairs and communion table, was made from the old oak timbers in the roof. The completed building, which cost about $31,000, was dedicated on September 13, 1892.

Trinity Parish was organized on May 31, 1828. The first church was erected on Court Street in 1833 and destroyed in the 1849 fire. This photograph is of the second church, which was designed by Richard Upjohn of New York City and was built on Court Street, beginning May 14, 1850. The church, referred to by parishioners as Old Trinity, was consecrated on January 23, 1851, and served the congregation until 1890.

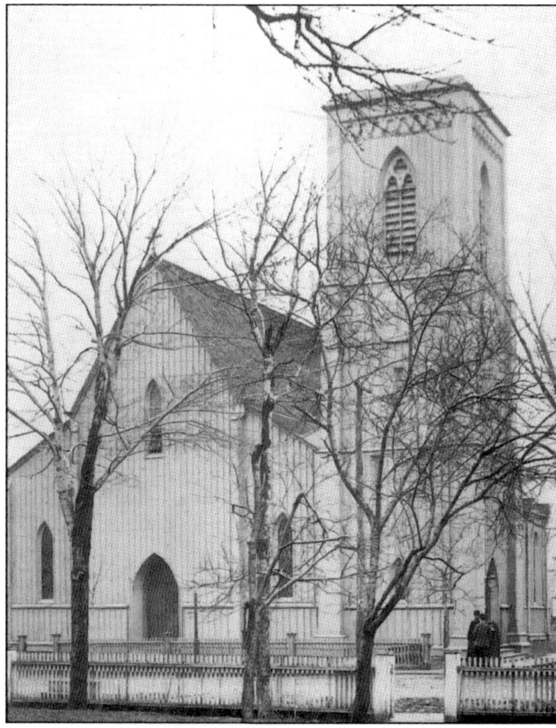

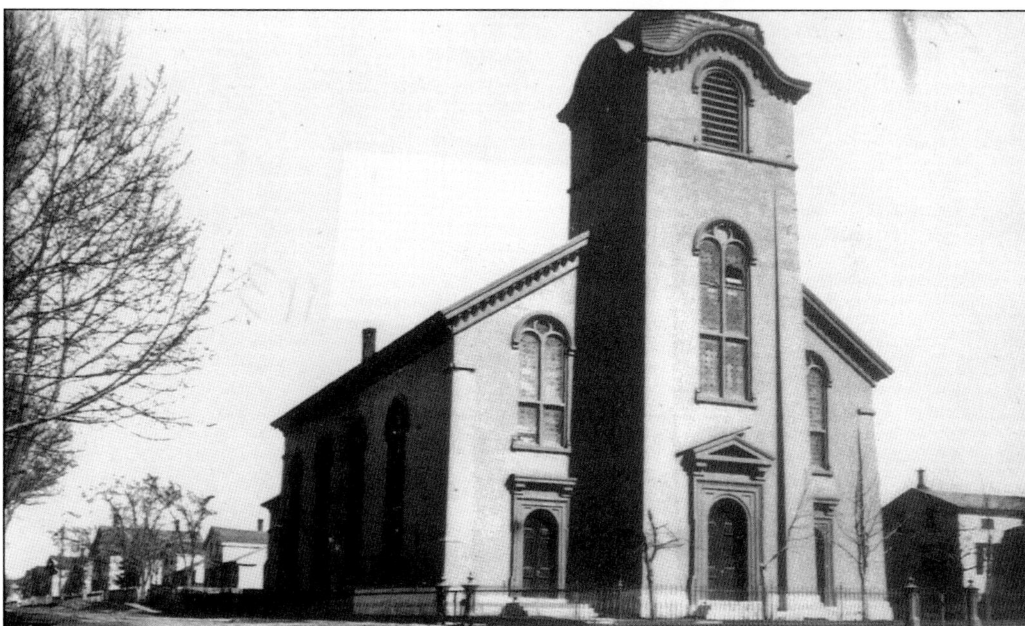

The two-story First Presbyterian Church, with an impressive domelike tower over the entrance, was erected in 1821. It was the first house of worship in Watertown. The members of the congregation saw a need for a larger church and started construction of a new building, largely of brick, at the same site in 1851. Throughout the years, renovations were made. In 1892, a front portico was erected and additions were made to the narthex at each side of the main entrance to provide new stairs to the balcony.

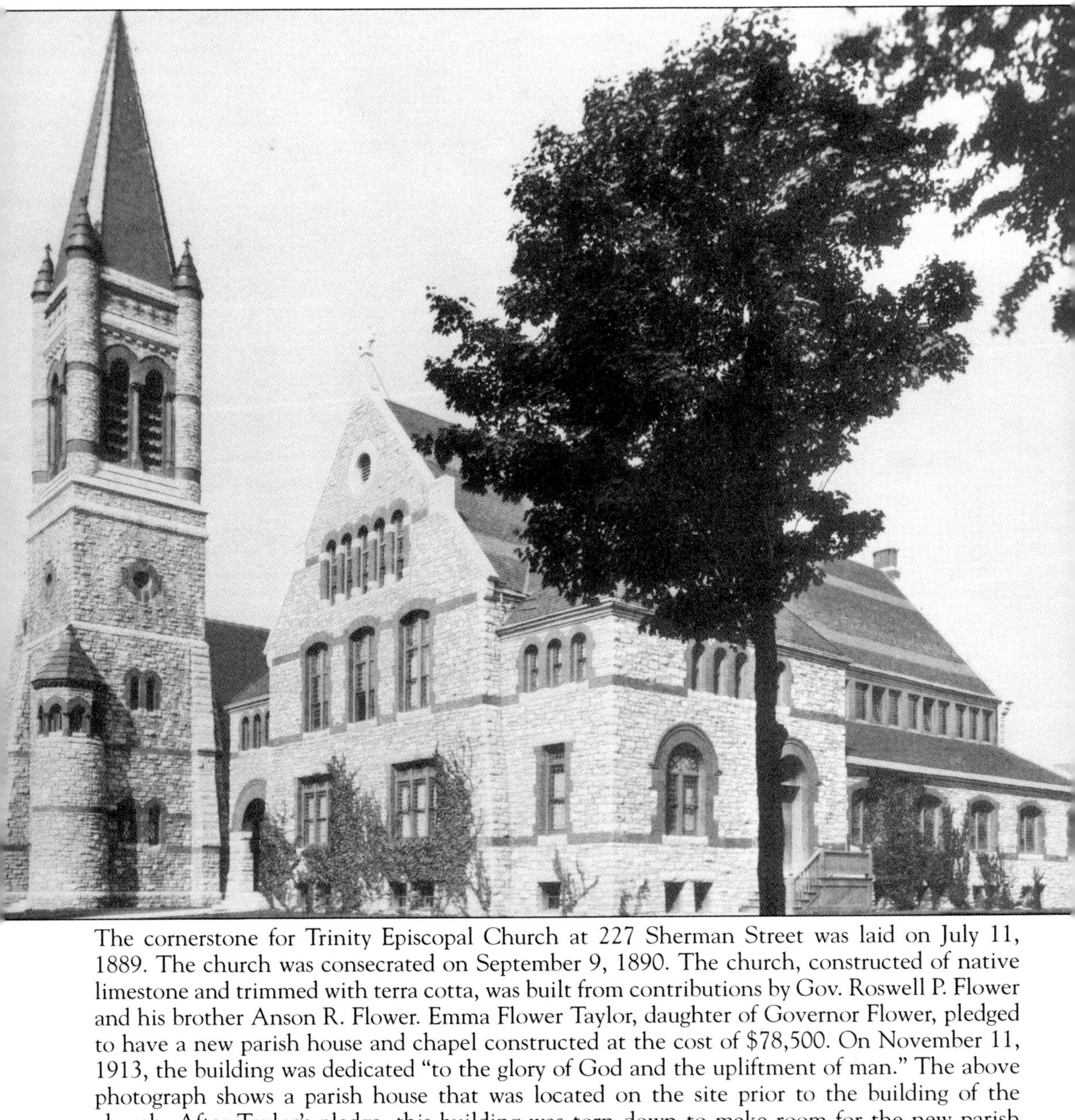

The cornerstone for Trinity Episcopal Church at 227 Sherman Street was laid on July 11, 1889. The church was consecrated on September 9, 1890. The church, constructed of native limestone and trimmed with terra cotta, was built from contributions by Gov. Roswell P. Flower and his brother Anson R. Flower. Emma Flower Taylor, daughter of Governor Flower, pledged to have a new parish house and chapel constructed at the cost of $78,500. On November 11, 1913, the building was dedicated "to the glory of God and the upliftment of man." The above photograph shows a parish house that was located on the site prior to the building of the church. After Taylor's pledge, this building was torn down to make room for the new parish house, which still stands on the site.

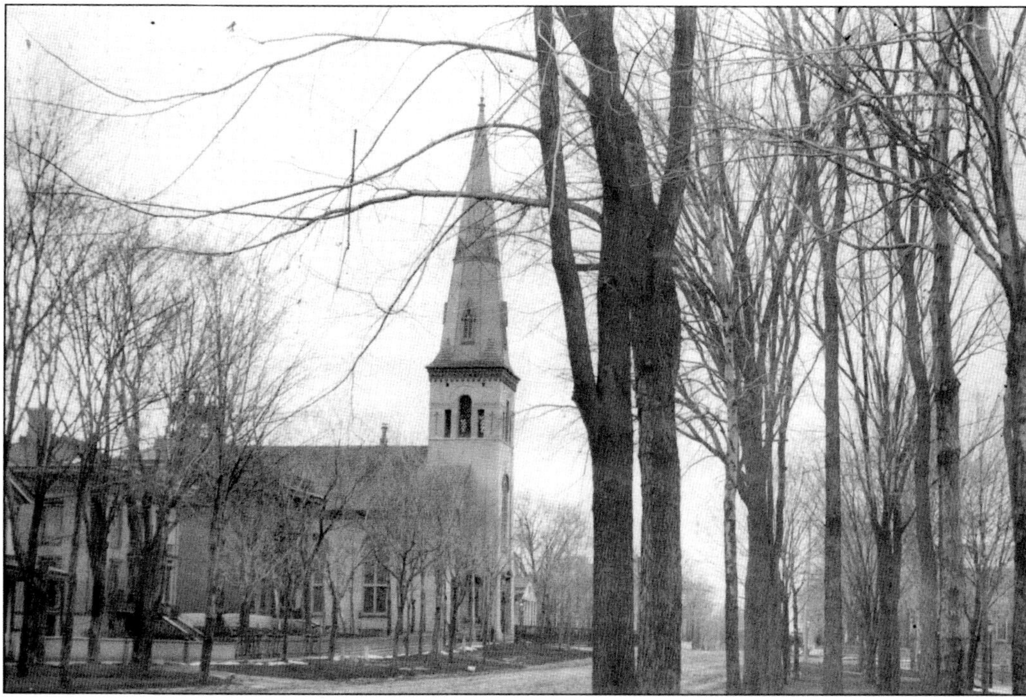

A later view of the First Presbyterian Church shows the church steeple.

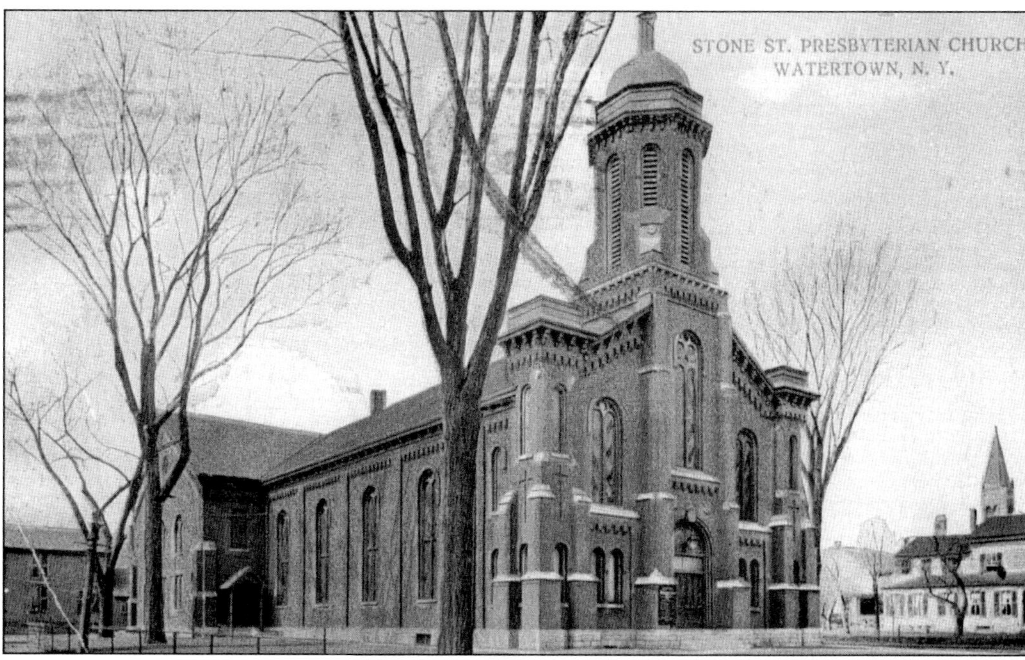

In 1831, the Second Presbyterian Church was formed. Services were held in a wooden church located at the corner of Factory and Mechanic Streets. A new site, shown here, was chosen on Stone Street, and the church was renamed Stone Street Presbyterian Church in 1864. Services were held there until 1982, when the church burned. The Stone Presbyterian Church rebuilt on Chestnut Street following the fire.

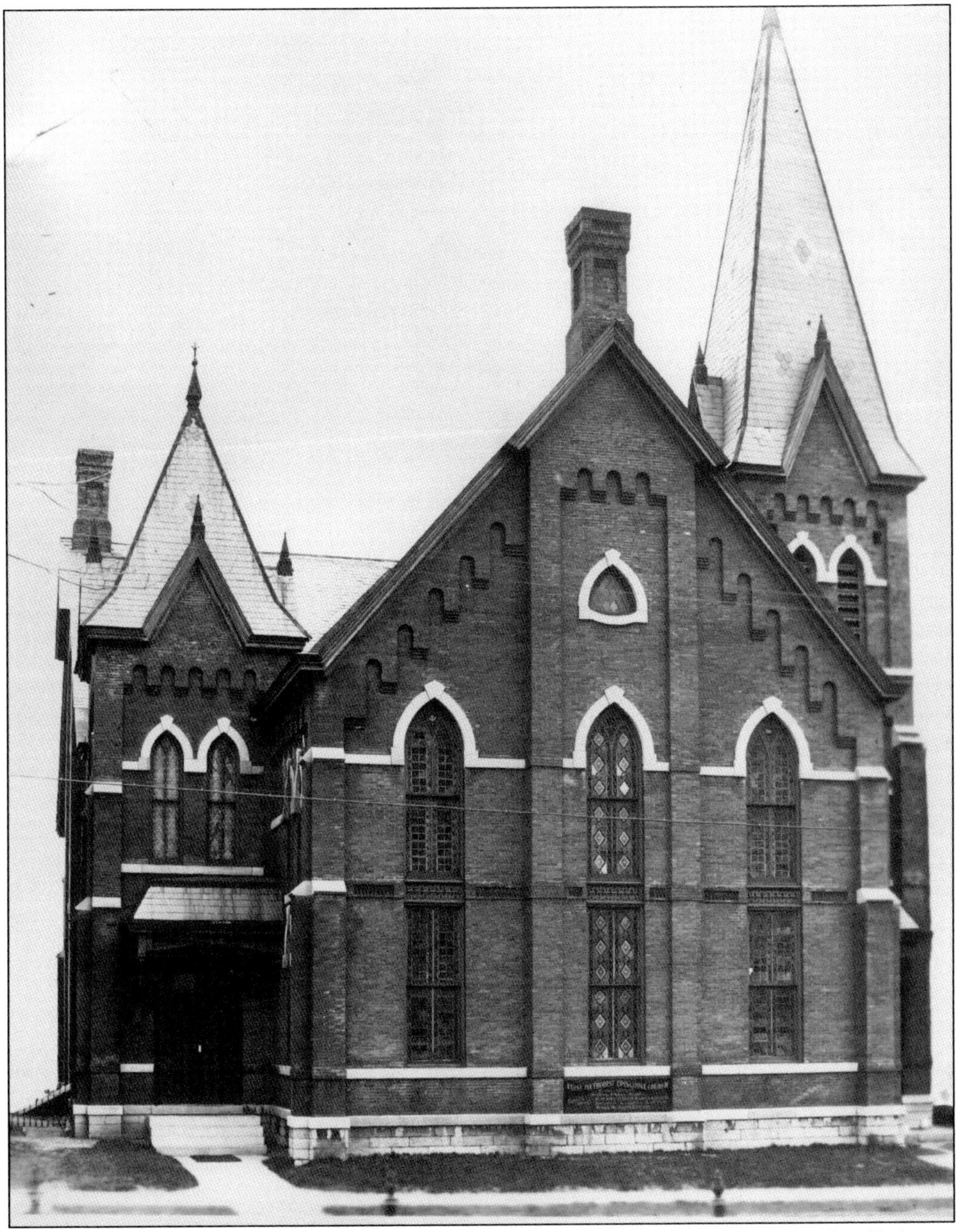

The First United Methodist Church held the first class meeting at Simeon Woodruff's home in 1804. Itinerant preachers served Watertown until 1821, when John Dempster was appointed preacher. The membership in 1821 was 391, and the First Methodist Episcopal Society was organized on November 21, 1821. The annual meeting of 1822 was in a stone church on the corner of Arsenal and Massey Streets, later the site of the Arsenal Street School. In 1849, the society was divided into two congregations, with the newly formed organization (State Street Methodist Episcopal Church, later Asbury) deciding to erect a new church in the rapidly growing eastern section of the village to serve the families residing east of Washington Street and Public Square. In 1851, the original First United Methodist Society built a new building at 180 Arsenal Street, which burned in 1880. In 1881, a brick building was built at a total cost of $18,816. Fire destroyed that building on February 22, 1942.

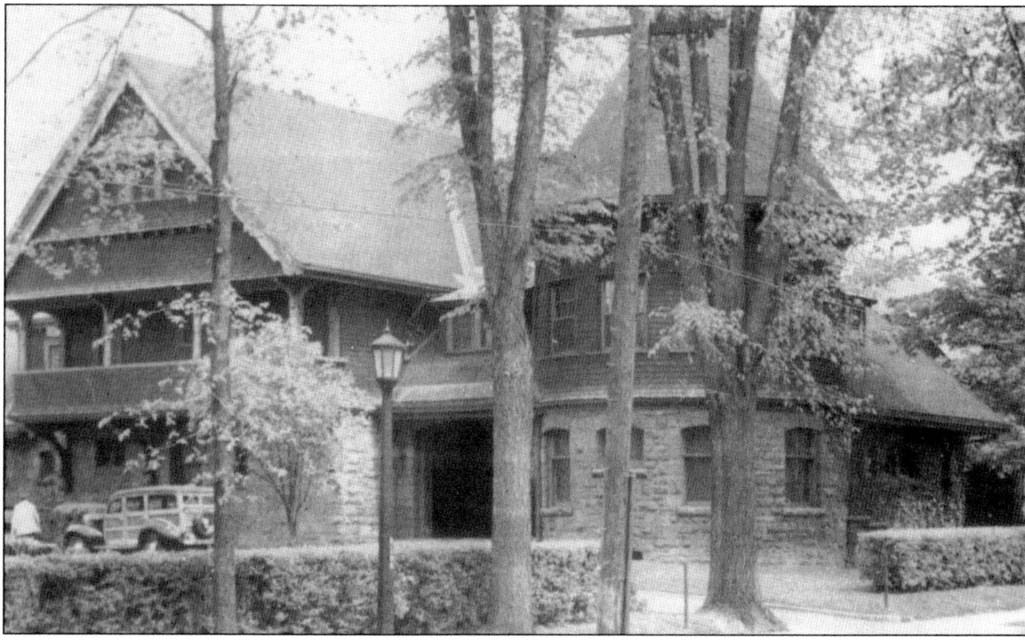

On June 27, 1943, a new building for the First United Methodists was dedicated at 236 Mullin Street. This was the horse stable and carriage house from the Emma Flower Taylor estate, which was originally built in 1896. The renovation and remodeling of the temporary sanctuary and church schoolrooms cost $42,000. The stable windows were saved with a Christian symbol placed in the middle glass. There was a kitchen, assembly room, and office on the first floor. On the second floor were classrooms, a church parlor, and kitchenette. In 1958, a new church sanctuary was added to the present building. (Photograph courtesy of FUMC.)

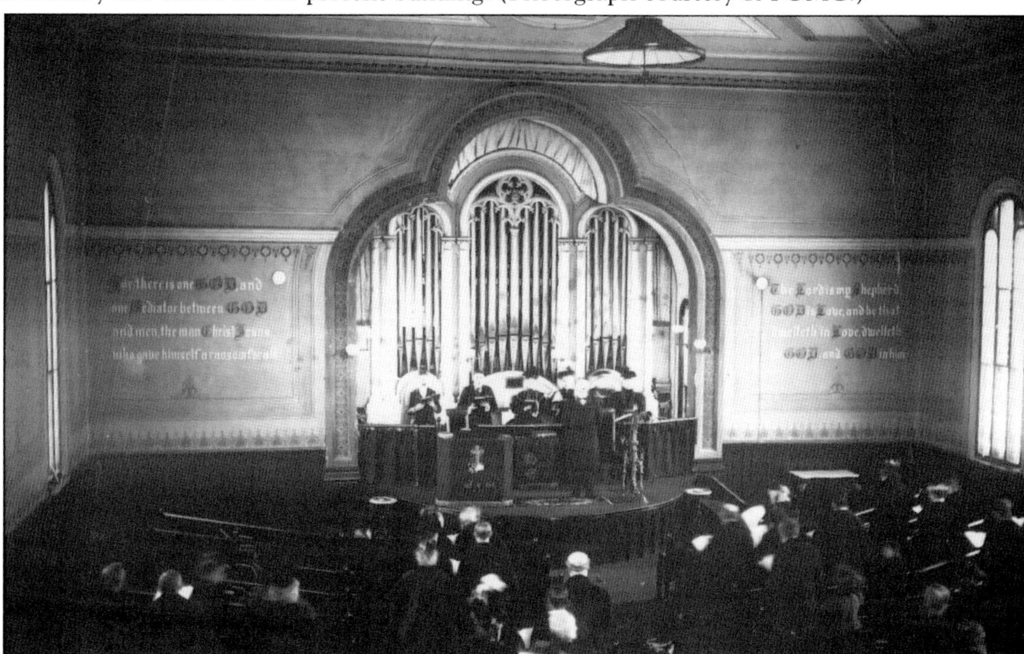

The congregation of State Street Methodist Church worship during a Sunday service.

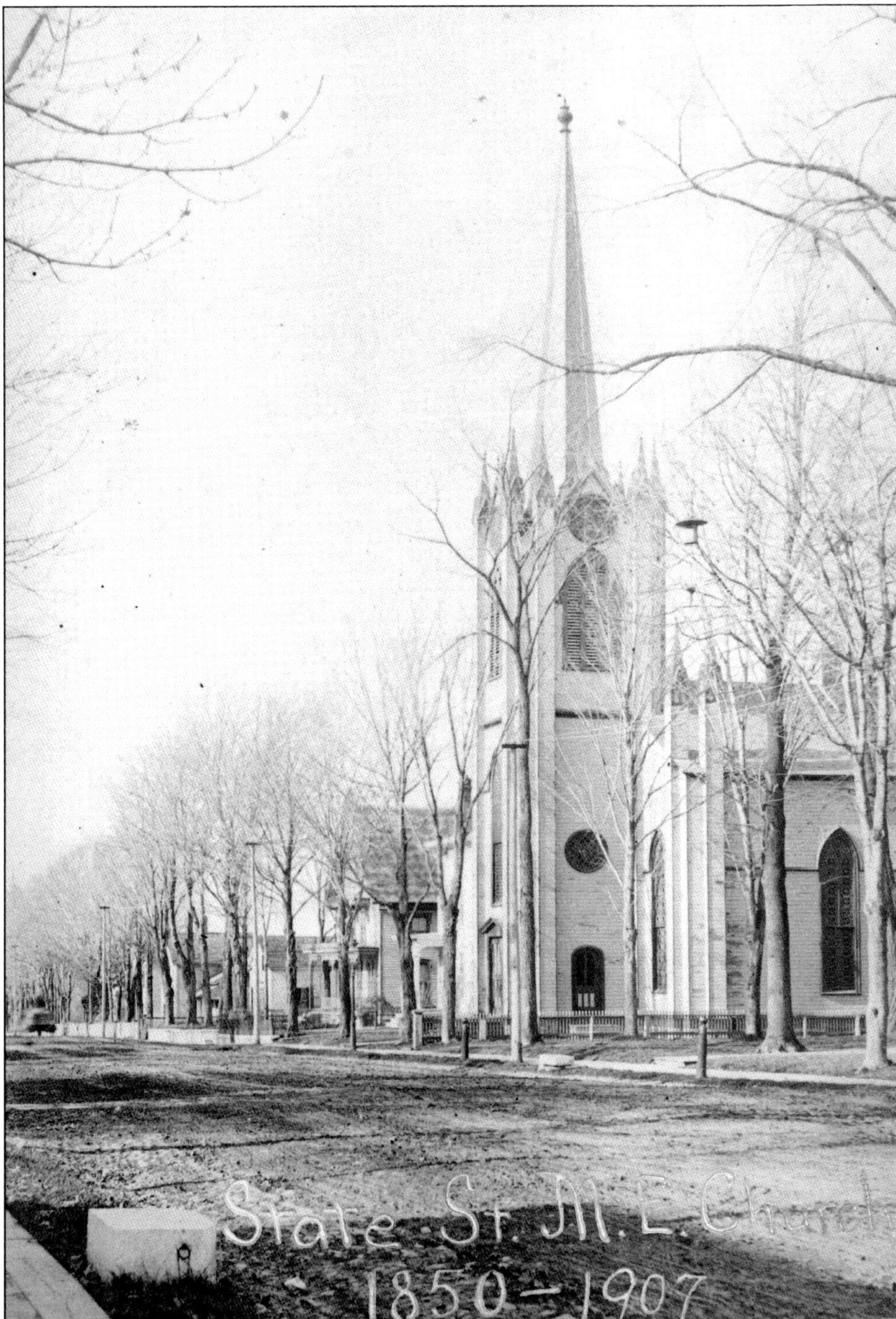

The State Street Methodist Episcopal Church erected a wooden edifice on the north side of State Street on a lot adjacent to the brick building of the Black River Academy which stood at the corner of Mechanic Street. The new church seated about 600 and was completed and dedicated on June 6, 1850. In 1876, a chapel was added. Seven years later, a bell and bell tower were erected above the front of the edifice. After 50 years, there was a desire for a better building and a quieter location. Services were disturbed by the noise of the trolley line.

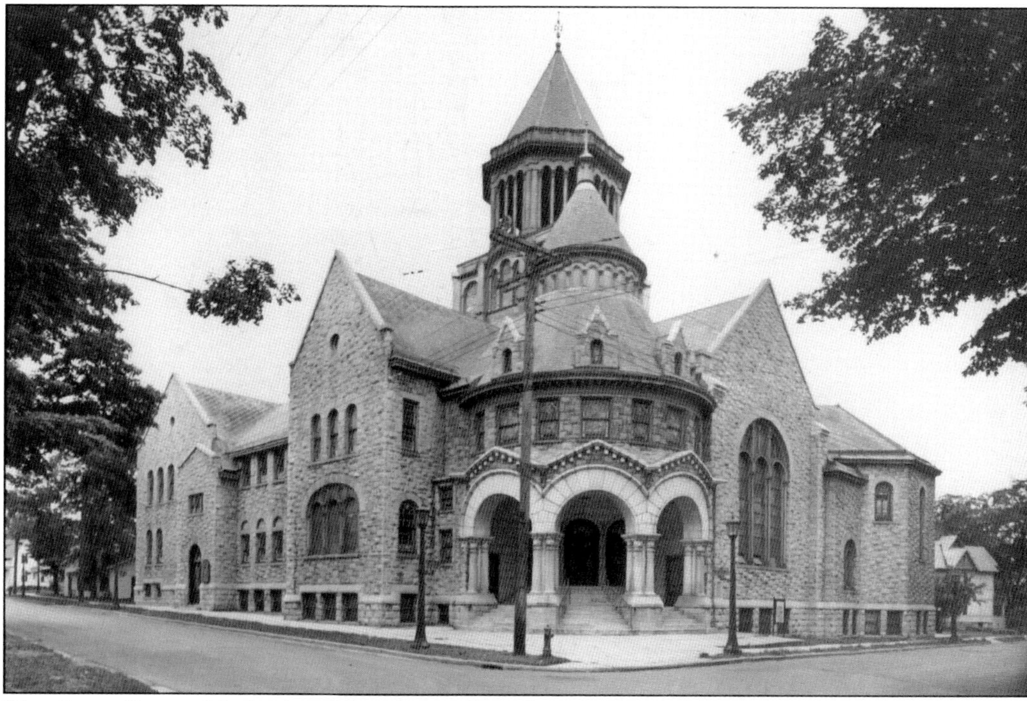

The State Street Methodist Church purchased property at the corner of Sterling and Park Streets on January 19, 1908. The name of Asbury was selected to replace the former name in honor of Bishop Francis Asbury. The new church was dedicated on December 12, 1909. This photograph was taken in 1920.

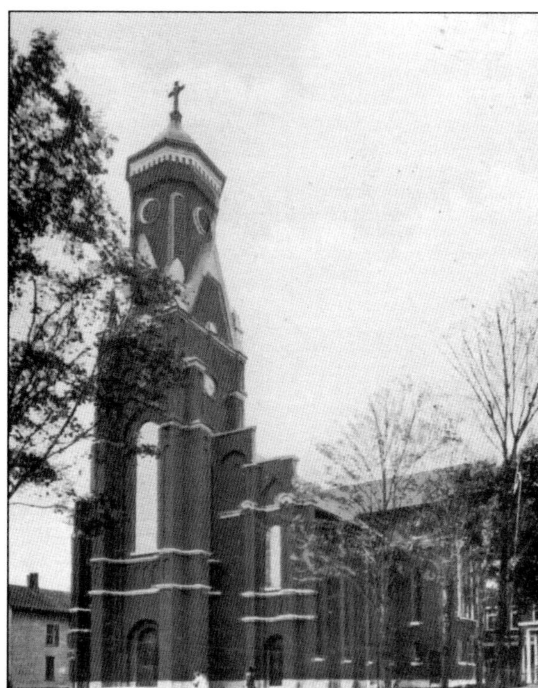

This photograph shows St. Patrick's with the addition of the steeple.

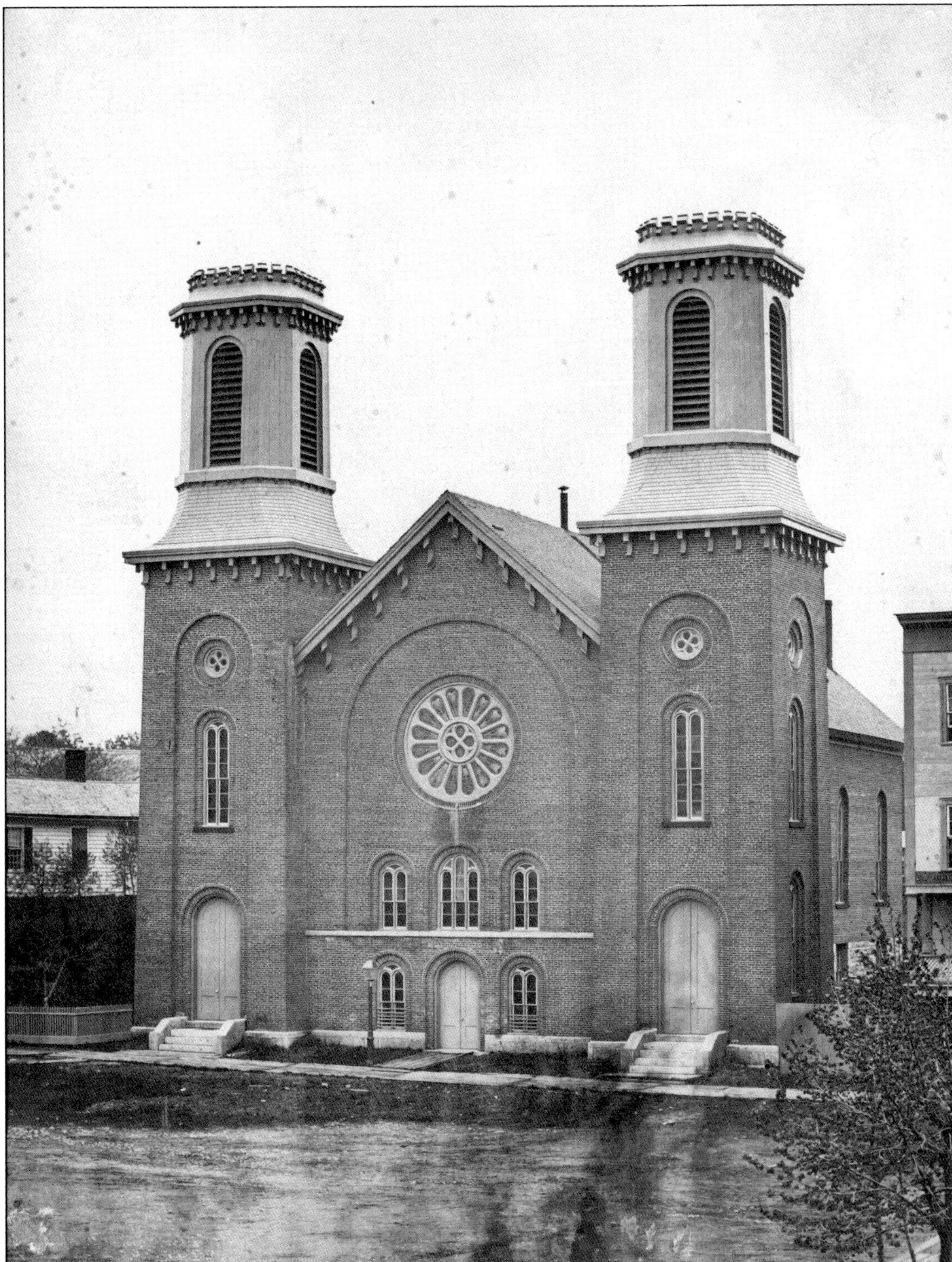

All Soul's Universalist Church had its beginnings on April 26,-1820, when the first society in Watertown was organized in the courthouse. The church building, a stone structure located on Public Square, was the first Universalist church in the village; it was dedicated on November 10, 1824. The building was destroyed by fire on September 29, 1850, resulting from a flying ember from a fire on Beebee Island. A new brick church was erected on the same site. Worship continued there until 1905, when it was sold for the construction of the Hotel LeRay.

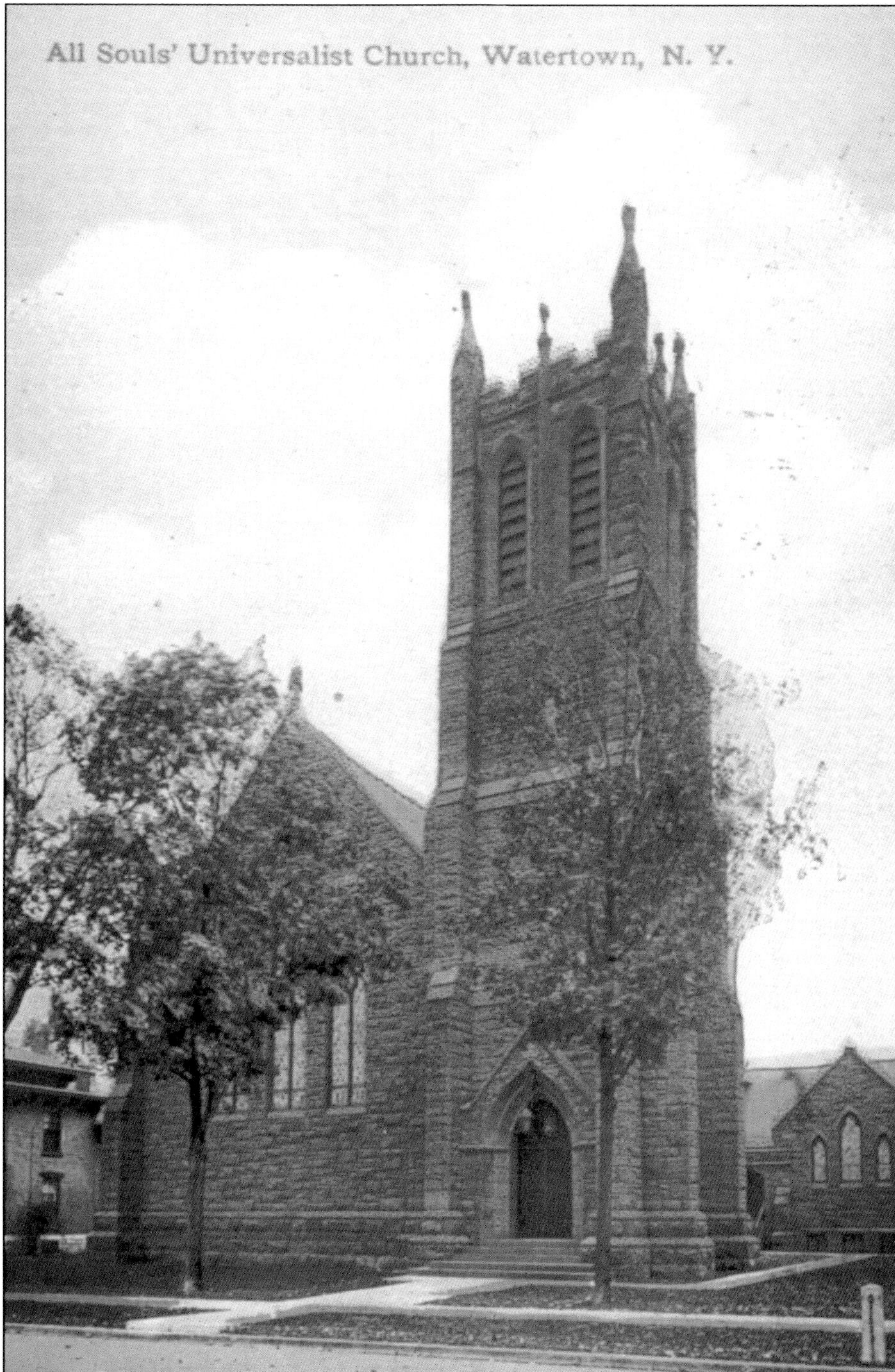

This photograph is of the brownstone All Soul's Universalist Church, which was constructed in 1906 and was located on Washington Street. When the church was dedicated, there was still a mortgage of $24,000. This debt was cancelled by Emma Flower Taylor and her mother, Mrs. Roswell Flower, in memory of Mrs. Flower's mother, Roxanna Woodruff Strong, who was a member of the Universalist Church.

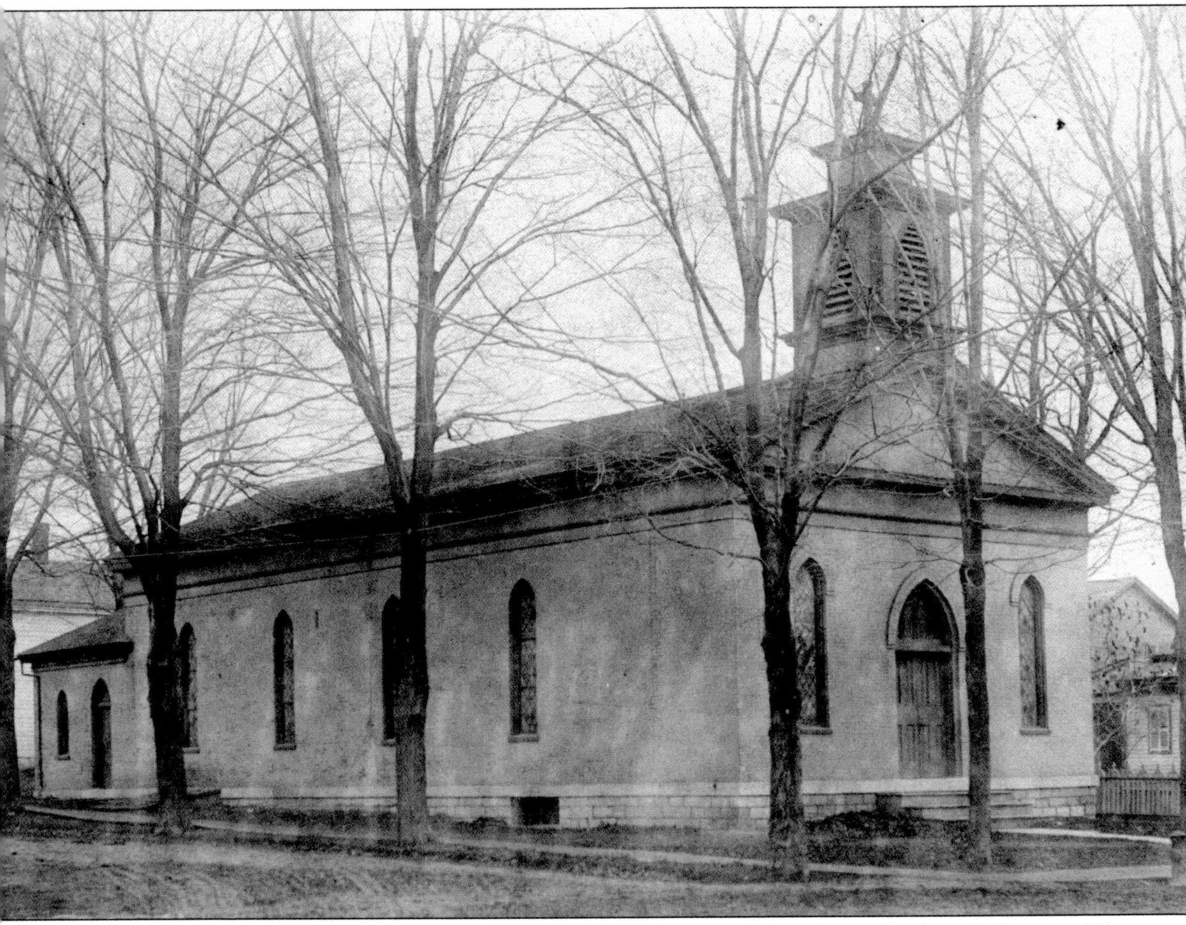

Grace Church was located on the corner of Sterling and Jay (now Gotham) Streets. The congregation consisted of former members of Trinity Church who had been given permission to organize a new parish in Watertown. What is now St. Paul's Episcopal Church was organized on July 21, 1867, and the first services were held at the courthouse until July 1868, when the little brick schoolhouse was purchased and remodeled for use as a church. Grace Church purchased land at the corner of Sterling and Clay Streets and a new building was dedicated on January 13, 1891. L.B. Valk and Son of New York were the architects for the church. Most of the building was erected under the supervision of John Hose of Watertown. Harvey & Parker were the contractors for the furnishing of the interior, with the exception of the furniture that came from J&R Lamb of New York City. The Grace congregation voted to change the name of the church to St. Paul's in 1901. (Photograph courtesy of *Watertown Daily Times*.)

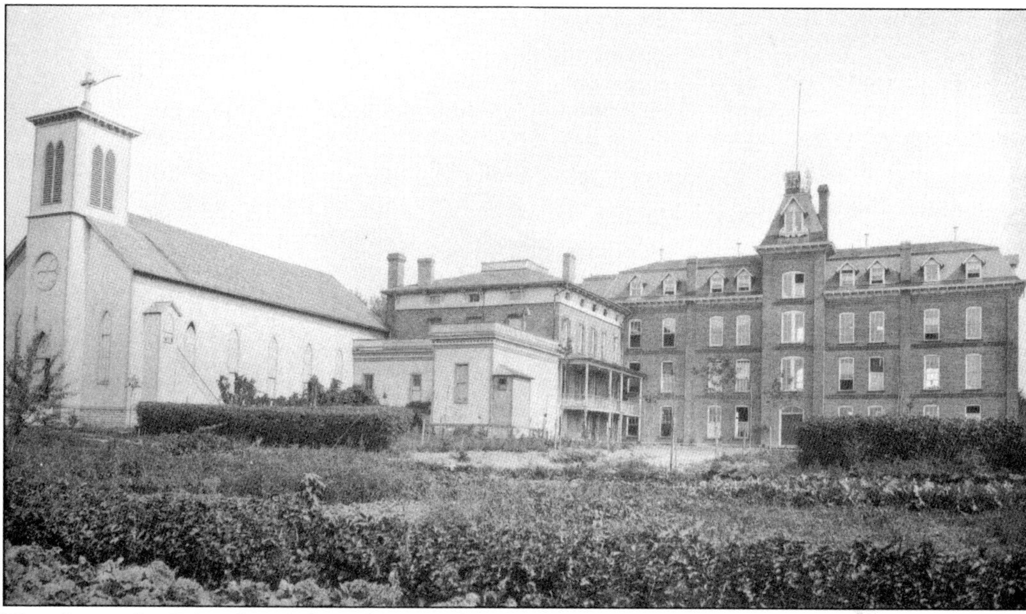

The Apostolic School and the Old Sacred Heart Church are shown in this early photograph.

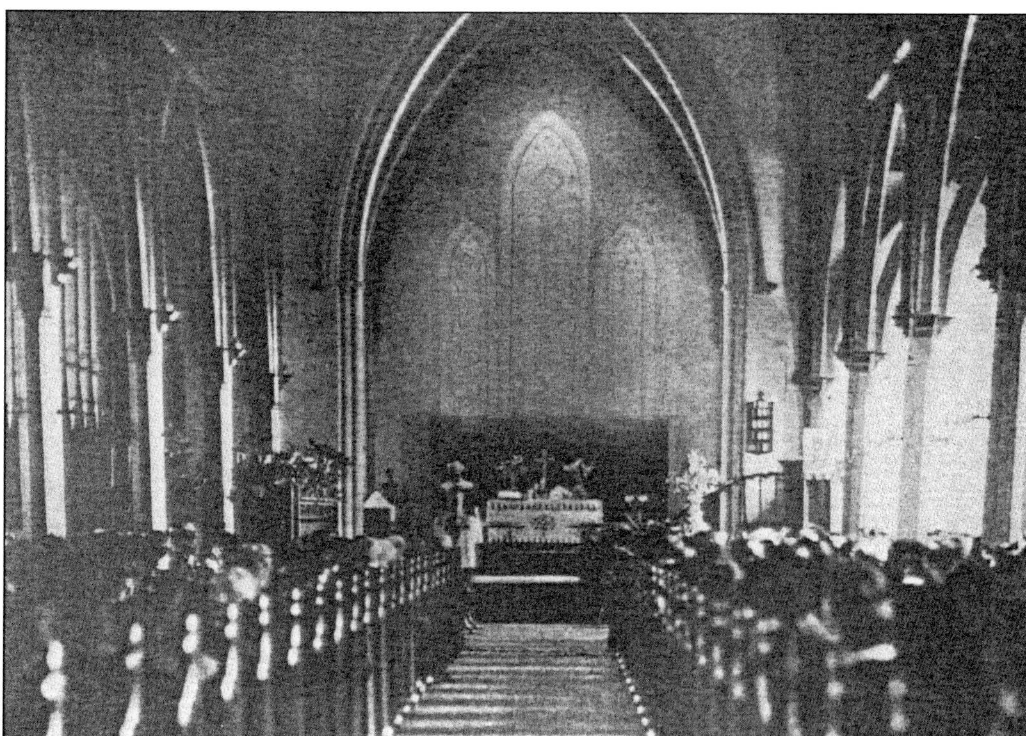

The interior of Old Trinity is shown here.

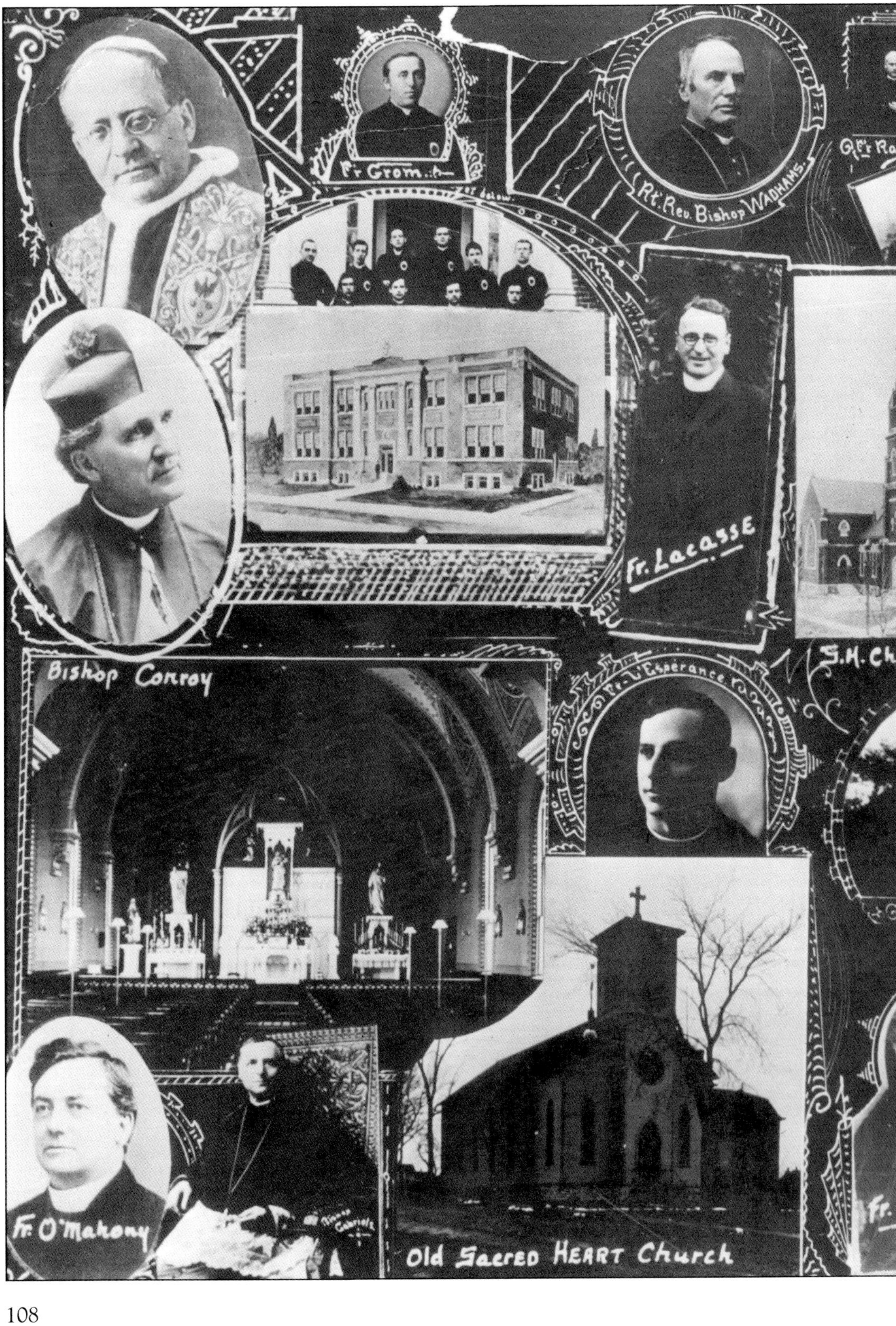

Rt. Rev. Bishop WADHAMS
Fr. Lacasse
Bishop Conroy
Fr. O'Mahony
Old Sacred HEART Church

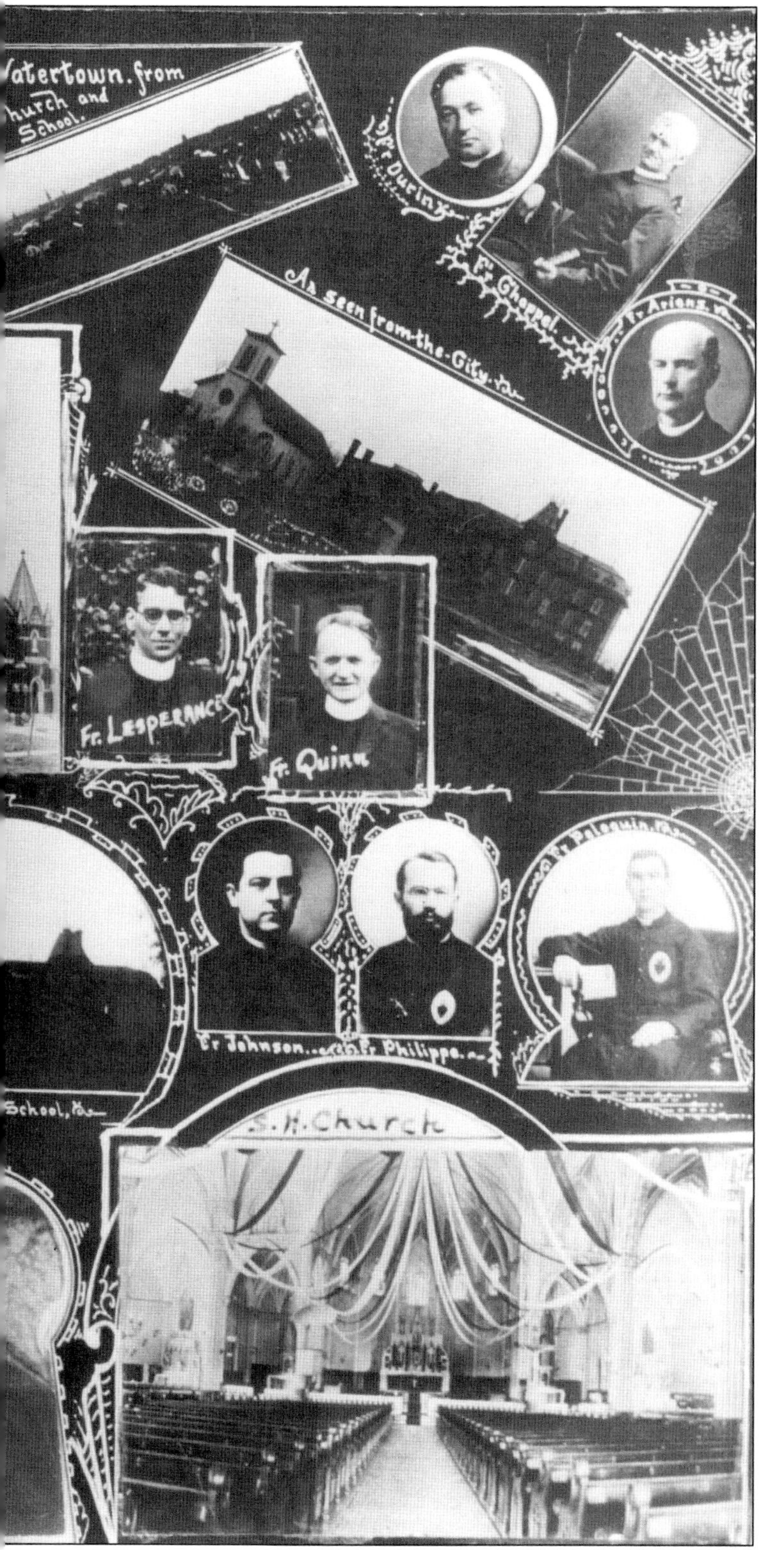

A collage of photographs shows the history of Sacred Heart Parish. Sacred Heart was the first church built on Watertown's north side. Four more south-side churches established churches or missions on the north side over the next 20 years. This was due to the tremendous influx of factory workers and their families into the north side at that time. When Irish members of St. Mary's left to attend St. Patrick's, the French-speaking Catholics remained. On July 5, 1857, St. Mary's was reorganized as the Societe Catholique Francaise de Watertown, New York. This parish served some 50 families totaling about 300 people, in and around Watertown. In 1878, a new church building was constructed on the north side.

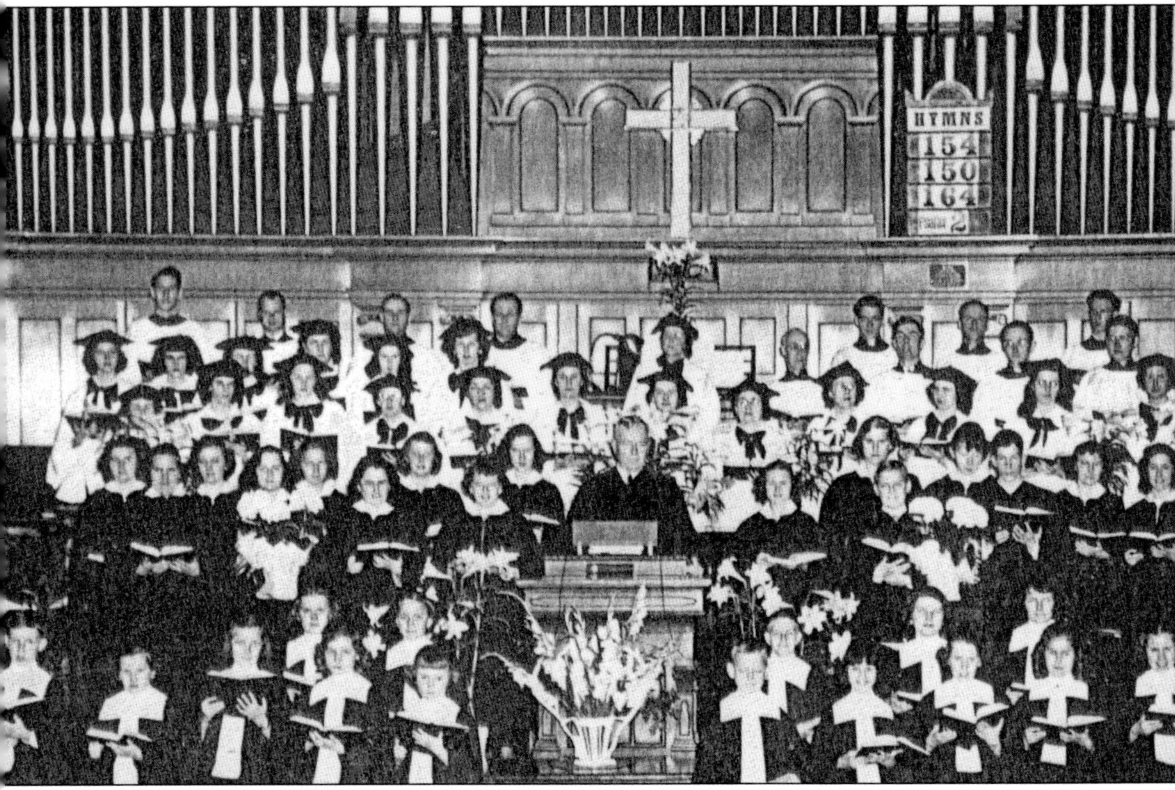

Asbury's Choir performs during the 1949 Easter service.

Nine

A Potpourri of Memories

Webster's Dictionary defines potpourri as "a miscellaneous anthology or collection," and that is exactly what this chapter is. The following photographs are sure to bring back memories of another time. It has often been said that while buildings line city streets, it is the people that make up the fabric of a community. All of the people in this book are part of our heritage. The photographs in this chapter are a tribute to our recent past. Take a walk down memory lane. Mardi Gras parades, downtown movies theaters, Newberry's, and Woolworth's all bring back wonderful memories.

The policeman on the American Corner always had a greeting for everyone who passed by. The smells of the Karmel Korn Shop in the Arcade filled the air. The glass counters in the Beehive Store, the revolving door at Empsall's, Newberry's pet shop, and the creaky floor of Fishman's are sights and sounds that many of us grew up with. The aromas and tastes from the Crest and Crystal Restaurants and the Fannie Farmer's Candy Store can be vividly remembered. Soda fountains at Whelan's, Newberry's, and Woolworth's and dances at the armory were great places to meet friends. These places and events are all pieces of a puzzle which, when put together, create the mural of our community.

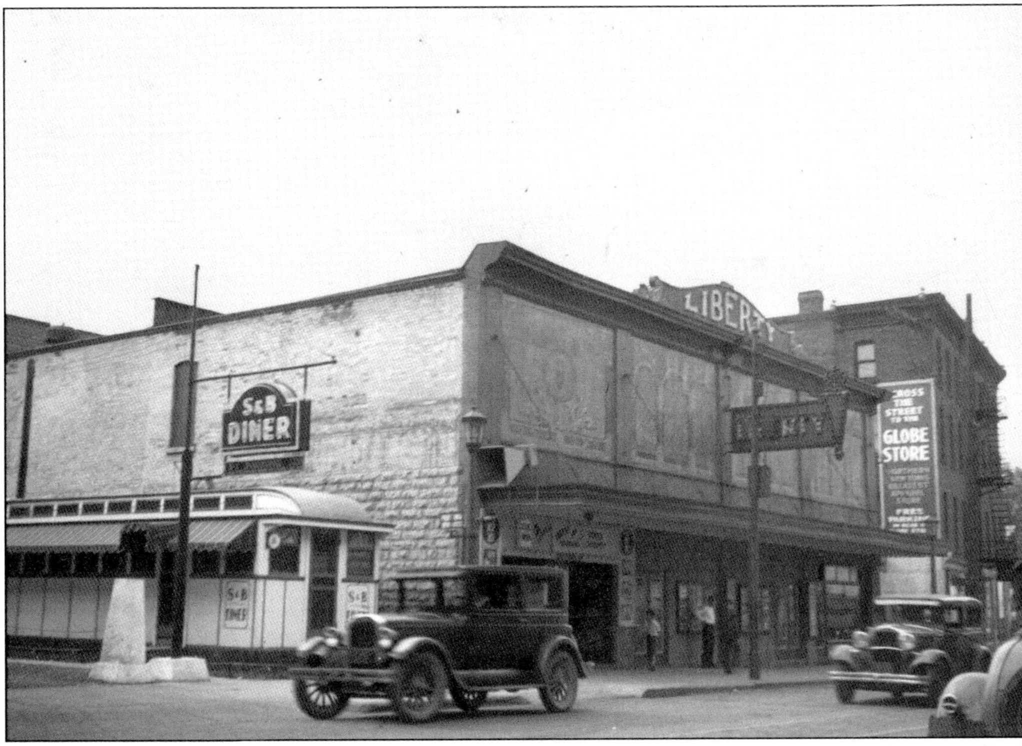

The Liberty Theater and the S & B Diner were located on Court Street. The theater, which began as the Antique Theater in 1908 and became the Liberty in 1921, closed on September 3, 1959. It was torn down to make room for a parking lot.

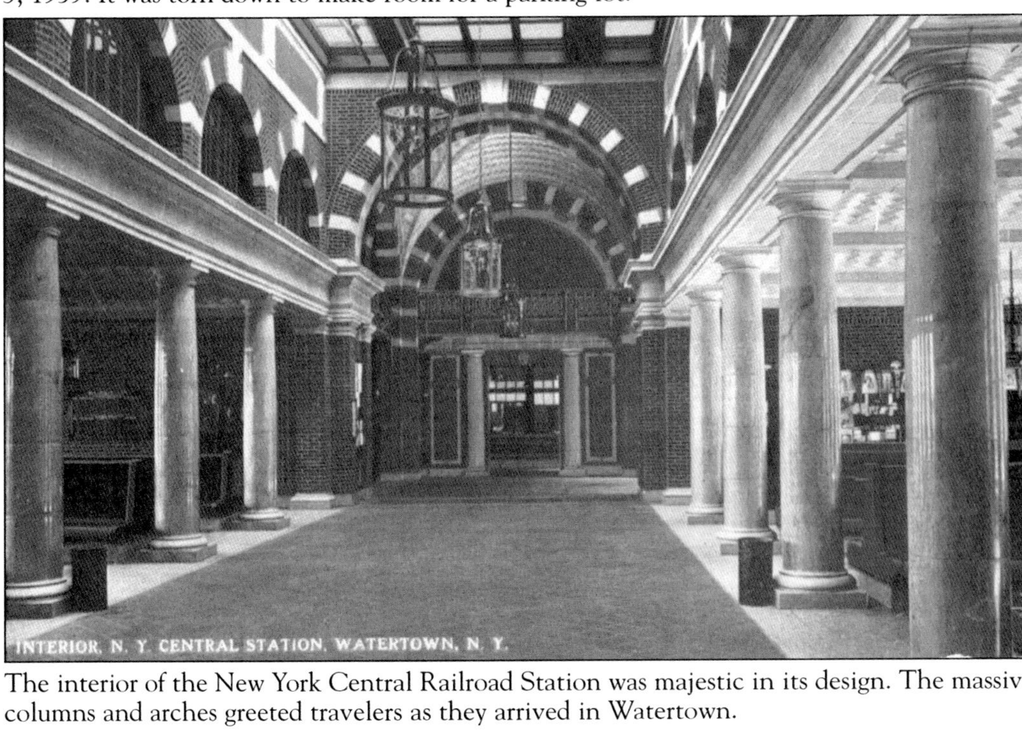

The interior of the New York Central Railroad Station was majestic in its design. The massive columns and arches greeted travelers as they arrived in Watertown.

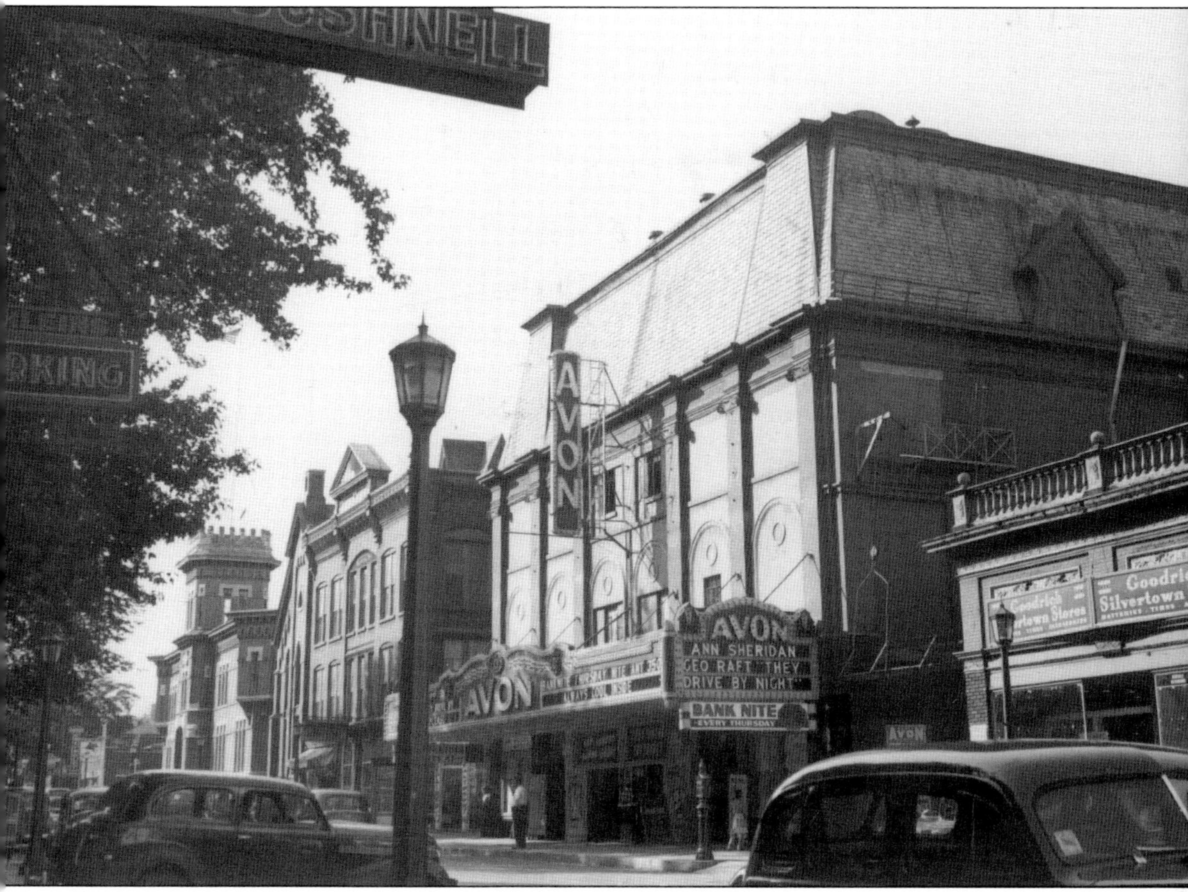

The Avon Theater was originally the City Opera House. Located on Arsenal Street, the theater was renovated in 1919. The Avon hosted vaudeville and stock companies for many years. Attendance records were shattered in September 1921, when there were 26,700 paid admissions in one week to see *The Great Moment,* starring Gloria Swanson, and *Now or Never,* starring Harold Lloyd. The theater continued to show movies until 1966, when the city purchased the building and demolished it during urban renewal.

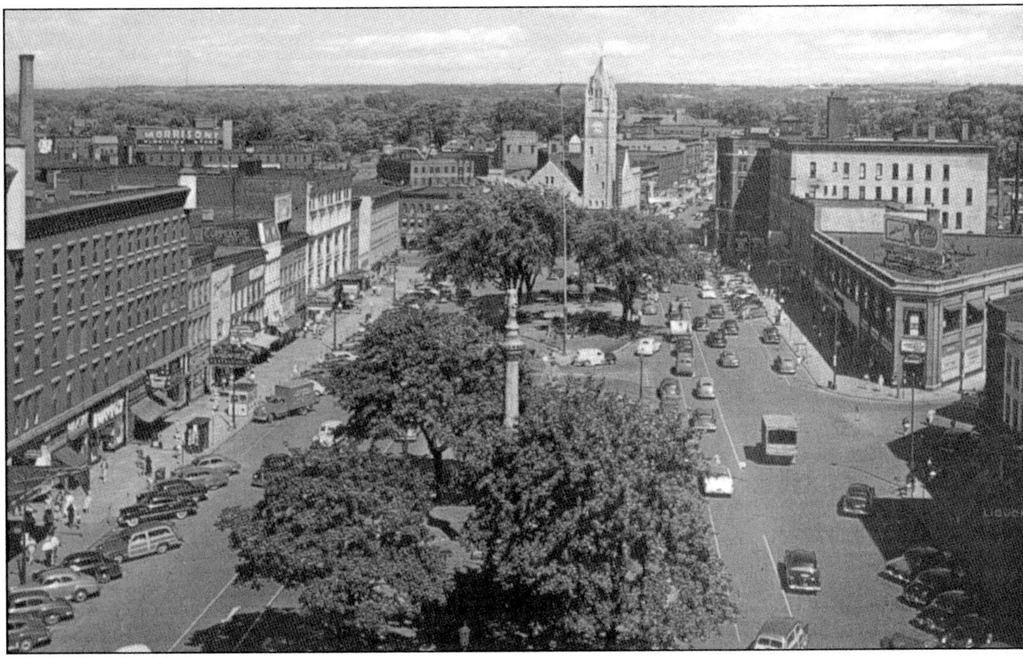

Public Square was a hub of activity in the 1950s. The traffic pattern allowed vehicles to cross over between the islands.

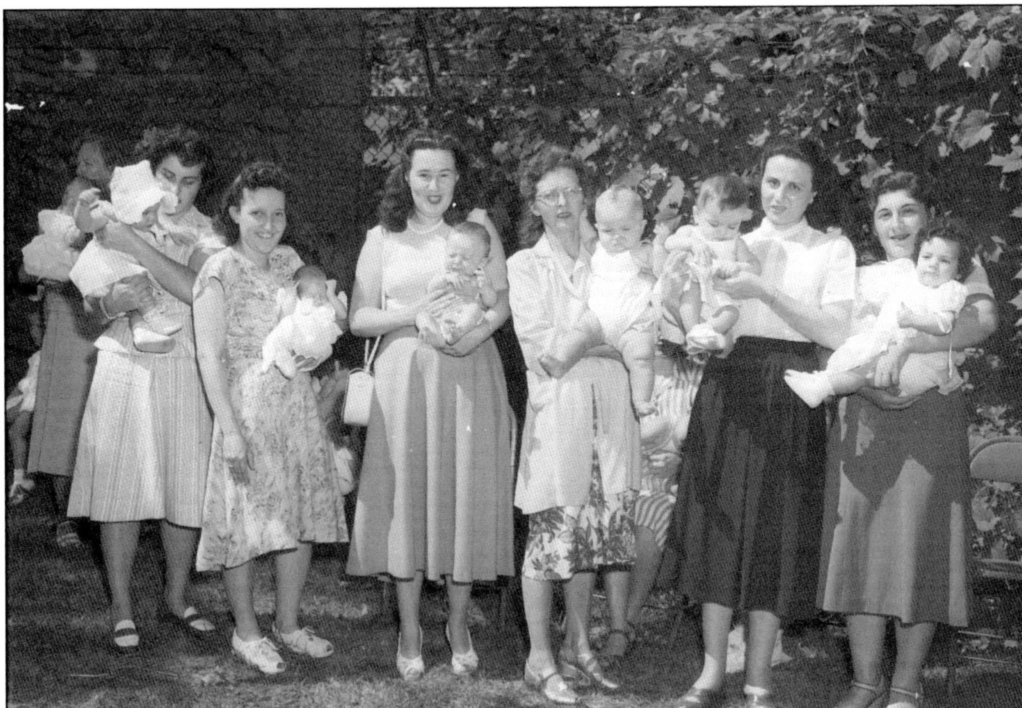

Mothers and babies line up for a citywide baby show in 1948.

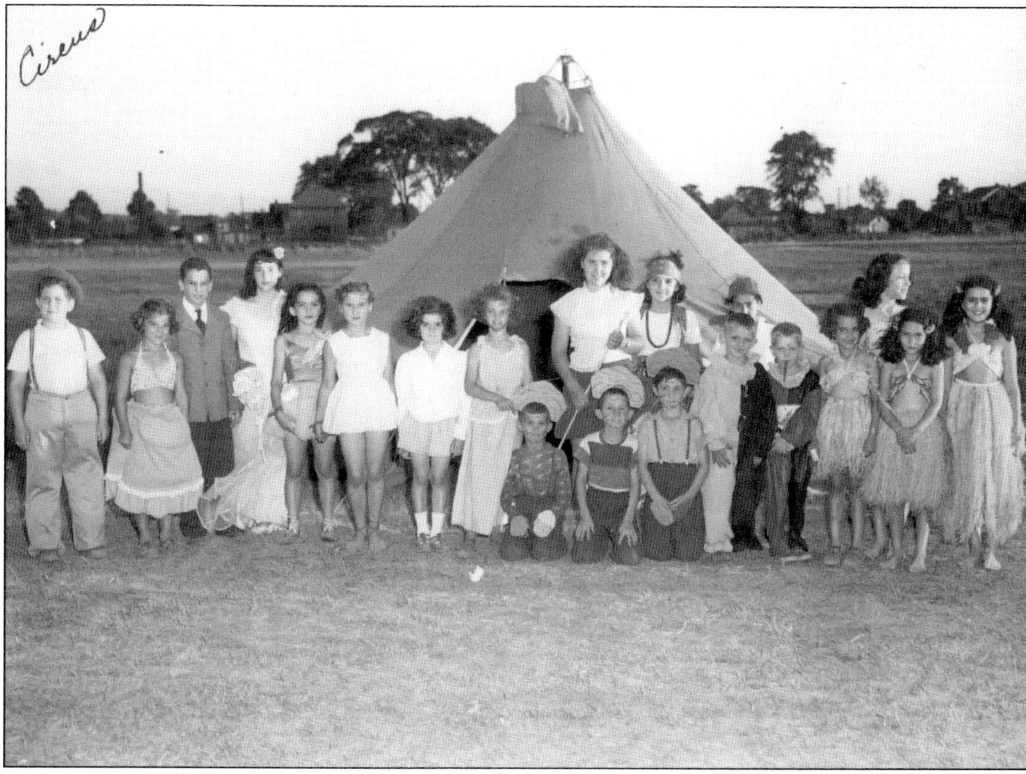

Young people participated in the summer recreation program's Circus Day at Kostyk Field in 1949.

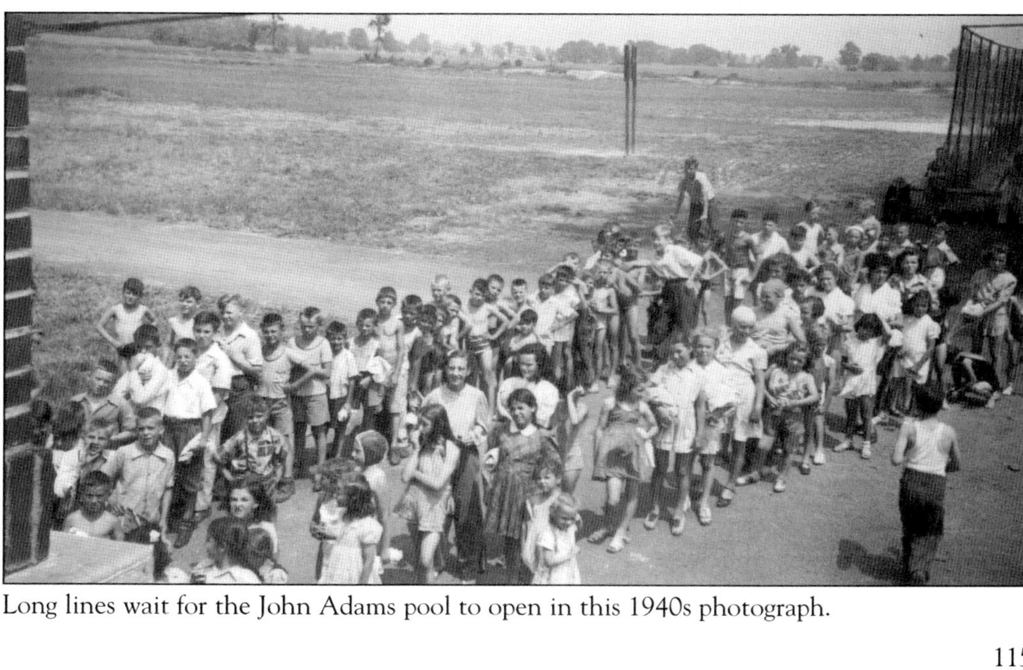

Long lines wait for the John Adams pool to open in this 1940s photograph.

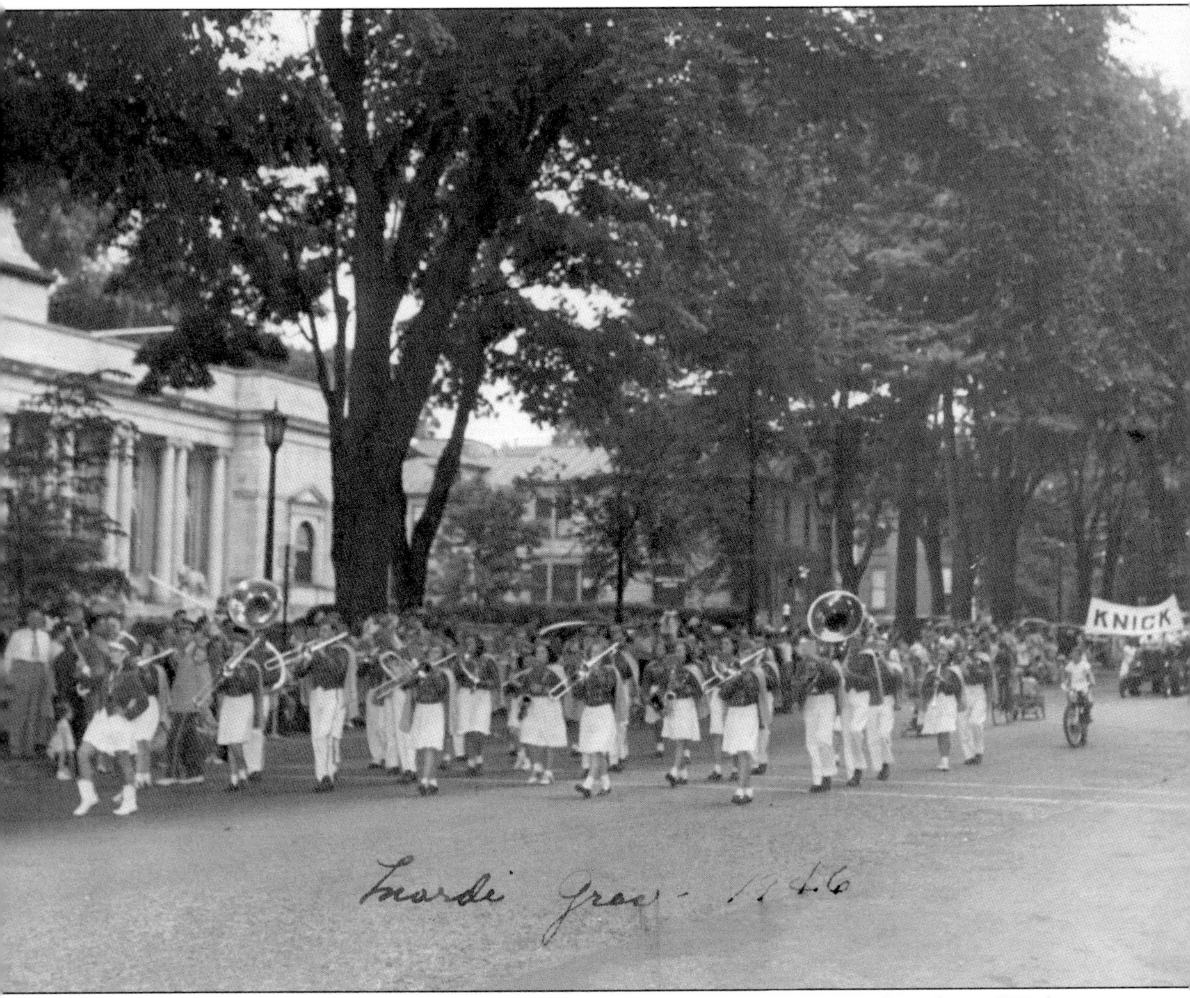

The 1946 Mardi Gras Parade for the summer recreation program marches down Washington Street in front of the Flower Memorial Library. The Mardi Gras Parade was an annual event for all of the city's playgrounds. Large crowds always lined the parade route to cheer for the youth of our community.

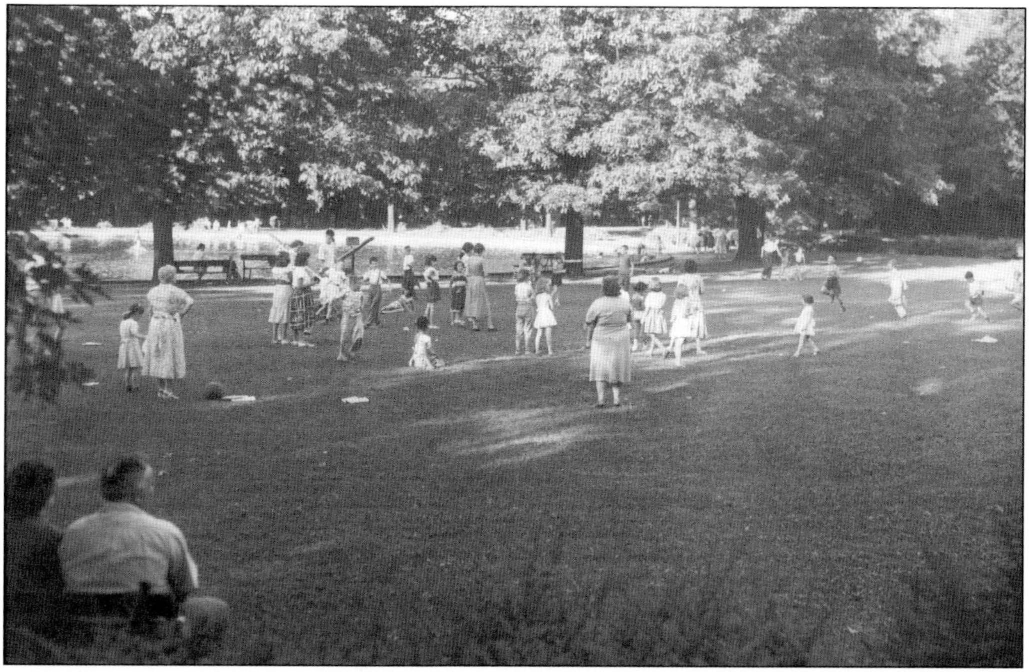

Everyone enjoyed the day in Thompson Park at the first annual Fresh Air Outing in 1951.

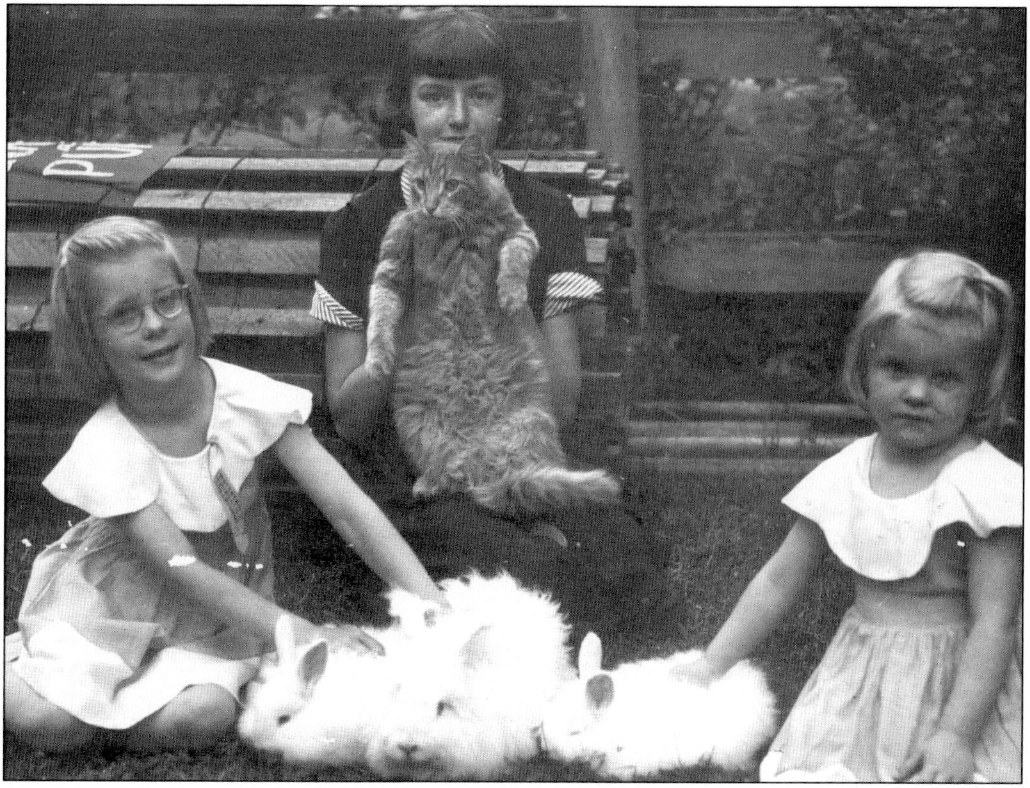

Annual pet shows were also held in Watertown. The 1951 winners are shown here with their young owners.

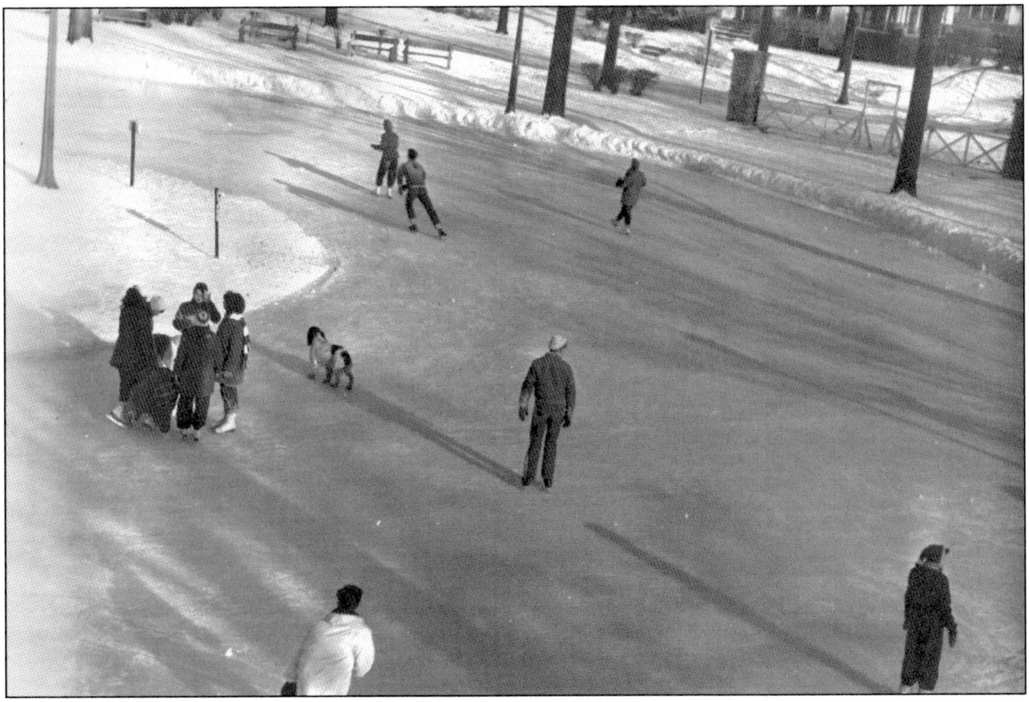

Winter in Watertown was a time when the Park Circle would be flooded for skating, as seen in this 1956 view. Even pets came out to try their skills on the slick surface.

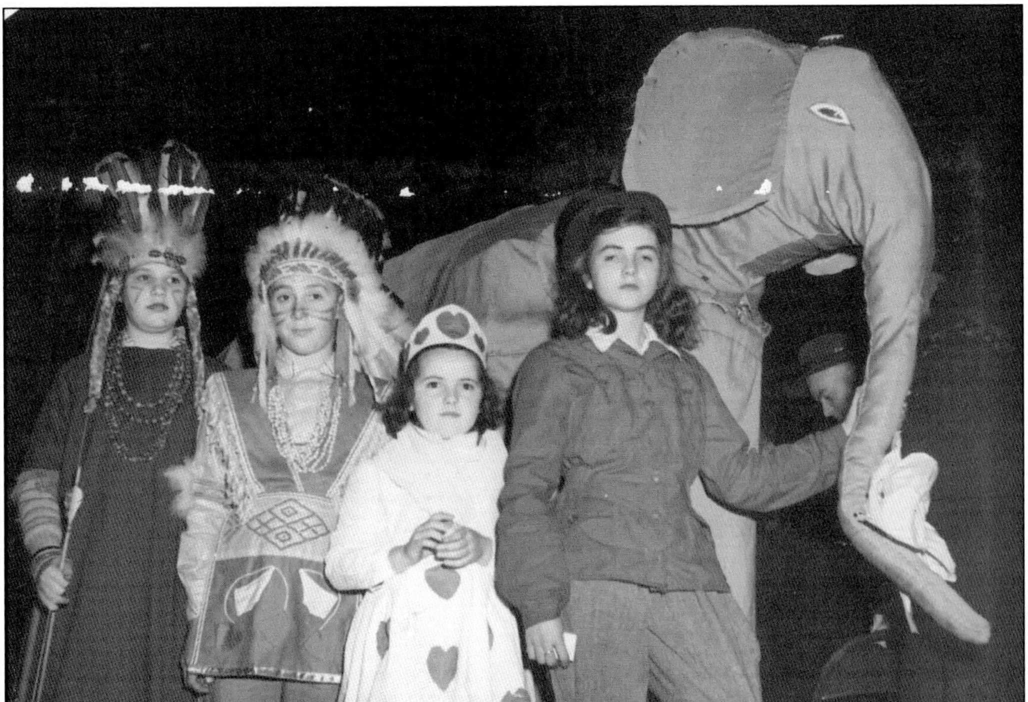

"Always Ready for a Parade" was the motto in the 1940s and 1950s. The winners for outstanding costumes pose during the 1944 Halloween parade.

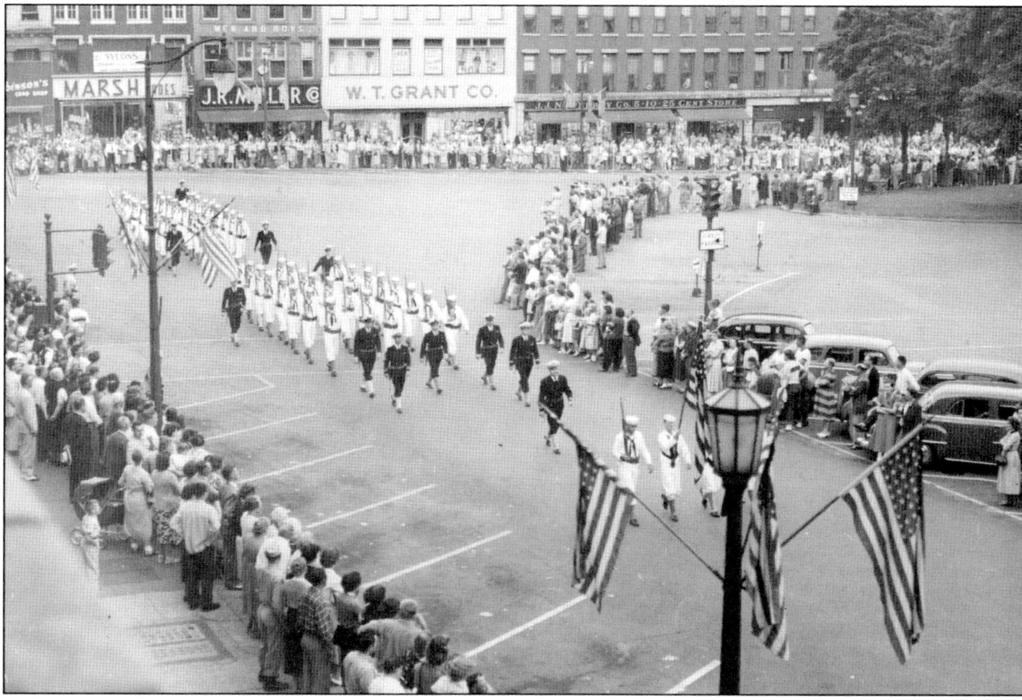

The Naval Reserve Unit marched in the combined V-J Day and Mardi Gras Parade held in 1951. The businesses in the background will likely bring back memories for some readers. Parking patterns around the square were quite different then.

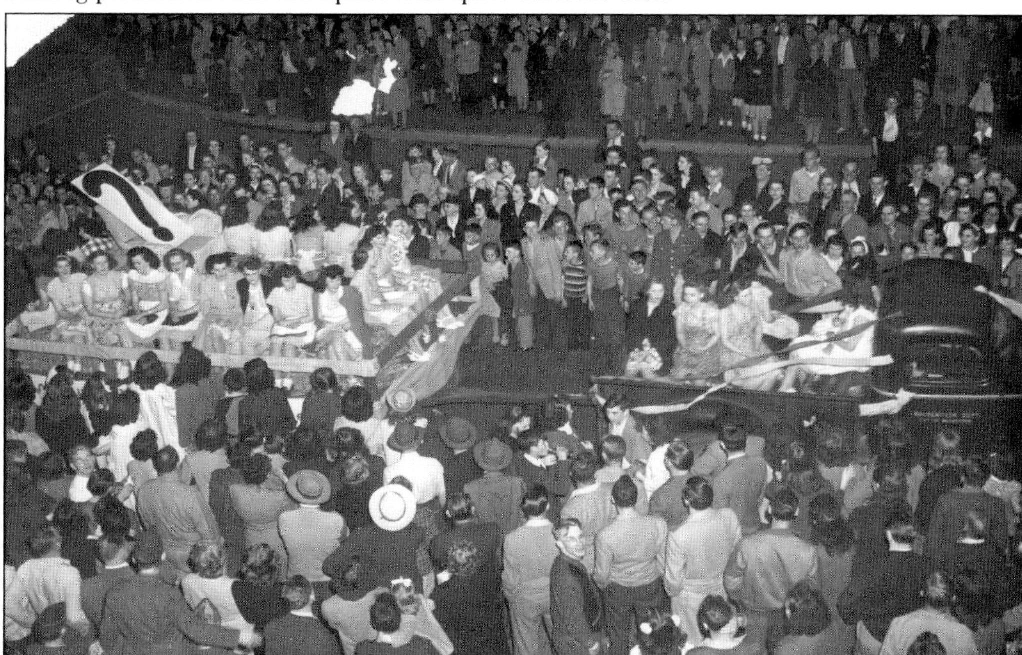

The Dairyland Festival was always a time for great celebration in Watertown. This 1946 photograph shows the Queen's Float lined with all the princesses. The large question mark asks who would be named the Dairy Queen.

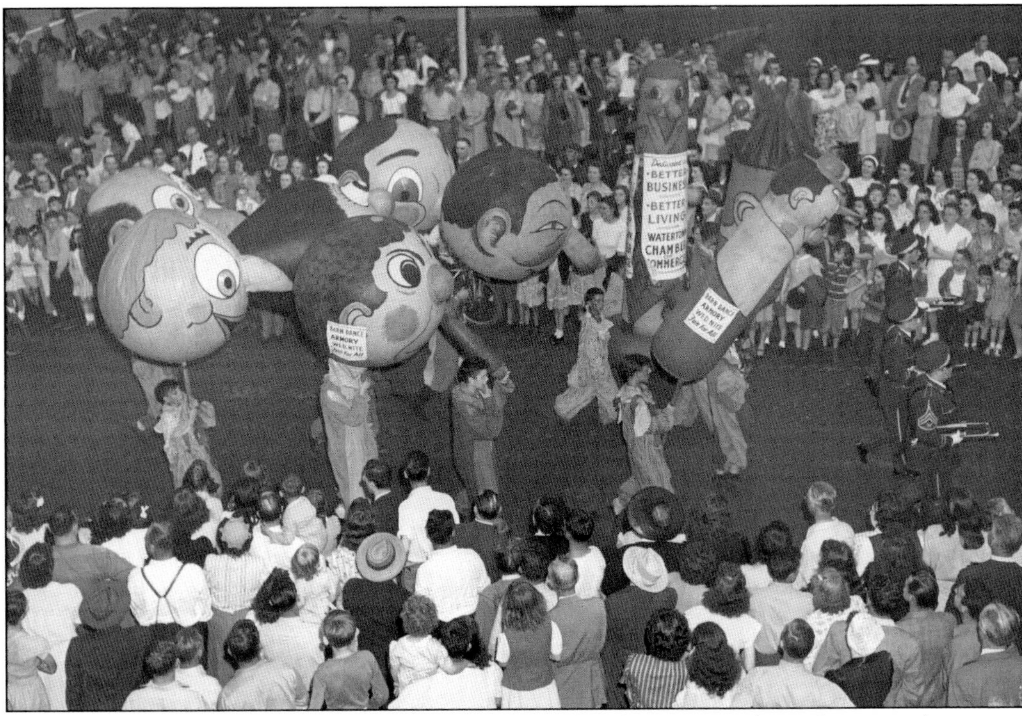

Clowns march in the 1947 Dairyland Festival Parade advertising a barn dance at the armory on Wednesday night.

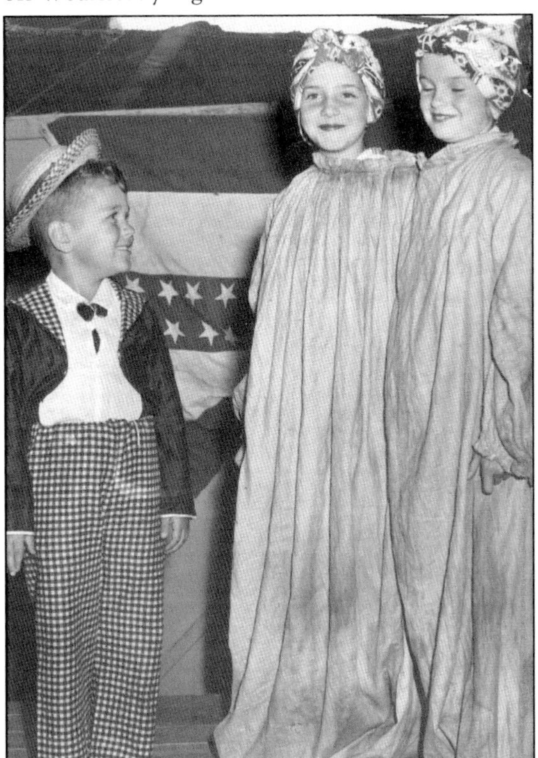

Costumes played a big part in growing up. Here John Fredenburg is dressed as Tom Thumb. Anne Fortin and Sharleen Jennette are dressed as Siamese twins.

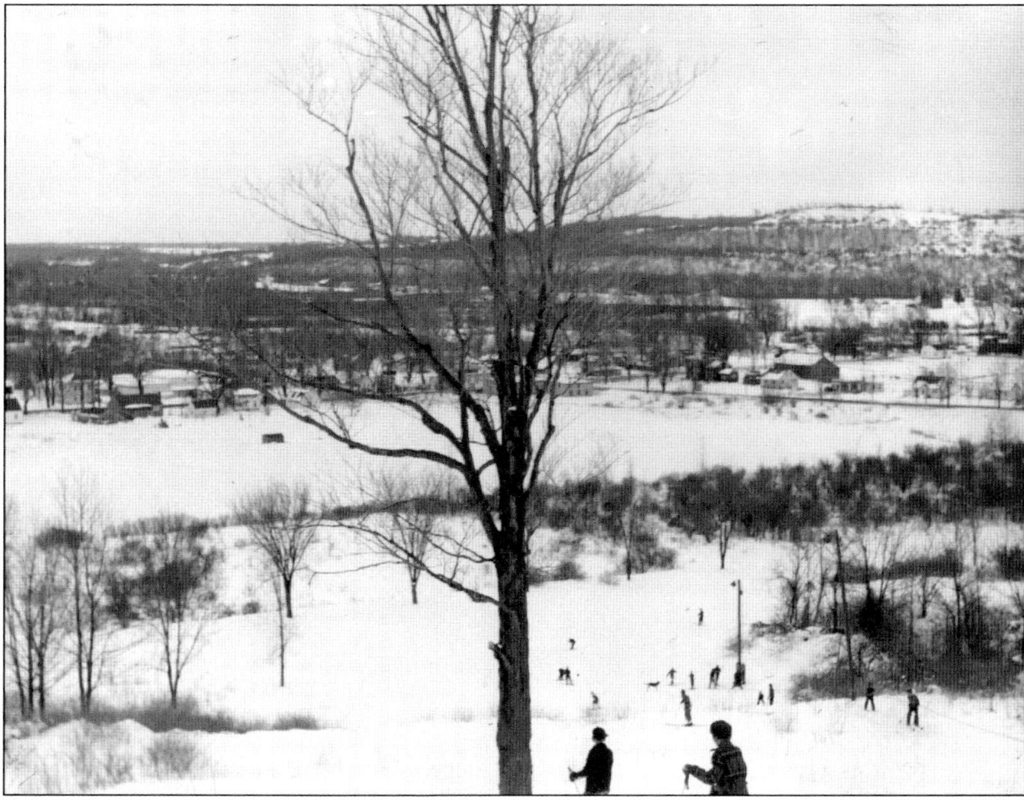

The ski tow at Thompson Park was a great place to spend a February day in 1955.

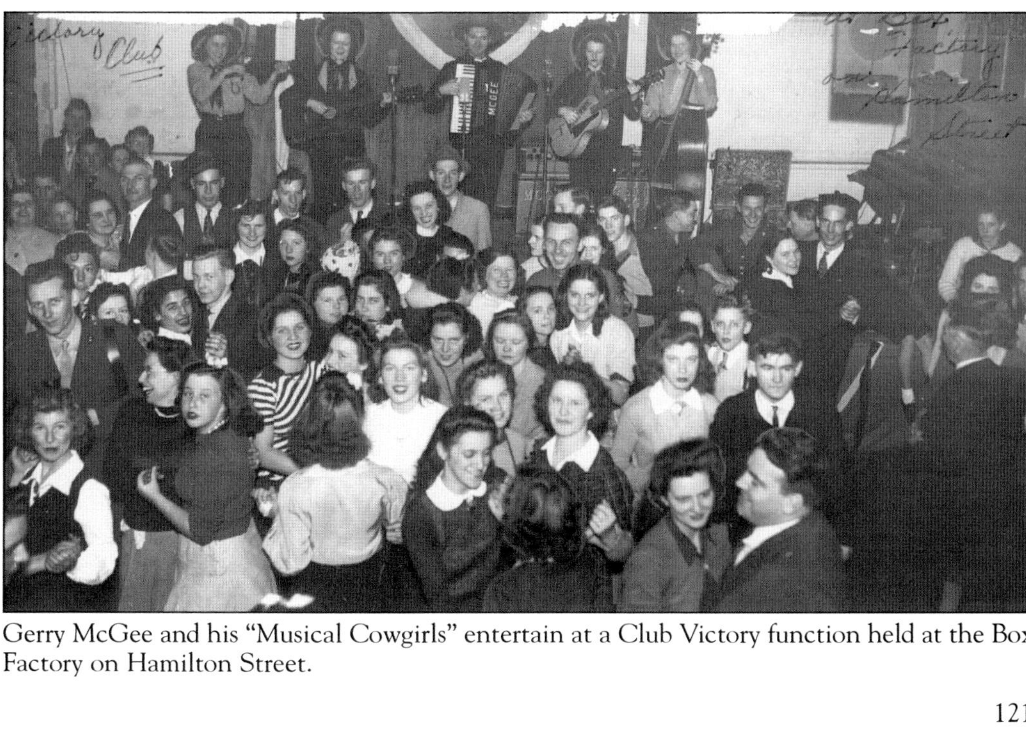

Gerry McGee and his "Musical Cowgirls" entertain at a Club Victory function held at the Box Factory on Hamilton Street.

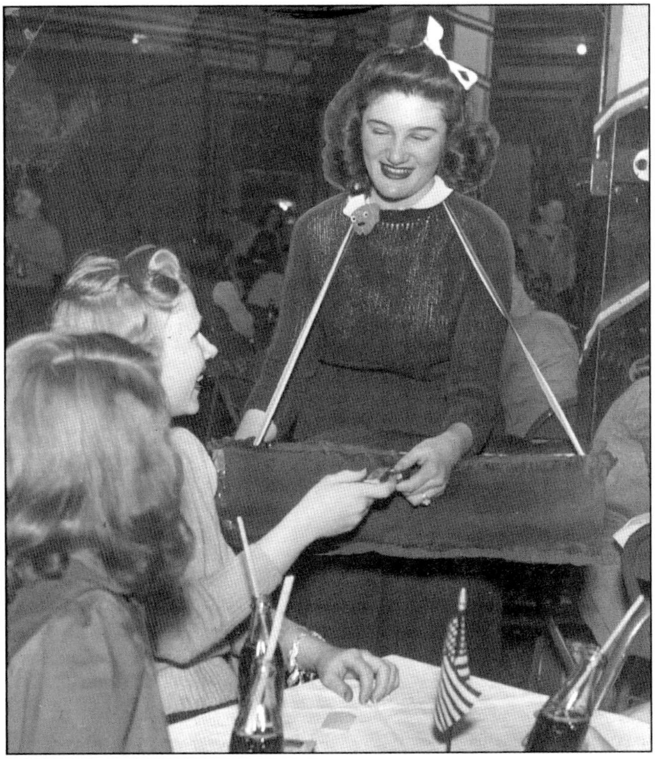

Kay Alexander was the "candy lady" at Club Victory's first cabaret event.

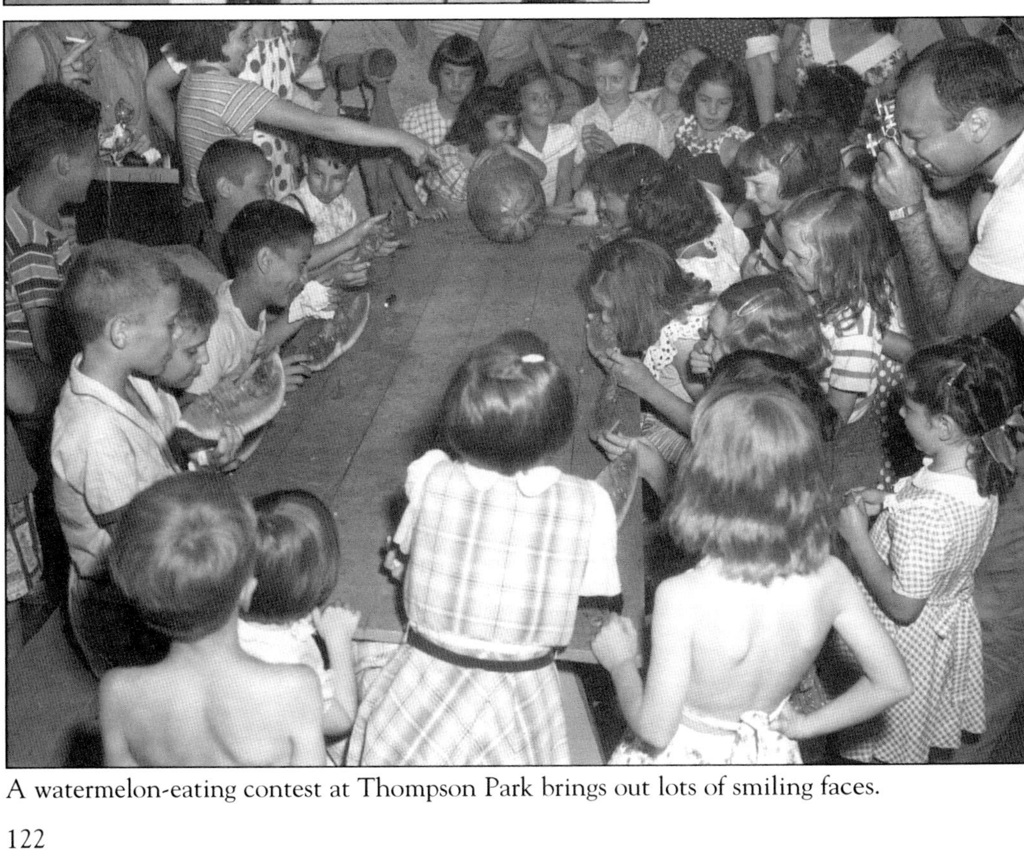

A watermelon-eating contest at Thompson Park brings out lots of smiling faces.

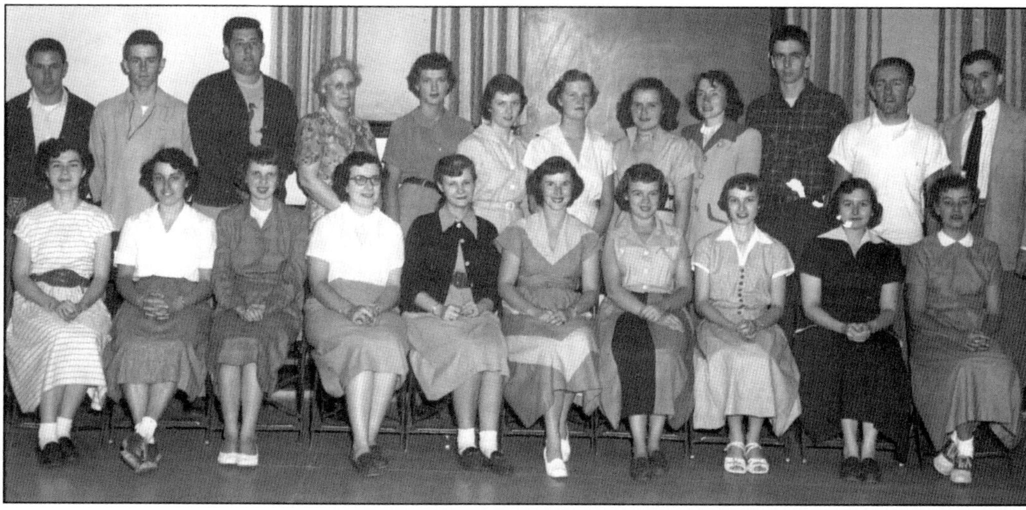

Members of the 1951 Playground Training Institute pose for a class photograph. Classes were held at the YMCA for city playground staff.

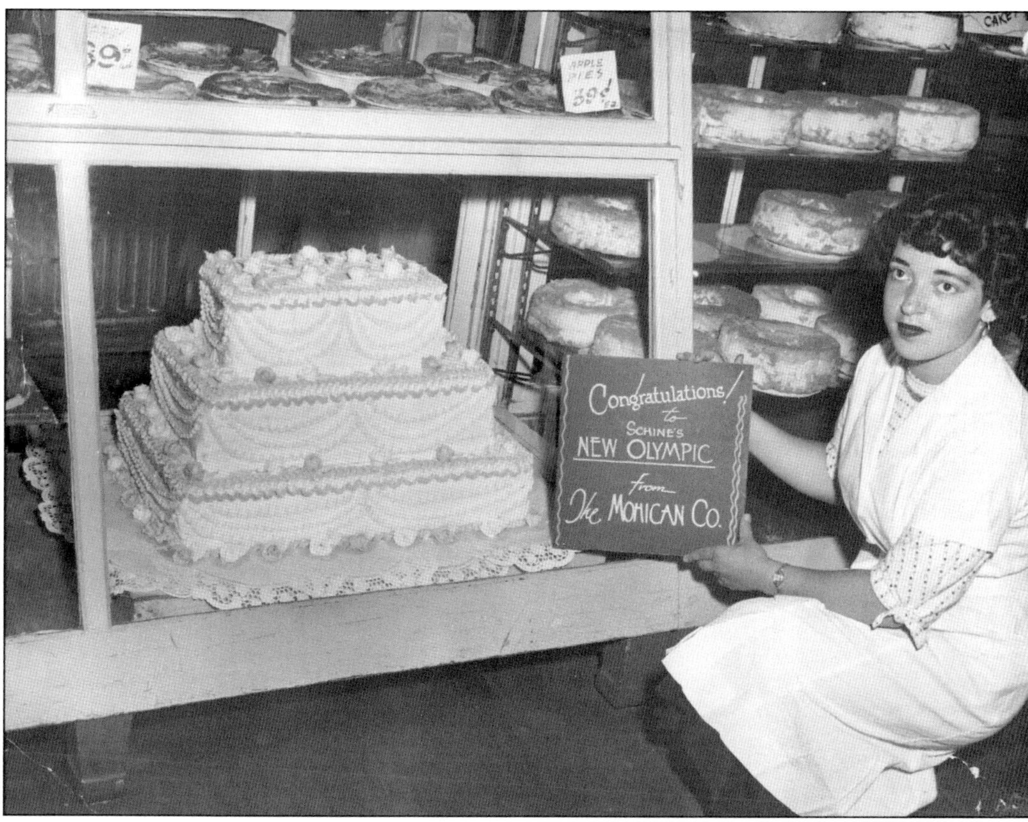

Doris Barrisford Petersen was employed by the Mohican Market. This photograph was taken c. 1949.

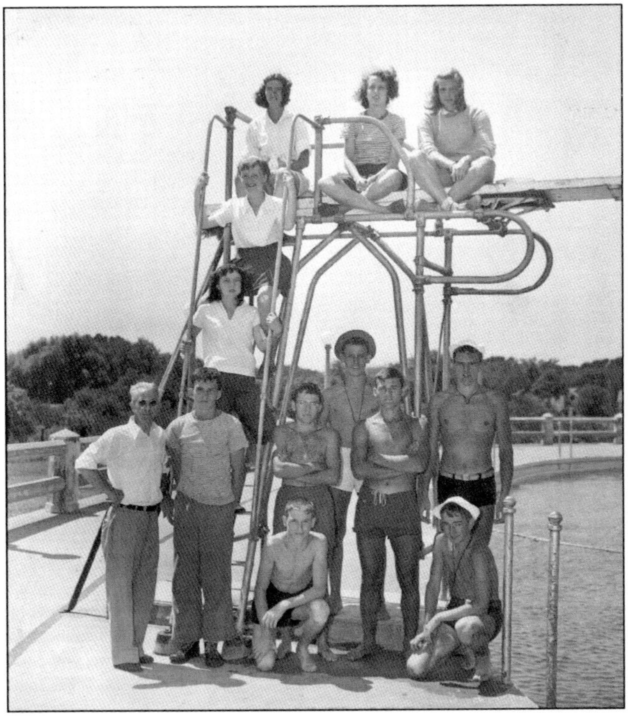

Members of the 1944 pool staff pose here. From left to right are the following: (kneeling) Bill Gaffney and Paul Plante; (standing) Howard Neal, Fred Daily, Charles Willis, Marcel Rouchard, Robert Whalen, and Hank Schultz. Posing on the ladder are Kay Williams (bottom) and Mary Lephart (top). On the diving board are Caroline Whitney (left), Muriel McClement (center), and Barbara Eldrige.

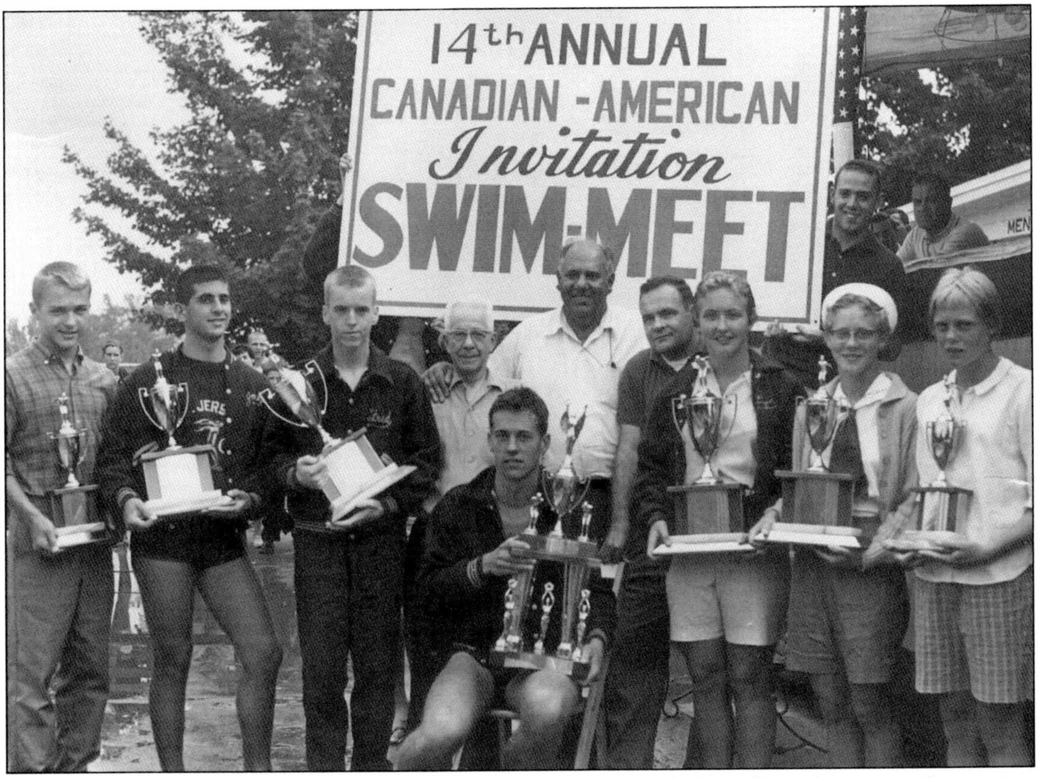

Winners show off their trophies following the 14th Annual Canadian-American Invitation Swim Meet in 1961.

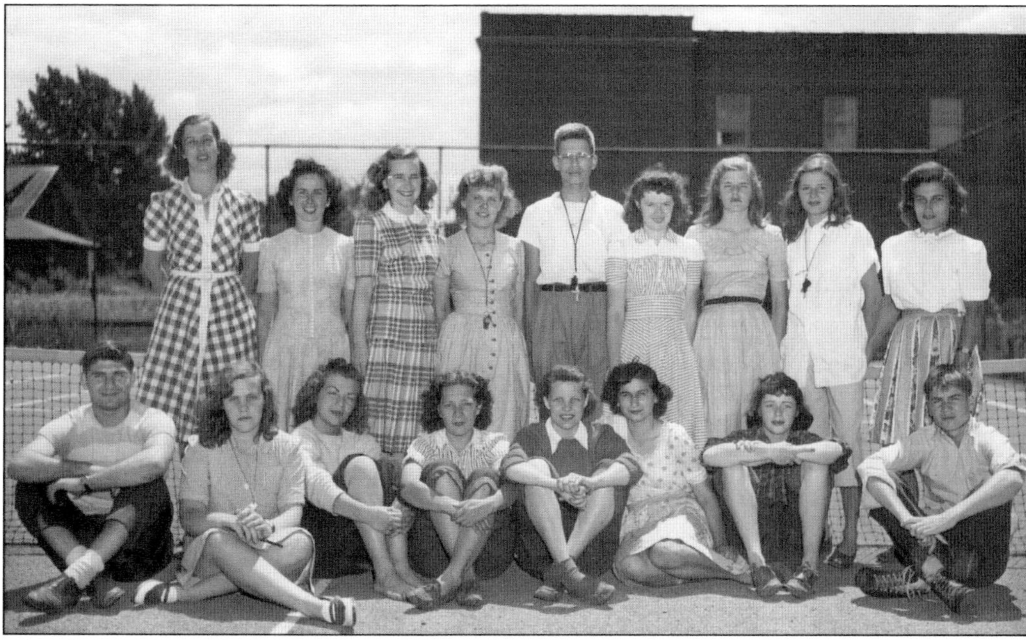

The playground staff of 1943 included, from left to right, the following: (front row) Joe Guardino, Bethyl Vincent, Eileen Aiken, Eunice Gerber, Ruth Chisamore, Rose Capone, Patty Reilly, and Fred Exley; (back row) Doreen Kirkland, Janet Greenizen, Helen Gossman, Peggy Brown, Bernard Yablin, Catherine Barben, Janet Inglehart, Martha Dunlay, and Sally Walrath.

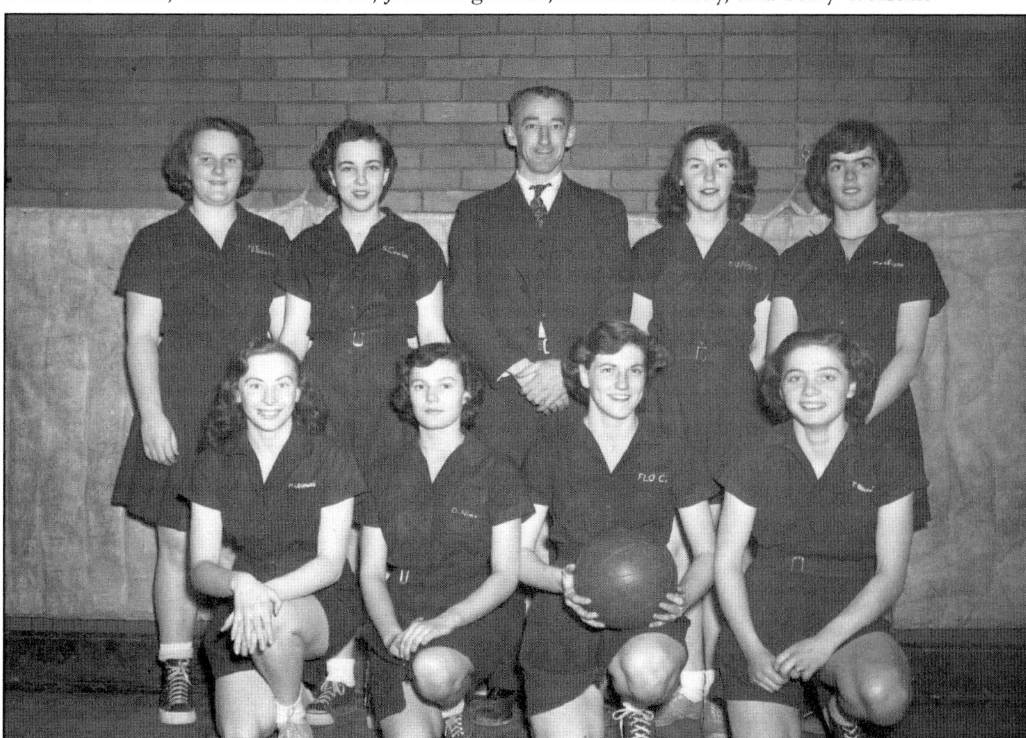

The North Side All Stars took the championship in 1949.

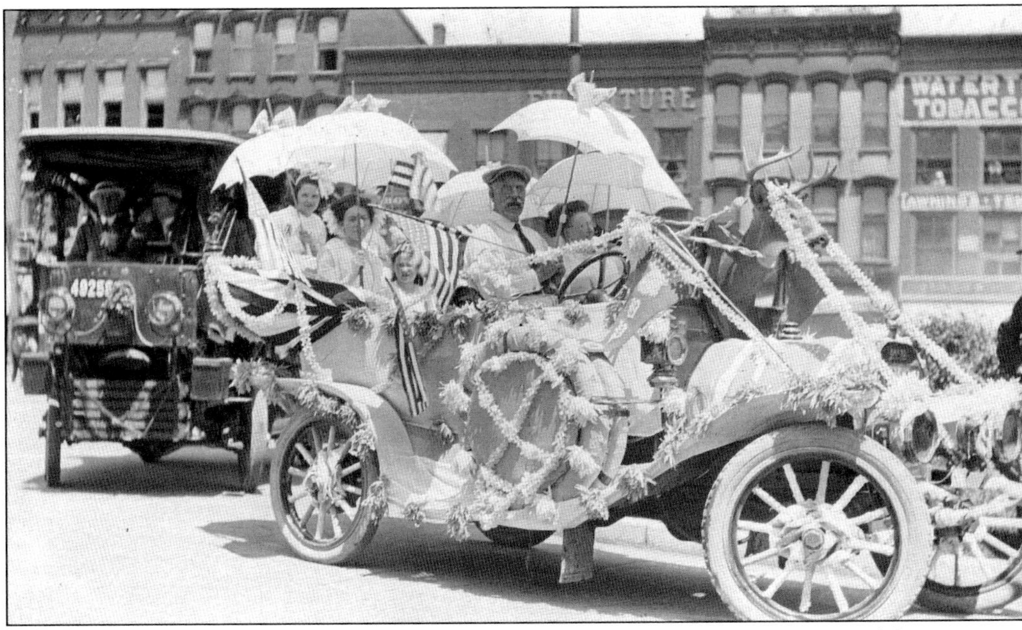

The car parade around Public Square featured vehicles adorned with all types of decorations.

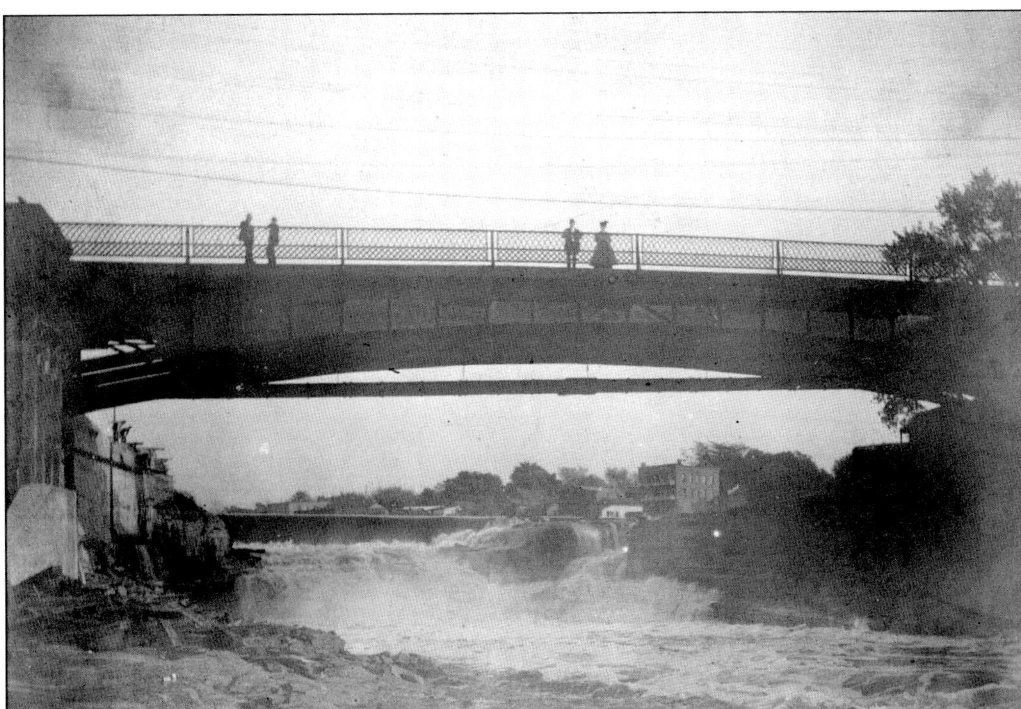

People observe the whitewater of the Black River from the Mill Street Bridge.

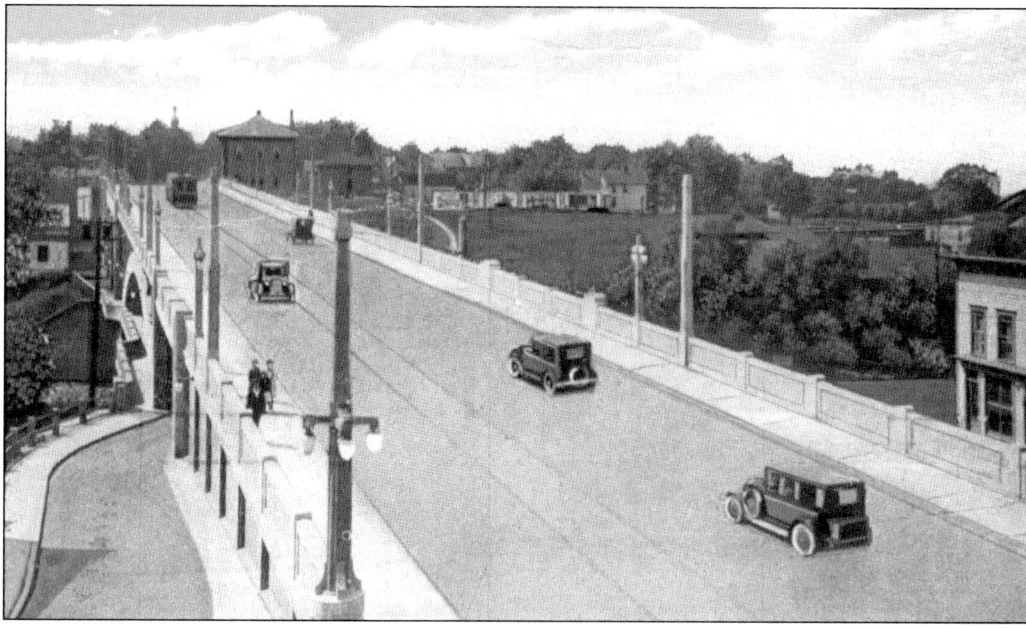

This postcard view is of the Court Street Bridge. Note the trolley in the center of the bridge.

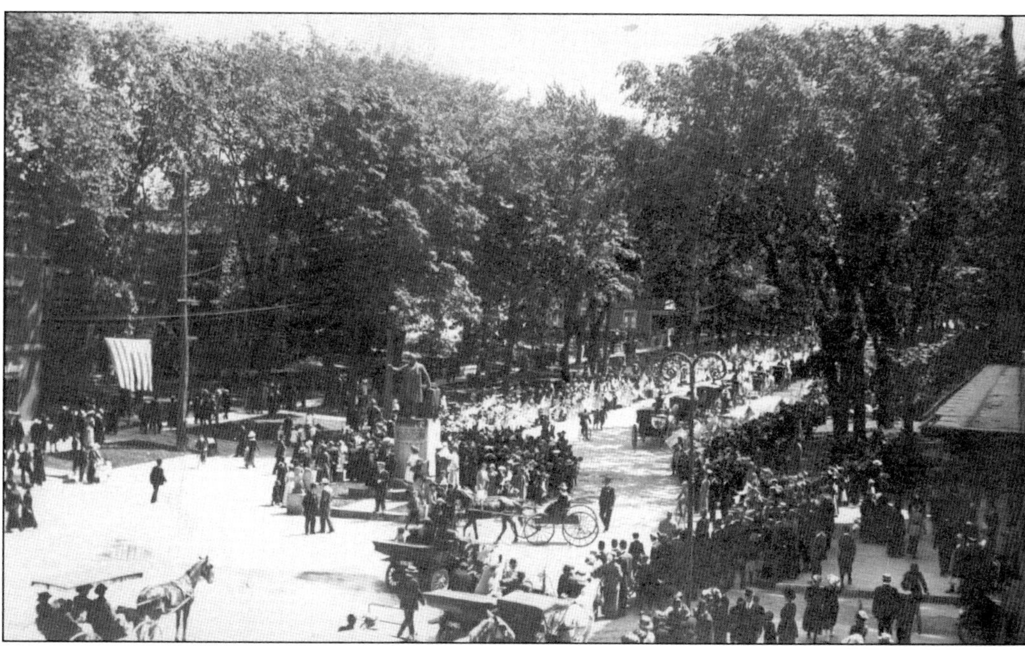

Flags fly during this festive celebration as a parade travels up a tree-lined Washington Street in this 1911 view.

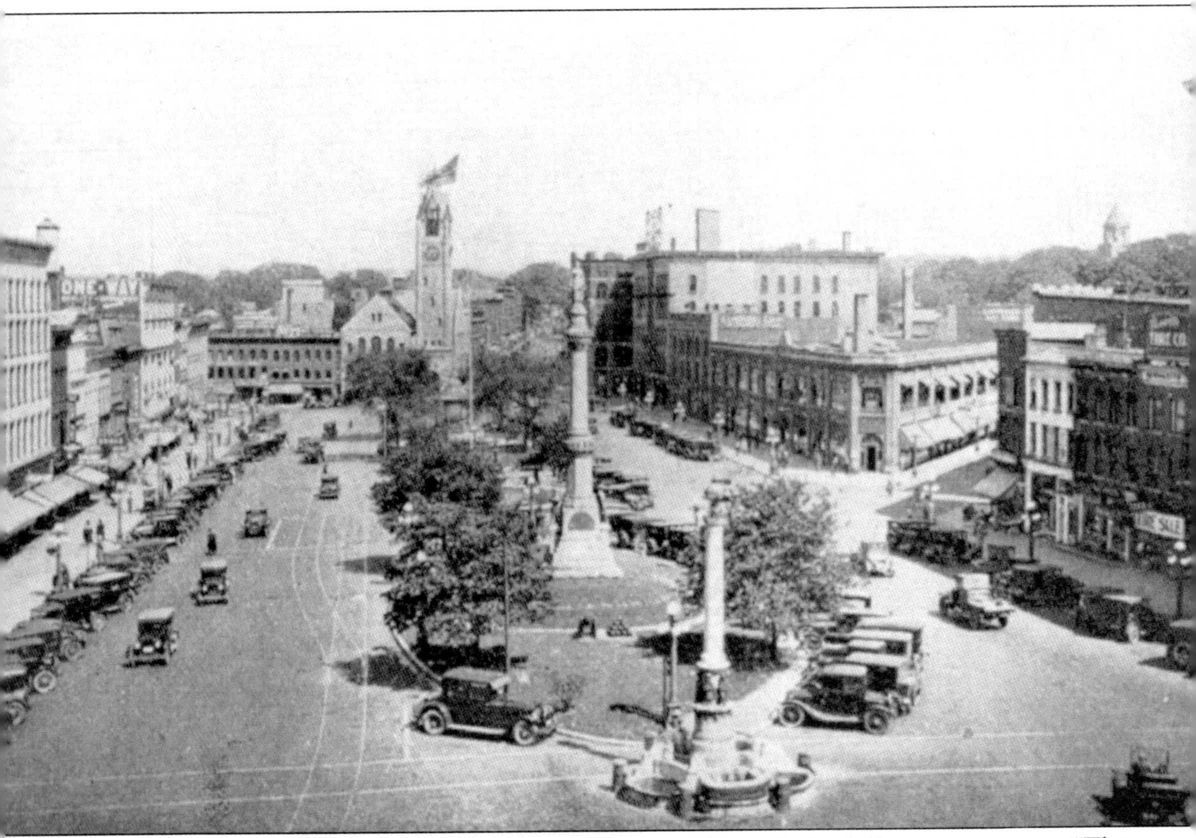

Watertown was named "the Ideal American City" in 1939, with the following statement: "This characteristic of the ideal city was handed down from its first settlers who in 1805 deeded the land now occupied by Public Square for public purposes. Parks, libraries, monuments, hospitals, and community welfare institutions have been contributed by successive generations. Watertown stands out as a standard for others to emulate."